The WAC Journal

Writing Across the Curriculum
Volume 29
2018

© 2018 Clemson University
Printed on acid-free paper in the USA
ISSN: 1544-4929

Editor

Roy Andrews

Managing Editor

David Blakesley, Clemson University

Associate Editor

Cameron Bushnell, Clemson University

Editorial Board

Art Young, Clemson University
Neal Lerner, Northeastern University
Carol Rutz, Carleton College
Meg Petersen, Plymouth State University
Terry Myers Zawacki, George Mason Univ.

Copyeditor

Jared Jameson

Review Board

Jacob S. Blumner, Univ of Michigan, Flint
Patricia Donahue, Lafayette College
John Eliason, Gonzaga University
Michael LeMahieu, Clemson University
Neal Lerner, Northeastern University
Meg Petersen, Plymouth State University
Mya Poe, Northeastern University
Carol Rutz, Carleton College
Joanna Wolfe, University of Louisville
Terry Myers Zawacki, George Mason Univ.
David Zehr, Plymouth State University

Subscription Information

The WAC Journal
Parlor Press
3015 Brackenberry Drive
Anderson SC 29621
wacjournal@parlorpress.com
parlorpress.com/wacjournal
Rates: 1 year: $25; 3 years: $65; 5 years: $95.

Submissions

The editorial board of *The WAC Journal* seeks WAC-related articles from across the country. Our national review board welcomes inquiries, proposals, and 3,000 to 6,000 word articles on WAC-related topics, including the following: WAC Techniques and Applications; WAC Program Strategies; WAC and WID; WAC and Writing Centers; Interviews and Reviews. Proposals and articles outside these categories will also be considered. Any discipline-standard documentation style (MLA, APA, etc.) is acceptable, but please follow such guidelines carefully. Submissions are managed initially via Submittable (https://parlorpress.submittable.com/submit) and then via email. For general inquiries, contact Lea Anna Cardwell, the managing editor, via email (wacjournal@parlorpress.com). The WAC Journal is an open-access, blind, peer-viewed journal published annually by Clemson University, Parlor Press, and the WAC Clearinghouse. It is available in print through Parlor Press and online in open-access format at the WAC Clearinghouse. *The WAC Journal* is peer-reviewed. It is published annually by Clemson University, Parlor Press, and the WAC Clearinghouse.

Subscriptions

The WAC Journal is published annually in print by Parlor Press and Clemson University. Digital copies of the journal are simultaneously published at The WAC Clearinghouse in PDF format for free download. Print subscriptions support the ongoing publication of the journal and make it possible to offer digital copies as open access. Subscription rates: One year: $25; Three years: $65; Five years: $95. You can subscribe to The WAC Journal and pay securely by credit card or PayPal at the Parlor Press website: http://www.parlorpress.com/wacjournal. Or you can send your name, email address, and mailing address along with a check (payable to Parlor Press) to Parlor Press, 3015 Brackenberry Drive, Anderson SC 29621. Email: sales@parlorpress.com

Reproduction of material from this publication, with acknowledgement of the source, is hereby authorized for educational use in non-profit organizations.

The WAC Journal
Volume 29, 2018

Contents

ARTICLES

WAC Seminar Participants as Surrogate WAC Consultants: Disciplinary Faculty Developing and Deploying WAC Expertise — 7
BRADLEY HUGHES AND ELISABETH L. MILLER

Writing across College: Key Terms and Multiple Contexts as Factors Promoting Students' Transfer of Writing Knowledge and Practice — 42
KATHLEEN BLAKE YANCEY, MATTHEW DAVIS, LIANE ROBERTSON, KARA TACZAK, AND ERIN WORKMAN

Building Sustainable WAC Programs: A Whole Systems Approach — 64
MICHELLE COX, JEFFREY GALIN, AND DAN MELZER

Inclusion Takes Effort: What Writing Center Pedagogy Can Bring to Writing in the Disciplines — 88
SARAH PETERSON PITTOCK

WAC Journal Interview of Asao B. Inoue — 112
NEAL LERNER

Getting Specific about Critical Thinking: Implications for Writing Across the Curriculum — 119
JUSTIN K. RADEMAEKERS

A Tale of Two Prompts: New Perspectives on Writing-to-Learn Assignments — 147
ANNE RUGGLES GERE, ANNA V. KNUTSON, NAITNAPHIT LIMLAMAI, RYAN MCCARTY, AND EMILY WILSON

More Than a Useful Myth: A Case Study of Design Thinking for
Writing Across the Curriculum Program Innovation   168
JENNA PACK SHEFFIELD

How Exposure to and Evaluation of Writing-to-Learn Activities
Impact STEM Students' Use of Those Activities   189
JUSTIN NICHOLES

Preparing Writing Studies Graduate Students within
Authentic WAC-Contexts: A Research Methods Course and
WAC Program Review Crossover Project as a
Critical Site of Situated Learning   207
MICHELLE LaFRANCE AND ALISA RUSSELL

"Stealth WAC": The Graduate Writing TA Program   230
CAMERON BUSHNELL AND AUSTIN GORMAN

REVIEWS

*Reframing the Relational: A Pedagogical Ethic for Cross-Curricular
Literacy Work* by Sandra L. Tarabochia   247
Reviewed by C.C. HENDRICKS

What We Mean When We Say "Meaningful" Writing:
A Review of *The Meaningful Writing Project*   252
MARY HEDENGREN

Contributors   257

WAC Seminar Participants as Surrogate WAC Consultants: Disciplinary Faculty Developing and Deploying WAC Expertise

BRADLEY HUGHES AND ELISABETH L. MILLER

For decades, writing across the curriculum (WAC) programs have aimed to open up conversations with disciplinary faculty across the curriculum about teaching with writing, and various researchers—including Anderson, Anson, Gonyea, and Payne (2015); Eodice, Geller, and Lerner (2017); Melzer (2014); and Walvoord, Hunt, Dowling, and McMahon (1997)—have studied the effects of those efforts and identified the characteristics of successful writing assignments in the disciplines.[1,2] In this article, we present new research about what instructors learned from participating in a semester-long faculty development seminar and learning community that our WAC program has led for the past six years at a large public research university. This research study offers both a way to define WAC knowledge for disciplinary faculty and a mixed-methods approach for discerning that kind of knowledge in action. In its findings, this study offers a powerful form of program assessment, providing evidence that the investment WAC programs and disciplinary faculty make in creating faculty learning communities pays off. At the same time, this research reveals some limits of what disciplinary faculty learn, reinforcing the value of the deep, specialized knowledge that WAC specialists possess.

The seminar in our research study, "Expeditions in Learning: Exploring How Students Learn with WAC," enrolls ten to twelve faculty, post-docs, and graduate teaching assistants—intentionally from diverse disciplines and various stages in their teaching careers. In addition to discussions of foundational WAC readings, this seminar engages participants in "expeditions," or active learning experiences, which range from observing peer workshops in an intermediate, writing-intensive biology course to talking in-depth with faculty across campus who teach writing-intensive courses in the arts and humanities, sciences, and social sciences. In the spring of 2015, we collected three kinds of data to help us understand what instructors learned from that particular seminar, especially from its unusual combination of learning activities. Using a mixed-methods design, we gathered (a) surveys of participants explaining what they learned and evaluating various components of the seminar; (b) draft assignment sequences they developed for a course they will teach; and (c) videos of their small-group peer-review discussions about those draft assignments with other seminar participants.

To understand what instructors across the disciplines learned from participating in this ten-week WAC seminar, in this article we view our data through three analytical lenses: first, Anderson, Anson, Gonyea, and Paine's (2015, 2016) extensive empirical work identifying key features of WAC assignments that engage students; second, Anson's (2015) six threshold concepts for WAC from the much-discussed collection *Naming What We Know* (Adler-Kassner & Wardle, 2015), concepts that offer an ambitious measure of learning goals for WAC faculty development; and third, an analysis of the interaction occurring in these peer workshops—the ways that faculty communicate and take on what we call "consulting methods." Through that analysis, we show how the instructors in our study demonstrated—at the end of this ten-week WAC seminar—some impressive understanding of Anderson et al.'s assignment principles that engage students and an understanding of many of what Anson identifies as the threshold concepts of WAC. With that knowledge, disciplinary faculty participating in this study practiced within their peer discussions some interactions characteristic of WAC consultants. From our analysis, we argue that these immersive learning contexts and peer-to-peer learning engage disciplinary faculty in surrogate WAC consulting roles, deepening their understanding of key WAC concepts and their commitment to teaching with writing. In this article, we first offer an overview of our seminar's "expedition" model, review literature that situates our study in work on faculty learning and learning about WAC, and sketch the research design for our study. We then analyze our survey data and the small-group discussions of draft assignments through the three lenses. We close by complicating these findings—interrogating what these surrogate consultants may overlook when a WAC specialist leaves the room.

The Expedition Model

This article focuses on one of the University of Wisconsin-Madison's longer-term WAC seminars, "Expeditions in Learning: Exploring How Students Learn with Writing Across the Curriculum." We offer this seminar every spring semester, and we're discussing one iteration of the seminar facilitated by one of the co-authors when she was in the graduate-student leadership role of assistant director of writing across the curriculum, in Spring 2015. As illustrated in the syllabus (see Appendix A), this seminar takes place over ten meetings with roughly ten participants. We deliberately want the group to be small to encourage discussion and community-building. We conduct this particular seminar in partnership with our university's Delta Program, a well-established and highly successful professional development program focused on teaching. The Delta Program is one of the founding members of the national Center for the Integration of Research, Teaching, and Learning (CIRTL) network. This program works especially with graduate students and faculty in the sciences to help them develop and prepare as teachers in their faculty careers. For that reason, our participants skewed toward graduate students and the sciences, but not exclusively. We did not offer financial incentives to participants. They participated for a variety of reasons—above all, because they wanted to learn more about teaching with writing. Some graduate student teaching assistants (TAs) joined our seminar to fulfill requirements for a teaching-focused certificate offered through the Delta Program (the seminar now offers one graduate credit). Many of the faculty and academic staff had consulted already with our WAC program or attended other WAC events, and they wanted to participate in a faculty learning community, exploring WAC more extensively and developing writing activities that aligned with teaching and learning goals in their courses.

Several of the topics featured on our syllabus look familiar from most WAC seminars, with readings from Bean (2011) and other favorites from WAC faculty development programming focused on understanding connections between writing and learning and on principles for designing effective writing assignments, giving feedback on student writing, exploring best practices for peer review and conferencing, supporting multilingual writers—and more. With such a small group of participants, much of what we do is discussion based. As a group, we also analyze successful assignments and series of assignments from courses across the curriculum at our own campus.

One of the most distinctive features of the seminar is what the Delta Program calls "expeditions"—active, immersive learning opportunities for participants. In our seminar, those expeditions offer participants chances to observe writing-intensive courses as they're being taught across the curriculum. They include four "mini field trips" to observe and experience WAC work firsthand:

1. Attending a TA meeting for a writing-intensive course or interviewing a professor or course coordinator for a writing-intensive course across the curriculum;
2. Observing in the Writing Center;
3. Watching some videotaped student writing conferences with instructors from writing-intensive courses;
4. Observing a class session focused on writing—a peer review session or writing workshop, for example.

Our seminar culminates with participants designing or revising and developing their own writing assignment or sequence of assignments for a course they are teaching or would like to teach in the future—to try to apply some of what we've talked about throughout the seminar. Participants workshop those assignments in groups of three and then integrate that feedback into a revised assignment that they submit to the seminar instructor in the final session. Throughout, we aim to expand instructors' perspectives about teaching with writing and to build their teaching repertoires. Our expedition model is intended to go beyond theory and advice in readings, examples, and discussions—to see and experience how writing instruction works on campus.

Faculty Learning and WAC Knowledge: A Brief Review of the Literature

Our research study builds upon important previous research about two key concepts. The first is faculty learning about teaching in general and about WAC in particular—what do faculty learn from participating in WAC faculty development programs? The second area of research that informs ours is what we call "WAC knowledge and practice"—that is, what constitutes key WAC instructional concepts and WAC consulting methods?

Even though one-time workshops about teaching and learning have long been staples in faculty development programs, including WAC programs, the semester- or year-long faculty learning community (FLC) model has proven to lead to far more learning and more change in actual teaching practices (Desrochers, 2010). As Beach and Cox (2009) defined them, "FLCs consist of a cross-disciplinary community of 8–12 faculty (and, sometimes, professional staff and graduate students) engaged in an active, collaborative, yearlong curriculum focused on enhancing and assessing undergraduate learning with frequent activities that promote learning, development, SoTL, and community" (p. 9). From a dissemination study about FLCs across six research-intensive or -extensive universities, Beach and Cox offered persuasive evidence that as a result of participating in a FLC, faculty incorporated into their teaching, for example, more active learning activities, student-centered learning, discussion, cooperative or collaborative learning, and writing. The faculty participants in FLCs reported gains in their own attitudes about teaching and in their students' learning and improvement in their own attitudes about teaching. Our research study gives us a chance to assess the power of a faculty learning community with a more specific WAC focus.

In what is still one of the most important research studies about faculty learning within and knowledge about WAC specifically, Walvoord, Hunt, Dowling, and McMahon (1997) conducted a groundbreaking longitudinal study of what faculty learned from participating in WAC programs. Walvoord et al. asked an open-ended question about what "WAC's role [is] in teacher-directed, multi-faceted, career-long development" (p. 16) of teachers. Built on deep respect for the complex career paths of disciplinary faculty, this study reminded us of the many factors that influence how WAC affects faculty. Because of those complex factors (for example, competing priorities for time, shifting teaching assignments, family responsibilities), we should never expect all instructors who participate in WAC programming to implement WAC principles and methods quickly and according to a particular orthodoxy. Thaiss and Zawacki (2006), too, examined the perspectives of faculty and students across disciplines as they learned to write within their disciplines and as they learned to teach writing. Their insights deepened our understanding of WAC learning in multiple sites, including the observation that disciplinary faculty often use the same terms, but mean radically different things.

In order to analyze the video data to see which WAC concepts our research participants demonstrated that they understood, we turned to both research and theory from the past decade that offered some clear centers of gravity about what constitutes core WAC principles and knowledge. In his study of 2101 assignments from courses across the disciplines at one hundred colleges and universities, Melzer (2014), for example, identified core WAC knowledge when he chose to analyze three main features of disciplinary assignments: rhetorical situation, genre, and discourse community. For most assignments in his sample, Melzer found limited purposes and audiences and genres (most often research papers or exams). As we will describe, our research participants had much more varied purposes and audiences and genres for the assignments they designed and discussed. Using data from the National Survey of Student Engagement, Anderson et al. (2015) identified three keys to designing WAC assignments that engage students: (1) "interactive writing processes," (2) "meaning-making tasks," and (3) "clear writing expectations" (pp. 206-07). As we will describe, the instructors in our study consistently focused on all three of these elements in the assignments they designed and discussed. In an important new study, *The Meaningful Writing Project*, Eodice, Geller, and Lerner (2017) also focused on students' experiences with writing assignments, asking students to describe a meaningful writing project and to explain what made that project meaningful to them. From 707 survey responses from seniors at three different universities, interviews with 27 of those seniors, surveys from 160 faculty who taught the courses for which those students wrote the projects, and interviews with 60 of those faculty, Eodice, Geller, and Lerner found that "meaningful writing projects offer students opportunities for agency; for engagement with instructors, peers, and materials; and for learning that connects to previous experiences and passions and to future aspirations and identities" (p. 4). The fact that in both Anderson et al. and in Eodice et al. *students*, from such a large number of universities, confirmed these hallmarks of engaging WAC assignments in these studies gives us confidence that these are important elements of core WAC knowledge for faculty to learn.

For a more theoretical perspective on WAC knowledge, we draw from Anson's (2015) "Crossing Thresholds: What's to Know about Writing Across the Curriculum." Anson identified six threshold or foundational concepts for WAC knowledge and practice, "concepts critical for continued learning and participation in an area or within a community of practice" (Adler-Kassner & Wardle, 2015, p. 2). The metaphor of threshold concepts, which by definition are initially troublesome and then transformative for those entering a new discipline, offers a powerful lens to analyze the multiple ways that our research participants demonstrated their understanding and application of core WAC knowledge. Anson drew his six WAC threshold concepts from "both the scholarly and the instructional literature on WAC" (p. 204). Within that literature these ideas appear so often, Anson explained, that "they have risen to the level of threshold concepts" (p. 204). Characteristic of WAC threshold concepts is a "metaknowledge that brings together fundamental principles of discipline-based communication with principles of writing instruction and support" (p. 204). According to Anson, understanding these intersections of knowledge requires:

1. defining writing as a disciplinary activity;
2. reconceptualizing the social and rhetorical nature of writing;
3. distinguishing between writing to learn and writing to communicate;
4. establishing shared goals and responsibilities for improvement;
5. understanding the situated nature of writing and the problem of transfer; and
6. viewing student writing developmentally. (p. 205)

We found that these specific WAC threshold concepts, which we explain in detail in our analysis below, offer a persuasive distillation of key WAC knowledge and a compelling way to interpret the rich data in our study.

In addition to knowledge about writing and teaching with writing embodied in Anderson et al. (2015, 2016) and in Anson's (2015) WAC threshold concepts, WAC consultants amass and hone expertise in the methods of consulting with others about writing and teaching. A range of work supports WAC practitioners as they develop this expertise (e.g., Anson, 2002; Bazerman et al., 2005; McLeod, 1988; McLeod et al., 2001). Among this work, Jablonski's *Academic Writing and Consulting in WAC: Methods and Models for Guiding Cross-Curricular Literacy Work* (2006) focused on developing "a systematic body of knowledge on how writing specialists actually negotiate, sustain, and assess successful relationships in CCL [cross-curricular literacy] contexts" (p. 4). Jablonski argued that WAC experts' skills at working across disciplines go beyond being friendly and collaborative and constitute a broader "procedural knowledge" that brings together knowledge of writing and rhetoric with pedagogical contexts across disciplines. What defines and complicates such consulting work is what Sandra Tarabochia (2013, 2016) examined in a number of studies of the interaction that occurs between WAC consultants and disciplinary faculty. Tarabochia focused on the role that language, power, and gender plays in the collaboration between disciplinary faculty and WAC experts. In her extensive study of and theorizing about CCL consulting work, *Reframing the Relational*, Tarabochia (2017) offered a powerful argument for basing that work on a pedagogical ethic, one that involves reflexive practice, reciprocal learning, negotiated expertise, change, and play. Our study follows both Jablonski and Tarabochia, focusing on interdisciplinary collaboration and interaction between the disciplinary faculty themselves as they participated in our ten-week seminar.

Research Design

In designing this IRB-approved study, we aimed to deepen our understanding of what works in interdisciplinary WAC faculty development. Analyzing seminar participants' survey responses and their interaction as they workshopped drafts of assignments, we sought to answer the following interrelated questions:

1. Which WAC concepts from the seminar do instructors report that they have learned?
2. Which WAC concepts do they apply in their assignment designs and in their discussion of instructor-peers' assignments?
3. What characterizes instructors' interaction in the workshops as they offer each other advice about draft writing assignments?
4. What are some of the limits of instructors' WAC knowledge?

This research design raises the important question of whether or not disciplinary instructor-participants in fact already knew these concepts before the seminar. We did not conduct a pre- and post-test to assess learning, and admittedly participants were likely to be motivated by a genuine interest in or even prior knowledge about teaching with writing that may have led them to enroll in this seminar in the first place. Although one of the participants was already familiar with John Bean's *Engaging Ideas*, almost all of the others were entirely new to these concepts. The instructor in this seminar clearly remembers from the weekly discussions that many of the principles participants reported learning were new to them. We also deliberately framed our first survey question to ask what participants believe they learned from the seminar and expeditions.

Participants

Table 1 provides basic demographic information about the ten participants in the seminar and research study. Participants came from a range of disciplines and phases of careers. Two of the participants were faculty (one in the Medical School and one in Astronomy), one a post-doc in biology, and one an instructional staff member in technology support services. Six were doctoral students (five of them teaching assistants—one was not yet teaching).

Table 1

Instructors Participating in This WAC Seminar and Research Study

Department	Teaching Position	Course Topic	Course Level	Course Size (# of Students)	Brief Description of Their Draft Writing Assignment
Comparative Literature	Graduate student	Literature & Theory	Advanced undergraduate	25	Exploratory paper: pose questions and explore answers by applying a theory to literary works; invites creative approaches and non-linear arguments
Biology	Post-doc	Science & Society	Intermediate undergraduate	20-25	Present both sides of a current scientific controversy and offer your opinion for an audience of scientists; then revised into a letter to the student newspaper
OBGYN, Medicine	Faculty	Disparities in health care	Introductory-level undergraduate	15	Critical thinking paper: evaluating factors that account for diverse opinions about what is fair and equal, fair and unequal

Department	Teaching Position	Course Topic	Course Level	Course Size (# of Students)	Brief Description of Their Draft Writing Assignment
Communication Arts	Graduate TA	Digital Design	Introductory-level undergraduate	20	Creating GIFs, memes, and posters using Photoshop—with critical reflection
Ethnobotany	Graduate TA	Ethnobotany	Advanced undergraduate	100	Scholarly literature review
Biology	Graduate TA	Environmental Toxicology	Graduate	15-20	Government report
Astronomy	Faculty	Intro to Astronomy	Introductory-level Undergraduate	30	Letter to students' home-town school board, urging that their high school incorporate the origin and evolution of the universe into the curriculum
Zoology	Graduate TA	Intro to Animal Development	Intermediate Undergraduate	115	Short reading responses and explanations of course concepts addressed to various audiences
Environmental Studies	Graduate TA	Environmental Studies Capstone	Advanced undergraduate	15	Critical reflections, addressed to next year's students
Academic Technology	Instructional staff	N/A—did not participate in workshop	N/A	N/A	N/A

Data Collection

We designed a mixed-methods study to triangulate toward understanding the knowledge that faculty develop from participating in a WAC seminar and the ways they use that knowledge (Johnson & Onwuegbuzie, 2004). To collect participants' self-reports of learning—including what they say they learned from, and thought of, the various learning activities in the seminar—we gave participants a brief survey (nine participants completed the survey) two weeks after completing the WAC seminar. We also videotaped the roughly one-hour peer workshops in which participants provided feedback to one another on their draft assignments. Nine of our participants engaged in this workshopping: three groups of three participants each, resulting in approximately three hours of video for analysis. This video data offers us insight into not only self-reported learning (as in the surveys) or the perceived products of learning (the assignment drafts themselves), but also the in-practice ways that groups of cross-disciplinary faculty talk about their own teaching with writing and how they engage with other faculty talking about writing. That is, the video allows us to interrogate how faculty put WAC knowledge into practice within interaction.

Data Analysis

In this article, we analyze (a) participants' self-reports of learning provided by the surveys and (b) the interaction around teaching with writing and designing writing assignments featured in the workshop video data. To analyze both the survey and video data, we first followed the open coding practices of grounded theory (Charmaz, 2006). We coded for WAC knowledge and interaction, including codes such as those we feature in the survey analysis section below: incorporating talk, process, and instruction; expanding repertoire and awareness of the variety of ways to incorporate writing; importance of and methods for giving effective feedback; understanding connections between writing and learning goals; incorporating peer review; learning about and using WAC resources; and discussing the importance of individual conferences. This open coding of survey results allowed us to offer a picture of instructors' self-reported learning (see Table 2)—and to keep those perceptions of learning grounded closely to participants' own responses. After performing open coding of our three hours of video from the assignment design workshops, we decided to further analyze the workshopping video by using Andersen et al.'s (2015, 2016) three major findings and Anson's (2015) six WAC threshold concepts. We organize our analysis into these categories—which represent centers of gravity in current WAC research. These categories offered an effective way to analyze much, but not all, of our data. For instance, to account for how some of our data exceeded categories developed from the WAC literature, our open coding approach led us to add the sections "WAC Consulting Methods" and "Complicating Our Claims: Why We Need a WAC Expert in the Room."

It is important to note that in our analysis of the video data, we focused on what we both perceived to be interesting trends in learning or implementation of WAC principles. These trends and moments from the workshops are not intended to represent learning for all seminar participants. Instead, they are compelling examples that most clearly reveal particularly evocative moments when participants draw on knowledge of WAC principles or use effective consulting methods. In our analysis, we did not pursue inter-rater reliability, but shared our open coding, came to agreements about survey codes, and then collaboratively determined that we would analyze the video using Andersen et al.'s (2015, 2016) and Anson's (2015) categories.

Survey Results: Instructors' Self-Reports of WAC Learning

One approach we took to answering our first research question was a straightforward one: after the seminar was over, participants responded to a twelve-item online survey (see Appendix B). After gathering some demographic information—about faculty roles and academic discipline, for example—the survey zeroed in on our primary research question, asking directly what participants had learned, from the seminar, about teaching with writing and which of these concepts, practices, or theories they planned to implement in future teaching. Other questions asked participants to evaluate how effective the design and various elements of the seminar were in helping them learn—we asked about particular readings, about the learning activities in the seminar, including the expeditions, and about the interdisciplinary group of participants. Nine of the ten participants who participated in the seminar completed surveys, and their responses to open-ended questions totaled about eleven pages of single-spaced text.

Concepts and Methods Learned

Table 2 summarizes, following our coding system, the responses to the first two questions—"What are 3 or 4 important things you've learned about teaching with writing through this course?" and "What are 2 or 3 concepts, practices, or theories from this course that you plan to implement in your future teaching?"

Table 2

Responses from Participants about What They Had Learned from the Seminar and Expeditions, Combining Responses to Survey Qs 1 and 2

Topics	Explanation and Sample Language from Respondents	# of responses across 2 questions
building process, interaction, and instruction into writing assignments	*scaffolding assignments, outlining, incorporating rewrites, intervening early, giving formative feedback, having discussions "to further projects"; "teaching with writing should be teaching the process of writing" (14 responses)* *peer review (5 responses)* *conferences (4 responses)*	23
expanding repertoire of assignments	*awareness of the great variety of ways to incorporate writing, especially short, low-stakes writing ("Writing assignments don't have to be long"); also writing for pre-discussion, multimodal assignments, discipline-specific assignments like posters and medical pamphlets ...*	11
giving effective, efficient feedback	*differentiating between broad and local issues, managing time, avoiding counter-productive feedback, developing a rubric in advance ...*	6
understanding connections between writing and learning goals and student engagement	"I first learned that writing is one of the most important course components leading to student engagement"	5

discovering and using WAC resources	for assignment design and WAC teaching (UW-Madison WAC faculty sourcebook, locally developed software for designing close-reading activities, Bean's *Engaging Ideas*...)	4
considering cultural dimensions of writing	awareness of contrastive rhetoric, for example, from Robertson (2005), *Writing Across Borders*	2
developing rhetorical understanding	understanding the importance of audience and purpose in writing	2

As shown in Table 2, in what were by far their most frequent responses, participants emphasized that they had learned how important it is to integrate process, interaction, and instruction into writing assignments, reflecting how central those topics were to the readings and discussions in the seminar and how visible these practices were in the expeditions. This strong emphasis on an interactive writing process aligns powerfully with findings from Anderson et al. (2015), which we discuss below in the analysis of video data. Given that the survey questions asked participants to identify *the most important things they had learned* from the seminar and the top concepts, practices, and theories that they planned to implement in their teaching, these responses clearly signal participants' growing understanding of process and social models of writing. Although they mentioned it less than half as often as the most common category of responses (11 times compared to 23), in their next most frequent responses, participants explained that they had expanded their repertoire of possible kinds of writing they can assign, including low-stakes WTL, WAC, WID, and multimodal assignments. A smaller number of responses (6) focused on feedback: respondents reported that they not only learned methods for developing evaluation criteria and responding to and evaluating student writing effectively but also learned to re-conceptualize feedback as a way to help students learn. And in five responses, seminar participants focused on something more theoretical that they had learned from the seminar and expeditions—they had learned to see writing activities as a means to help students learn the content of a course. As one instructor explained, "Teaching writing doesn't have to come at the expense of teaching material"; another asserted, "[W]riting greatly improves student engagement." In their lists, a few participants also reported that they had discovered a wealth of local and published resources for learning more about WAC and had come to appreciate cultural and rhetorical dimensions of writing. Taken as a whole, these survey responses create a vivid image of seminar participants' taking on some of the knowledge and the language of WAC consultants, which is especially impressive given that they are responding in their own words to open-ended questions, not choosing from a menu of options. In fact, many of their comments and explanations sound strikingly like the discourse of WAC professionals.

Valuing the WAC Expeditions

To understand how the WAC expeditions may have contributed to learning in the seminar, we asked participants which of the four expeditions—(a) interviewing a course coordinator or instructor in a writing-intensive course across the curriculum, (b) observing a writing center session, (c) watching video of one-to-one conferences of writing-intensive course instructors across the curriculum meeting with student-writers, or (d) observing a writing instructional session (e.g., peer-review workshop) within a writing-intensive course across the curriculum—was most beneficial and why. Respondents identified the interview with a writing-intensive course instructor as the most beneficial (5 responses), then the observation of writing instruction within a writing-intensive course (3 responses), and then the observation of a writing center tutorial (2 responses). One respondent said that all four were beneficial and "showed me new things." Their explanations of their rankings reveal genuine enthusiasm for what they learned from the expeditions and a variety of reasons for their rankings, illuminating just how varied learning goals can be for participants in a WAC seminar. One participant who identified observing a writing-intensive biology course session as the most beneficial explained, "Seeing Biocore [a writing-intensive honors biology sequence of three courses] in session was great. They seem to have a well-oiled machine of a class that actually teaches writing in an extremely integrated way." Another participant noted how crucial it is to have a discussion with an experienced course instructor in addition to visiting a class: "I liked having a discussion [with the course instructors] rather than just observing. The others were valuable, but without having read the assignment that was being discussed it was difficult to have the context to fully understand what was going on." A respondent who chose the observation of a writing center tutorial as the most beneficial explained why: "I really found the writing center session observation to be helpful. I plan to do a lot of one-on-one conferencing with students in the future, and it provided a really useful model (e.g., having the client read their writing out loud, and identify what they did well and what they could have done better)."

Valuing the Mixed Group of WAC Co-learners

When we asked how the mix and range of participants (graduate students, instructional staff, postdocs, and faculty from a variety of disciplines) influenced learning in the seminar, the respondents universally and enthusiastically endorsed having such a variety of participants in the WAC seminar. Most focused on the benefits of having participants with a wide range of teaching experience (from none to decades of experience), while a few focused on the benefits of cross-disciplinary discussion. As one respondent explained, "Multiple perspectives and a diversity of experience are key to enriching the types of discussions that we had. I didn't always agree with every view shared, but I appreciated them all." Another identified a valuable difference from discussions among instructors within a department: "It [the WAC seminar] disrupted the group-think that occurs in departments (i.e., this is how you teach this class—that's how we've always done it). The people in our course didn't have those assumptions, so it really opened up discussion." Several respondents explained how the mix of seminar participants mirrored the diversity of student perspectives within the courses they teach and how, within seminar discussions, instructors could be surrogates for varied student perspectives: ". . . [Having people from a variety of disciplines was useful because] we got to hear a wider variety of assignment planning ideas and think about how they would work in different types of classes (STEM people have to teach to a broad audience sometimes, like in a freshman seminar, and humanities people may have to discuss STEM-related topics)." "This [the varied levels and disciplines represented by seminar participants] was great. I teach students who tend to come from a variety of disciplines (and therefore a variety of writing styles/expectations), so having natural scientists and other non-humanists provided an opportunity to more deeply understand how different disciplines—and different minds—approach the writing task."

The Video Data: WAC Concepts and Methods in Interaction

The survey responses helped us answer our first research question in clear and convincing ways—the seminar participants reported that they had learned key WAC principles and methods. But too often in our experience survey responses are disappointingly thin. As researchers and as WAC professionals, we wanted to probe beyond brief written responses, to explore the depth and the limits of disciplinary instructors' knowledge of WAC. We wanted to explore how this developing WAC knowledge manifests itself through interaction among disciplinary instructors. We wondered how deeply our research participants had taken up these concepts, how they applied that knowledge in planning their courses and assignments, and how they used that knowledge as they interacted with each other in discussions about WAC assignments. To answer those additional research questions, we wanted to have a window into the unstructured talk of disciplinary instructors discussing their draft assignments and assignment sequences with seminar colleagues. To analyze this video data, we first used research findings from Anderson et al. (2015) to see which of their WAC constructs were in evidence in the workshop conversations. We then further analyzed the content of the video data through the lens of Anson's (2015) threshold concepts of WAC. We focused on the interactions among disciplinary instructors using concepts about procedural WAC knowledge from Jablonski (2006), and we close by analyzing some of the limitations of the WAC knowledge that disciplinary instructors displayed in these workshop conversations.

Evidence of WAC Knowledge: NSSE Findings

Recent WAC research based on student-engagement surveys offers an important lens for viewing what our WAC seminar participants learned from their seminar. From their extensive study of 72,000 students' responses to the writing questions in the National Survey of Student Engagement, Anderson, Anson, Gonyea, and Paine (2015,

2016) identified three keys—what they call "constructs"—for designing effective writing activities across the curriculum. Assignments engage undergraduate students and enhance student learning when they involve (a) "interactive writing processes" (Anderson, Anson, Gonyea, & Paine, 2015, p. 206); (b) "meaning-making tasks, such as ones that ask students to analyze, synthesize, apply or otherwise do more than just report" (p. 207); and (c) "clear writing expectations" (p. 207). To enhance student learning and development, Anderson, Anson, Gonyea, and Paine (2016) urge WAC/WID specialists to emphasize these three empirically supported strategies—over other familiar WAC principles—in their work with disciplinary faculty.

Anyone analyzing the workshop discussions of our WAC seminar participants could not miss how central *all three* of these constructs were within the discussions. The draft assignments themselves sounded, in fact, much like Anderson et al.'s (2015) "meaning-making tasks," and the instructors talked frequently about the challenging learning goals they had for their assignments, using the language of analysis, synthesis, application, argument, and critical thinking. One of the draft assignments from an introductory astronomy course, for example, called for students to persuade a skeptical public school board to incorporate into the high-school curriculum some instruction about the big bang, dark matter, and black holes. As they offered advice to each other about ways to revise draft assignments and as instructors planned their revisions, the seminar participants frequently talked about incorporating into their assignments more interactive writing processes, such as in-class workshops about preliminary ideas, conferences with the instructor, or peer reviews. For an assignment in a toxicology course, workshop participants suggested that the instructor incorporate a complex two-stage peer review with different kinds of readers who represent different audiences for the paper assignment. No doubt echoing readings from the seminar and discussions, seminar participants frequently used an umbrella term—"scaffolding"—as a shorthand to refer to the stages, instruction, and interaction they were building into their writing activities.

The third construct—clear writing expectations (Anderson et al., 2015)—also figured prominently in their workshop discussions: the participants consistently asked questions about what instructors were looking for in an assignment, and they pushed each other to clarify instructions in assignments. In one workshop group, for example, a medical professor asked a biology instructor whose draft assignments required students to revise a six-page scientific paper into a two-page letter, "In going from the 6-page down to the letter, can you enunciate what you're looking for?" In another workshop group, as they discussed a series of reflection assignments for a senior capstone course in environmental studies, a colleague pushed for more precision in the assignments, suggesting a much clearer and more focused central question. In response to such questions and suggestions from colleagues, instructors regularly articulated plans for revising their assignments to clarify their expectations for students, to add examples to illustrate what they were asking for, to add additional questions to promote the kind of analysis they wanted, and to make their rubrics more specific in order to convey their expectations more explicitly. Given the variety of topics and the fluid movement among them within such long conversations, it's difficult to say for sure that they learned to prioritize those constructs above all other kinds of WAC knowledge and expertise, but those three constructs were cardinal topics throughout the workshop discussions.

Evidence of WAC Knowledge: WAC Threshold Concepts

"Writing in a discipline reflects the ways that knowledge is produced there" (Anson, 2015, p. 205). Of Anson's six WAC threshold concepts, "writing as a disciplinary activity" is one of the most salient within the workshop discussions. We found no shortage of examples of this disciplinary awareness. For example, when a postdoc in biology was designing an assignment for intermediate biology students to translate scientific concepts to public audiences, she explicitly identified a goal to bridge the gap between sciences and the public—highlighting her awareness of disciplines' insider language. Similarly, a medical school professor workshopping assignments with a humanities graduate student new to teaching referred to the writing center tutorial she observed in Expedition #2 for our seminar to make sense of disciplinary differences in writing assignments. The professor observed a philosophy student discussing a "non-traditional format" that she thought might be a model for the humanities graduate student instructor's assignment development.

While these are important moments of disciplinary awareness, we observed that workshop participants did not always fully or explicitly grapple with what disciplinary differences show up in writing—or consider how we may support students writing in our respective disciplines. As WAC experts know, making disciplinary differences in discourse apparent to disciplinary faculty is one of our primary challenges. Anson reminded us that this process is so challenging because much of "faculty members' extensive discourse knowledge resides at a level of behavioral consciousness" (p. 206). That is, "many faculty in academic disciplines don't routinely reflect on what they do to perform effectively: they 'know how' but don't always 'know that' (Ryle, 1949)" (as cited in Anson, 2015, p. 206)—that is, they don't explicitly know that writing relies on disciplinary conventions and epistemologies. One problem with disciplinary writing knowledge and conventions remaining tacit, of course, is the unchecked assumption of "good writing" being constant across disciplines and contexts.

The following excerpt features steps toward understanding this foundational threshold concept, but also some limits of that understanding. This discussion occurred between three teaching assistant instructors across disciplines (A in communication arts; B in ethnobotany; C in toxicology):

B: Something that I struggle with . . . inevitably students submit these "paper-parade" papers where it's just chronological introducing papers they've reviewed. So, teaching them to synthesize this stuff, I don't know how to effectively do that.

A: Cool. Right. And synthesis is kind of the core part of the assignment because it's, it's mostly lit review, or?

B: Yeah.

A: Okay, okay.

B: Yeah, but it's like they're completely oblivious to that even if we say it. Because it's just, maybe they don't know what it looks like to do.

A: Yeah.

C: Would it help to have them submit some kind of, like, thesis statement that forces them into some sort of synthesis instead of just, like, "Here's everything we know about this topic"?

B: Mmm...hmmm... "the data dump" [reference to Bean]

C: Yeah

A: I'll add, for me as an undergrad, I mean, I was in the social sciences. So this might be different, but it was helpful just to get, just to hear, number one that I wasn't supposed to just list it and number two, just to kind of like say like I have all of these articles and then to group them, so that each paragraph was like a group—so just looking for commonalities in your articles, like these four talk about this, but these four plus one mentioned in this group talk about this.

B: Oh yeah. I like that. [writes down notes]

A: Because then maybe it kind of gets you to the point where you're ready to make an argument. You start to see patterns emerging.

C: That might be a good like alternative to the outline.

A: Oh yeah! Totally.

C: Or, like, a version of an outline that's different than just, like, introduction, first point about whatever. Because I know that Bean was not really a big fan of starting out with an outline.

B: Oh yeah.

C: And I know that as a student, I don't like being told I have to start with an outline because I have to know what the paper's going to look like before I write it. So, if it was like starting out with grouping your different resources somehow...

B: That's a good idea [nodding, writing down notes]

C: ...like concept mapping. Instead of an a, b, c outline.

When Instructor B noted that "maybe they just don't know what it looks like" to synthesize published articles in a review like the one he assigns, he importantly challenged the notion that writing moves are transparent and equivalent across disciplines and contexts. From there, the three instructors worked together to strategize how to make synthesis attainable for student writers: that is, they emphasized how to support students "knowing how" and "knowing that." Much more than a transparent skill, synthesis, Instructor A clarified, is a "core part"—or a learning goal of the genre of a literature review that requires scaffolded support. Instructor C suggested guiding students toward synthesis by having them submit "some kind of like thesis statement," moving them from what Instructor B earlier referred to as John Bean's (2011) "all about" or "data dump" versions of papers (p. 27). Instructor A drew on her experience as a student herself, receiving explicit instruction in how to write literature reviews by grouping and making connections between various sources.

Beyond making writing moves like synthesis understandable to students, Instructor A encouraged the group to consider how synthesis is specific to disciplines, noting her own experience as an undergraduate "in the social sciences"—which, she reasoned, "might be different" than Instructor B's context of ethnobotany. Instructor A's suggestion of disciplinary differences is not one the group takes up explicitly: they do not discuss how their relative disciplines define "synthesis" or the genre of the literature review. Still, the three instructors are clearly talking about the kind of rhetorical work that needs to be done in effective writing and communication in the sciences and social sciences.

"Writing is a social and rhetorical activity" (Anson, 2015, p. 206). As Anson explains, WAC faculty as professionals within a discipline "know tacitly that when they write, they are usually participating in a socially rich activity system designed to convey and negotiate meaning" (pp. 206–207). But because of the imperatives for assessment within higher education, Anson argues, these same faculty often strip rhetorical context out of the assignments they give students. In response, "WAC leaders take great pains to help faculty to imagine more authentic kinds of writing situations and audiences" (p. 205) for their students' assignments. Within the draft assignments and the workshop discussions in our study, authentic writing situations and sophisticated discussions of audiences abounded. Instructors in this WAC seminar chose particular situations in order to focus communication tasks and to give students opportunities to use their developing expertise about course content to communicate what they know with *non-expert* audiences, as recommended in the Boyer Commission report on *Reinventing Undergraduate Education* (1998). They also created specific rhetorical situations to motivate students to care about their writing, which was a prominent concern in all of the workshop discussions, by making assignments more relevant to students' future professional work. Even if these instructors used the term *rhetoric* only occasionally and never used the term *social* to characterize their understanding of writing, it's clear that they were in the process of passing through this particular threshold WAC concept.

Most compelling about these workshop discussions of rhetorical situations and audiences were the varied and complex concepts of audience within their WAC assignments. In the case of the draft writing assignments for a graduate course in toxicology, the instructor explained that she has created a professional rhetorical situation and audience to motivate students who are not toxicology majors to care about the assignment and the course content. In the workshop conversation about this draft assignment, a colleague zeroed in on audience, asking "Can you talk [with us] about who the audience is?"—a question that led to the recommendation, mentioned above, about building in two stages of peer review for two different audiences. For an environmental studies capstone course built around a community-service project, the professor designed a series of writing-to-learn reflection assignments. With those assignments, whose audience typically would be the student-writer and the course professor, the instructor wanted to persuade students to be honestly critical about their often less-than-ideal experiences with community projects. The instructor felt that students understandably were reluctant to express their disappointments with projects and with the course. One suggestion from the workshop group was to define the audience for this reflection piece as students who will take the course the following year, so that students would be offering advice to a familiar audience in the form of an advice letter, and their role would be defined as helping future peers rather than criticizing the course. For a communications course in digital design, the instructor wanted students to design a poster about the course itself; the poster would be used to recruit future students into the course and into a new minor. In the WAC seminar workshop discussion of this draft assignment, disciplinary instructors had a nuanced discussion about the rhetorical situation and multiple audiences for these posters. For an intermediate-level course on animal biology, an instructor designed a 100-word low-stakes assignment asking students to explain a biological concept to a friend. As a different workshop group discussed an assignment for an introductory astronomy course, mentioned above—a letter to the school board advocating for including key astronomy topics in the school curriculum—the workshop participants offered impressive insights into the complexities of having students write for dual audiences of the imagined school board *and* of the course professor who was checking students' understanding of course concepts. But, as we explain below, their discussion fell short of demonstrating a sophisticated understanding of what Anson and Dannels (2004) call "conditional rhetorical space."

"Writing can be a tool for learning or communicating" (Anson, 2015, p. 207). Anson's third WAC threshold concept addresses the well-known, "somewhat oversimplified but instructive distinction between writing to learn and learning to write" (p. 207) and the ways that both may be productively integrated into instruction. For disciplinary faculty new to WAC tenets, WTL, in particular, offers a new and exciting tool for deepening students' learning. Low-stakes writing assignments ask students to explore questions, synthesize ideas, respond to readings and ideas, refine their thinking, or otherwise grapple with course content. As such, Anson notes that WTL helps reinforce how writing need not "intrud[e] on coverage" of course content, "but becom[es] a way to ensure it" (p. 209).

While instructors in our workshop did not use the specific language or labels of "writing to learn" or "writing to communicate," their assignments demonstrated that they had internalized both strategies for teaching with writing. One instructor in toxicology, for example, was drafting a WTC assignment for graduate students to learn to write reports in a genre required for their future professional lives. Of course, many other assignments discussed by seminar participants combined elements of WTL and WTC, too. For instance, as mentioned above, a communication arts TA was planning to have students in a digital media course compose posters but also to do reflective writing on the process of creating those posters, a process that included learning to use Photoshop and other tools. In particular, though, one group demonstrated a strong commitment to WTL—a biology TA, for example, developed an assignment in which undergraduate students must write a series of short assignments explaining course concepts to lay audiences—parents, friends, etc. An environmental studies TA designed a series of reflection essays for students involved in a service course. A medical school professor likewise asked students to reflect in writing assignments about health inequity.

"Improvement of writing is a shared responsibility" (Anson, 2015, p. 209). When it comes to the curricular and pedagogical projects of WAC, no threshold concept seems more foundational than this: "[t]he entire WAC movement is founded on a belief that teachers of all subjects share responsibility for supporting the development of advanced student literacies" (p. 209). As all WAC specialists know, it's easy for faculty to resist accepting this responsibility—for a variety of reasons. But it is abundantly clear that the participants in our study have passed through this threshold concept and embraced this shared responsibility. Although in the workshop discussions no one said, "I know that it's my responsibility as a botanist to teach my students to think and write within my discipline," they in effect said so—over and over—through their actions.

The instructors signaled their responsibility by planning specific ways to revise and improve their assignments. The astronomy professor crystallized this responsibility in a striking comment: "Having graded these [papers in response to her assignment] recently, I now see every single thing I did wrong [in the design of my assignment]." The instructors displayed a strong commitment to clarifying their assignments, to detailed planning to incorporate interaction and scaffolding and discussions of model papers with future students, and to building in peer review. When the medical school professor, for example, explained that the undergraduate students in her course on health disparities did not understand the difference between *inequality* and *inequities*, she clearly saw it as her responsibility to teach this, so she designed a writing assignment and planned discussions to help students understand and to think critically about these concepts. Then she planned a reflection paper after the formal assignment to help students consolidate their learning. Similarly, in the discussion quoted above, when an instructor from an ethnobotany course wanted his students to learn how to synthesize published literature—that is to find commonalities and differences across published literature instead of writing what he called a "paper parade"—his workshop colleagues all eagerly brainstormed ways to design an assignment that would involve grouping research studies and concept mapping, looking for commonalities, and students submitting a draft thesis statement that "synthesizes," "that makes a point." No shirking of responsibility for advanced literacy instruction here. When our research participants did choose to limit responsibility, they were responding to the realities of instructors' workloads. While some of the courses under discussion were small (10–15 students), another, a biology course, was growing from 60–100 students with no increase in instructional staff. So understandably—and appropriately—these instructors acknowledged the limits of what any individual instructor can do and collaborated to look for efficiencies as they limited how many drafts and how many conferences they would require in such situations.

"**Writing in all contexts involves situated learning, challenging the 'transfer' of ability**" (Anson, 2015, p. 211). A corollary of almost all of the other WAC threshold concepts identified by Anson, this threshold concept—that because writing involves situated learning, student-writers often struggle to transfer what they have learned about writing in one context to a new one—has deep roots in theories and research about discourse communities and about the challenges that writers face when they transition into new writing situations or discourse communities, ones in which they are, in Joseph Williams' (1991) terms, not yet "socialized." In recent research, this concept has become known as *the problem of transfer*—the difficulty that both student and expert writers have when they write in new disciplines, in new genres, at new levels, for unfamiliar audiences. If WAC faculty recognize "that no amount of prior knowledge from a generalized composition course will help students know how to cope with new genres...," faculty consequently "understand the need to support students' writing experiences in every course, especially courses that involve unfamiliar genres and methods of discourse production" (Anson, p. 211).

Within their workshop groups, the instructors in our study demonstrated a limited understanding of this WAC threshold concept. They consistently recognized that many student writers struggle to do the intellectual tasks at the heart of various assignments and, as discussed above, they planned instruction to help students learn how to do those tasks. With the assignment for a comparative-literature course—a deliberately very open-ended assignment, one in which the instructor invited students to write a non-linear or creative kind of paper—the workshop group members peppered the instructor with clarifying questions ("When you say, 'Discuss two texts,' will students know what you mean? Might you want to be more precise about what you mean?" "What's your experience with students and non-traditional formats?" "Have you thought about scaffolding?"), questions that stem no doubt from their perception that student writers are likely to struggle to figure out this genre and the expectations for such an open-ended assignment. Despite this helpful push for clarification and support in the assignment, the questions and recommendations do not seem to be motivated by a deeper understanding of the challenges students will have with transfer from previous writing experience and instruction. The seminar participants never use the language of transfer, nor do they refer to students' previous writing instruction. As is typical of most instructors, these focus on their courses and assignments as autonomous. This finding is probably not surprising, given the content of the seminar. Although the seminar focused quite a bit of attention on viewing writers developmentally (with, for example, repeated discussions about which kinds of assignments were appropriate for different levels; see the next section of our analysis), the seminar did not focus specifically on the problem of transfer across courses and disciplines.

However, one exception—one fascinating moment when this threshold concept burst into the open—occurred when a medical-school professor was discussing her students' disappointing performance on a recent mid-term essay exam in a first-year seminar on health disparities. In this discussion, she explicitly traced her students' problems with her writing assignment to their misapplying or overgeneralizing advice they had received from an instructor in a prior writing course. In this excerpt, Instructor E is from the Medical School, and Instructor D is from biology.

E: So, I said to my students, if you have any insight into why this [the exam writing] is particularly difficult, please tell me. A gal came right up to me, and she said, "I had a writing instructor who told me that when you write, you should pick one topic and discuss it really well." Well, you're supposed to, in an exam, be showing me that you know *everything*

D: [nodding] Uh, hmm.

E: that I taught you. That was common sense to her, I think—it seemed a little bizarre to me—but I bet you a whole bunch of the students were on the same page. And then, as I thought about it, you know, nobody necessarily says at the outset that there are going to be very different kinds of writing.

D: Uh, hmm

E: There is the narrative. There is the rhetorical. There is [sic] variations for the public—who's your audience, who's your audience, who's your audience?

D: Right.

E: And, and I see this when we're recruiting [for the medical school], and when students write for professional school and for graduate school, oftentimes they consider themselves their audience. And they're especially pretty bad, you know, and it goes to what do I want you to say, what do I want you to know about me, you know, and then it comes to personality.... So, lots of students want to write a story. They use a middle-school model: has a beginning, middle, and end, and a theme. And nobody told 'em that that's not how you write professionally.

It's remarkable to see this professor illustrate her point with two very different examples at different stages of students' undergraduate studies, to hear her insightful observation that "nobody necessarily says [to students] at the outset that there are going to be very different kinds of writing," and to hear her subsequently coin the phrase "writing across a [student's undergraduate] career" to describe the experience students have as they write in varied disciplines and genres. There seems to be no doubt that at least one WAC seminar participant had internalized the WAC threshold concept of the problem of negative writing transfer.

"**Writing is highly developmental**" (Anson, 2015, p. 212). Anson's last WAC threshold concept emphasizes writing as developed over time, always building on "prior experience" (p. 212). As Anson summarizes, "learning to write effectively requires slow, steady development over many years of (diverse) practice" and "it continues to develop across the span of people's lives" (p. 212). WAC experts enact this well-known principle by making writing development visible to the faculty with whom we work: to shift "attention away from the writing itself and toward the development of the writer's knowledge, ability, and expertise at a particular learning or career stage" (p. 212). This threshold concept also reminds WAC experts and disciplinary faculty of students' diverse literacy backgrounds. Multilingual writers, students with disabilities, students with more or less access to literacy preparation all enrich and influence—in important ways—our pedagogical decisions.

Seminar participants demonstrated that they had internalized this threshold concept at a number of levels. As we have illustrated above, throughout their workshop discussions instructors were especially attentive to building in scaffolding and process-oriented tasks to support students in the incremental, challenging tasks of writing. Instructors frequently commented on their own—and other instructors'—work to "scaffold" assignment tasks. "I like how you sequence this, not just with due-dates, but with the logical progression/sequence for research" a botany TA responded to a TA designing a graduate-level toxicology assignment. Shortly after, he added that the assignment was especially well-suited for motivating students at a particular level. In the same workshop discussion, a communication arts TA told the botany TA that she "loves" the "timeline, and all of the opportunities for feedback" built into his assignment, which she saw as "steps reinforcing it [writing] as a process." Later the botany TA commented that his course has, to this point, not taught "writing as a process enough." Certainly, an instructor's desire to support students' process demonstrates an understanding of writing as developmental. Likewise, the same workshop group noted how students have a "huge variation in their preparation," as the botany TA put it, making it difficult to know how to pitch one's instruction: "to the lowest common denominator? The middle?" A particularly interesting discussion of "levels" was initiated by the medical school professor who, in the excerpt quoted above, observed that in addition to variations in writing across the curriculum, students will need different kinds of preparation and will be asked to work in a variety of genres across their professional lives.

WAC Consulting Methods

In addition to demonstrating that they knew and could deploy threshold concepts of WAC, seminar participants also employed productive consulting methods within their workshop conversations, methods that sound exactly like WAC professionals. Though these kinds of interpersonal approaches may seem characteristic of and necessary for any collegial discussion, we observed that participants consistently asked probing questions to understand their colleagues' complex instructional contexts, focused on learning goals, listened actively and critically, reinforced their peers' ideas, offered suggestions and cautions and encouragement, and demonstrated genuine interest in each other's teaching challenges. Virtually every workshop discussion began with inquiry into the pedagogical context for and specifics of colleagues' assignments, including information about class size, level of students, and more. Seminar participants went on to ask pointed questions to help colleagues refine assignment design, learning goals, and evaluation criteria. In a discussion of a comparative literature graduate student's (who had not yet taught) assignment design, a biology postdoc and veteran teacher and a medical school professor offered generative guiding questions: "Have you thought about scaffolding? How long would you give them to work on this?" the biology postdoc asked. "What's your experience with students and nontraditional formats?" the medical school professor asked, and later, "Are you going to have any peer evaluation?"

Alongside constructive questions, seminar participants also frequently offered concrete, specific praise—reinforcing what they appreciated about one another's pedagogy and simultaneously reinforcing many of the threshold concepts of WAC. Before leading in to the questions about scaffolding mentioned above, the biology postdoc first noted how much she appreciated the comparative literature graduate student's creative assignment design: "I like how you allow a lot of creativity, open… allow non-traditional…really allows students to feel ownership." "I love your built-in revision"; "I like how you sequence this, not just with due-dates, but with the logical progression, sequence for research," a biology instructor said to a toxicology instructor. "Progression is awesome; rhetorical situation is awesome. I dig," a communication arts instructor concurred. The same botany instructor, in fact, admired the communication arts instructor's organized and creative approach to writing assignments so much that he asked for a copy of her syllabus for his own future reference, even though he was in a significantly different discipline.

In their interactions with disciplinary faculty, WAC consultants do other important work: they often empathize with colleagues and acknowledge heavy teaching workloads and other teaching challenges. That empathetic work is central to the relationship-building required of WAC consults. The WAC consultant, however, must move from acknowledgement of challenges to problem-solving. We noted one particular interaction between workshop participants that compellingly did that complex work. Just as WAC experts need to do, workshop participants acknowledged challenges and then helped fellow instructors productively move on to address those challenges. The following excerpt features this generative balance between commiseration and problem-solving necessary in teaching and in WAC consultation work.

In addition to developing helpful strategies to encourage students' learning, this group of three graduate-student instructors (A in communication arts, B in ethnobotany, C in toxicology) strove to keep teaching workloads manageable:

A: Ooh yeah, yeah! And then maybe turning in at that stage in the project, turning in the thesis or the argument would be useful. So, just a one sentence, that's easy for you to grade then.

C: Yeah–that's easy to grade, one sentence!

A: Right

B: All of that, less grading!

A: Right?! If higher education has taught me nothing else . . . [laughing]

B: Right, just getting by with the bare minimum. That's the lesson that's taught to these students. These are all seniors, so they know how to skate by . . .

C: Well, yeah, they know how to skate by, but they also know, hopefully, how to read literature, kind of, no, not really . . . ?

B: Eh, unfortunately, there's such a huge range. That's what we've noticed is that some of them don't know what this looks like, and some of them really do, so I don't know if we should teach to the lowest common denominator, the middle, or?

C: Do you let them choose their groups?

B: Ah, yes. So that might make sense to mix it up based on experience.

C: I don't know how you would measure that ahead of time, but?

A: Maybe fill out a questionnaire? What other ethnobotany, botany classes have you taken? Are you a science major or a humanities major?

B: Well yeah, that's legit because half of them are . . .

C: And then that could be helpful to pair them with different experiences. And I know you were in some of the Biocore observations [Expedition 1 & 4], they do that—choose the groups, and I think that works well for them. I mean it's smaller classes, but . . .

B: And since ethnobotany is innately kind of a crossover discipline, there are going to be anthro students and bio students. And so, it would be cool to put them together and they can kind of create a new fusion, anew each time.

A: Totally. They can teach each other in the process!

Right after Instructor C mentions concept-mapping as one teaching strategy, Instructor A points back to Instructor C's initial suggestion—to "force" students to make some kind of synthesis, by turning in a one-sentence thesis or argument. Not only will that one sentence assignment move students toward synthesis, it will be relatively easy to grade.

It is clear throughout this excerpt that commiseration—about workload, about scarcity of resources, about perceived difficulty with students' preparation, etc.—was cathartic and generative for these teaching assistants. But what kept this commiseration from devolving into "student-bashing" or aimless complaining was the instructors' quick turn to problem-solving. For instance, when Instructor B suggested that seniors "know how to skate by," Instructor C immediately countered that they have also learned "how to read." Instructor B identified another problem: the range of student preparation. In turn, Instructor C asked how groups were assigned, drawing on her experience from an Expedition in the seminar to suggest that Instructor B could help form groups. Instructor A added that questionnaires may help group students by disciplines and experience with scientific writing. In turn, Instructor E re-saw that disciplinary diversity as a "cool" "fusion." And Instructor A noted how students with these diverse disciplinary experiences may come to "teach each other in the process." This reframing moved student problems into possibilities. WAC principles, here, were not part of the wider problems experienced by instructors—scarcity of resources, unreasonable workload—but simply best practices for teaching and learning. They were part of the solution and an asset in managing scarce resources and heavy workloads.

Complicating Our Claims: Why We Need a WAC Expert in the Room

Although the evidence we discuss above compellingly demonstrates how disciplinary faculty—especially the ones more experienced with WAC and with teaching in general—take on WAC knowledge and practice some of the pedagogical ethic that Tarabochia (2017) identifies in the methods of cross-curricular literacy professionals, we want to complicate any easy conclusions about the role of WAC consultants or the knowledge and actions of disciplinary faculty. In fact, observing disciplinary faculty take on WAC knowledge and consulting roles has further reinforced for us how unique and valuable the skill-sets of WAC specialists really are. In this way, we agree with Jablonski's (2006) conclusion that "in addition to their 'content' knowledge of rhetorical theory and composition pedagogy," WAC experts "possess a certain procedural knowledge of application" (p. 131)—that is, they know how to apply that knowledge to cross-disciplinary pedagogical needs. And like Jablonski, we assert that WAC specialists sometimes undersell their expertise when they assume that "nonwriting specialists can apply these pedagogical guides, or our more specialized published scholarship, without much difficulty" (p. 6). We found in our data that disciplinary faculty did have some noticeable limits in applying WAC knowledge and consulting practices. Below, we discuss three areas in which a WAC consultant's absence has clear consequences.

Erasing disciplinary differences. Even while seminar participants take on consulting roles and demonstrate their uptake of powerful WAC knowledge, they also often fail to appreciate fully some of the disciplinary differences in discourse. For instance, as Thaiss and Zawacki (2006) found, faculty often appeared to be using a shared vocabulary when they were discussing student writing but were, in fact, erasing disciplinary differences through ostensibly shared vocabulary. In one of this seminar's workshop discussions, illustrated in the excerpt analyzed above, when the three instructors spoke of "synthesis," what exactly did they mean? While the communication arts instructor acknowledged that her background was in the social sciences, the other two instructors in the physical and life sciences did not discuss their varied definitions of and experience with "synthesis." Not explicitly or deeply engaging with disciplinary differences no doubt also limits these instructors' abilities to consider how their students' previous learning about synthesis might transfer into doing these new assignments and might transfer beyond their particular courses and assignments. Concern about transfer is exactly the kind of knowledge that WAC consultant experts would likely bring to this conversation.

Similarly, within the workshop discussions among a new graduate student in comparative literature (who had not yet taught) and two experienced instructors (a postdoc in biology and a medical school professor), we observed how a clear disconnect occurred when they talked about a literary analysis assignment so central in the humanities. The instructors from the sciences seemed to understand "analysis" differently, and none of the instructors acknowledged any of these differences. These two veteran science instructors asked the humanities graduate student a series of questions about her assignment, warning her against risks of vagueness in directions. But their examples always referred to labs and science, never demonstrating any understanding of genres of literary analysis and rhetorical moves made in that field or fully appreciating this instructor's intentional choice to have students be creative in their interpretations of assignments and approaches to papers.

Not fully grappling with complexities of key WAC principles. Just as they sometimes conflated writing terms or overlooked disciplinary differences, seminar participants also sometimes failed to fully grapple with the complexities of WAC principles or threshold concepts. In his discussion of threshold concepts, Anson (2015) warned that reductive uptake can reduce subtle understandings of writing and learning to catchphrases. We observed participants talking around an important issue or WAC principle, but not quite pinning down or demonstrating full understanding of its meaning. For instance, instructors were often enamored of creating a rhetorical situation for their assignments—of invoking a "real" audience. However, pressing on that goal, we find a number of gaps and questions. When the astronomy professor's assignment asked students to write a letter to a school board, for example, many details of that rhetorical situation remained underdeveloped, potentially confusing students.

How well will students, for instance, understand the genre of a professional letter? What are the characteristics of school board audiences?

This example highlights how disciplinary faculty take up a WAC principle (Anson's [2015] threshold concept "Writing is a Social and Rhetorical Activity," for example) but then—without the support of a WAC specialist—fail to fully grapple with the complexities and implications of that approach to teaching writing. As Anson and Dannels (2004) observe, disciplinary faculty often end up creating "hybrid genres" and "conditional rhetorical space"—the complex and confusing results of assignments that mix "external or professional audiences and rhetorical situations" with "the more conventional-assessment-driven" assumptions of classroom contexts (Anson, 2015, p. 207). The result, for students, is a need to "navigate complex sets of expectations" as they understand their audience as both the teacher and an "imagined or sometimes real external audience" (207). Within their discussions, the disciplinary faculty in our study rarely considered some of these complexities.

Limiting feedback to an incremental level. Looking at these workshop discussions at a macro level, we observed that most of these discussions and recommendations were what we would call incremental: they focused on tweaks to existing assignment plans, and participants typically offered small suggestions. All of that feedback was genuinely helpful—and possibly all that was necessary. But missing in these discussions was what a WAC specialist might have offered in some cases—the intentional consideration of entirely different kinds of writing activities and assignments for achieving learning goals. In a recent WAC consultation, one of the authors of this article, for example, after lengthy discussion, encouraged a biomedical engineering professor to consider shifting from a major formal WID or WTC assignment due at the end of a course (a course in which there had previously been no writing assignments at all) to lower-stakes, informal, brief WTL writing assignments, done several times during the semester, for familiar audiences (such as fellow students who misunderstood an equation) to check and deepen understanding of key course concepts, which was a primary teaching-and-learning concern of the professor. This kind of consultant work no doubt requires the breadth of knowledge that WAC professionals have and the deep repertoire of the kinds of assignments and approaches in the process of consulting work that experienced WAC professionals have developed. Certainly, it also involves power relationships in some of the ways that Tarabochia discusses (2013, 2016). In a peer review, who has the authority to raise a big question that might suggest wholesale revisions or very different approaches? Unlike instructor peers, experienced WAC professionals may bring to their conversations with disciplinary faculty an authority as well as the experience to suggest more broad-based changes to assignments than we saw the disciplinary faculty offering in these assignment workshop discussions.

Implications and Closing Thoughts

Taken as a whole, our research provides evidence for how disciplinary faculty may take on WAC knowledge and interaction—acting as surrogate WAC consultants. In addition, we hope that this research study serves as a persuasive form of assessment for this model of WAC faculty development—a sustained, semester-long, interdisciplinary, mixed graduate-student and faculty cohort model of a faculty learning community focused on WAC, with excursions to observe and interact with WAC classes and instructors and to observe writing center consultations. As all WAC professionals know, creating and sustaining this kind of learning community requires substantial time both for the WAC program professionals who design and lead it *and* for the faculty and graduate students who participate, so it's important to demonstrate that this model of faculty development leads participants to understand and apply central WAC knowledge and principles. In our analysis of workshopping discussions of draft assignments, we found extensive evidence of in-depth conversations that crossed disciplines reasonably well, of collaborative problem-solving, of active listening, and of the learning that occurs in faculty learning communities (Beach & Cox, 2009; Desrochers, 2010). In their survey responses and in their conversations about the assignments they designed, instructors focused on links between writing and learning, learning goals for assignments, specific audiences and rhetorical situations for writing, disciplinary differences, multiple genres both formal and informal, student learning and developmental perspectives, interactive processes and scaffolding, ways to anticipate common problems, and approaches to increase student motivation. It's also important to recognize, as we have outlined, some of the limits of the knowledge that disciplinary faculty demonstrated.

We also hope that our theoretical approach—defining core WAC knowledge and principles by using the latest research about WAC assignments (Anderson, Anson, Gonyea, & Paine, 2015, 2016; Geller, Eodice, & Lerner, 2017; Melzer, 2014) and Anson's (2015) articulation of threshold concepts of WAC—avoids some of the risks of imposing a "WAC orthodoxy" that Walvoord et al. (1997) warned about and offers new directions for research about faculty learning in WAC. And we hope that our mixed methods—especially the video analysis of disciplinary faculty workshopping their draft assignments to augment survey results—offers valuable approaches for future research about faculty learning about WAC. In this case, the evidence of WAC learning that we see in the workshop discussions about draft assignments not only confirms the reliability of self-reports of learning in the surveys but also allows us to deepen our analysis beyond what surveys alone provide.

Like all research, this study raises intriguing new questions, ones that we are eager to explore ourselves and to have other WAC researchers pursue. Some of those questions involve more fine-grained analysis of the disciplinary faculty workshop conversations about their draft assignments: How often, for example, do the conversations move toward more complex understandings of WAC concepts? When that happens, what leads to sustained conversation and deeper understanding? What would happen to these workshop conversations about draft assignments if a WAC specialist participated along with the instructors? And most of our questions for future research require more longitudinal or follow-up case studies, some focusing on application and others on retention of WAC concepts: What, if anything, did instructors do with the suggestions that arose in their workshop conversations? What happens when instructors encounter inevitable roadblocks in their use of writing activities in their courses? To what extent do instructors retain this WAC knowledge beyond the seminar? Does some knowledge persist more than other types? In what ways do instructors use their WAC knowledge to influence colleagues within their disciplines as surrogate WAC consultants?

But before we try to address some of those questions, as WAC program directors *and* as WAC researchers we found it heartening to discover in our study persuasive evidence that disciplinary faculty engaged in our hands-on, intensive WAC seminar do indeed understand and apply many WAC threshold concepts. In framing these workshop participants as surrogate WAC consultants, we hope to underscore one of the central underpinnings of WAC work: WAC demands a blend of knowledge between, as Anson (2015) explains, the "fundamental principles of discipline-based communication" *combined with* "principles of writing instruction and support" (p. 204). Appreciating this ongoing accomplishment requires that we understand how complicated WAC work and partnerships really are, that "[t]hese two kinds of knowledge clearly overlap, *but neither is sufficient alone* to achieve hoped-for communication outcomes for student learning" ([emphasis added] p. 204)]. We offer our expedition-model WAC faculty development seminar and our research about it as a contribution to that ongoing work.

Acknowledgments

The authors wish to thank our research participants and the editor of *The WAC Journal* and the two anonymous *WAC Journal* reviewers for their generous critical engagement with this project.

Notes

1. Bradley Hughes and Elisabeth L. Miller are co-first authors.

2. This material is based in part on work supported by the National Science Foundation under Grant Nos. DUE-1231286 and through the Delta Program in Research, Teaching & Learning at the University of Wisconsin-Madison.

References

Adler-Kassner, L., & Wardle, E. (Eds.). (2015). *Naming what we know: Threshold concepts of writing studies*. Logan, UT: Utah State University Press.

Anderson, P., Anson, C. M., Gonyea, R. M., & Paine C. (2015). The contributions of writing to learning and development: Results from a large-scale multi-institution study. *Research in the Teaching of English, 50*(2), 199–235.

Anderson, P., Anson, C. M., Gonyea, R. M., & Paine, C. (2016, December 26). How to create high-impact writing assignments that enhance learning and development and reinvigorate WAC/WID programs: What almost 72,000 undergraduates taught us. [Special issue on WAC and high-impact practices]. *Across the Disciplines, 13*(4). Retrieved from https://wac.colostate.edu/atd/hip/andersonetal2016.cfm

Anson, C. M. (2002). *The WAC casebook: Scenes for faculty reflection and program development*. Oxford: Oxford University Press.

Anson, C. M. (2015). Crossing thresholds: What's to know about writing across the curriculum. In L. Adler-Kassner & E. Wardle (Eds.), *Naming what we know: Threshold concepts in writing studies* (pp. 203–19). Logan, UT: Utah State University Press.

Anson, C. M., & Dannels, D. P. (2004). Writing and speaking in conditional rhetorical space. In E. Nagelhout & C. Rutz (Eds.), *Classroom space(s) and writing instruction* (pp. 55–70). Cresskill, NJ: Hampton Press.

Bazerman, C., Little, J., Bethel, L., Chavkin, T., Fouquette, D., & Garufis, J. (2005). *Reference guide to writing across the curriculum*. Anderson, SC: Parlor Press.

Beach, A. L., & Cox, M. (2009). The impact of faculty learning communities on teaching and learning. *Learning Communities Journal, 1*(1), 7–27.

Bean, J. C. (2011). *Engaging ideas: The professor's guide to integrating writing, critical thinking, and active learning in the classroom* (2nd ed.). San Francisco, CA: Jossey-Bass.

Boyer Commission on Educating Undergraduates in the Research University. (1998). *Reinventing undergraduate education: A blueprint for America's research universities*. Stony Brook, NY: State University of New York.

Charmaz, K. (2006). *Constructing grounded theory: A practical guide through qualitative analysis*. Thousand Oaks, CA: SAGE Publications.

Desrochers, C. G. (2010). Faculty learning communities as catalysts for implementing successful small-group learning. In J. Cooper & P. Robinson (Eds.), *Small group learning in higher education: Research and practice* (pp. 1–17). Stillwater, OK: New Forums Press.

Eodice, M., Geller, A. E., & Lerner, N. (2017). *The meaningful writing project: Learning, teaching, and writing in higher education*. Logan, UT: Utah State University Press.

Jablonski, J. (2006). *Academic writing consulting and WAC: Methods and models for guiding cross-curricular literacy work*. Cresskill, NJ: Hampton Press.

Johnson, B., & Onwuegbuzie, A.J. (2004). Mixed methods research: A research paradigm whose time has come. *Educational Researcher, 33*(7), 14–26.

McLeod, S. H. (1998). *Strengthening programs for writing across the curriculum*. San Francisco: Jossey-Bass Publishers.

McLeod, S., Miraglia, E., Soven, M., & Thaiss, C. (Eds.). (2001). *WAC for the new millennium: Strategies for continuing writing-across-the-curriculum programs*. Urbana, IL: NCTE.

Melzer, D. (2014). *Assignments across the curriculum: A national study of college writing*. Logan, UT: Utah State University Press.

Robertson, W. (Writer & Director). (2005). *Writing across borders*. [DVD]. Corvallis, OR: Oregon State University.

Tarabochia, S. L. (2013). Negotiating expertise: A pedagogical framework for cross-curricular literacy work. *WPA: Writing Program Administration, 36*(2), 117–41.

Tarabochia, S. L. (2016). Investigating the ontology of WAC/WID relationships: A gender-based analysis of cross-disciplinary collaboration among faculty. *The WAC Journal, 27*, 52–73. Retrieved from https://wac.colostate.edu/journal/vol27/tarabochia.pdf

Tarabochia, S. L. (2017). *Reframing the relational: A pedagogical ethic for cross-curricular literacy work*. Urbana, IL: National Council of Teachers of English.

Thaiss, C., & Zawacki, T. M. (2006). *Engaged writers and dynamic disciplines: Research on the academic writing life*. Portsmouth, NH: Boynton/Cook Heinemann Press.

Walvoord, B. E., Hunt, L. L., Dowling Jr., H. F., & McMahon, J. D. (1997). *In the long run: A study of faculty in three writing-across-the-curriculum programs*. Urbana, IL: NCTE.

Williams, J. M. (1991). On the maturing of legal writers: Two models of growth and development. *The Journal of the Legal Writing Institute, 1*(1), 1–33.

Appendix A

Syllabus for **Expeditions in Learning: Exploring How Students Learn with Writing Across the Curriculum**, Writing Across the Curriculum Program, The University of Wisconsin-Madison, Spring 2015.

Instructor: Elisabeth Miller, The University of Wisconsin-Madison; Assistant Director of the UW-Madison Program in Writing Across the Curriculum

          Time: Tuesdays, 1:30 – 3:00 pm

Location: The Writing Center Commons, 6171 Helen C. White Hall

Overview

Research has shown that when students write more in a course, they learn course content more effectively. At UW-Madison, many faculty and instructors across the disciplines have taken up this approach by making writing central to their courses. This "Expeditions in Learning" Delta course allows participants to consider the opportunities and challenges of this Writing Across the Curriculum pedagogy. Through expeditions (or mini field trips), as well as readings and discussions, participants will deepen their theoretical and practical foundations for helping students learn with writing in a range disciplines.

Course Structure

This course follows an expeditionary learning model, grounded in adult learning theory, where participants can develop new questions about teaching and learning and create methods for exploring answers to those questions. The course fosters a community of peers that will work together during meetings throughout the semester. During the weeks we don't meet, you will head out on expeditions to observe teaching and learning. You may engage in expeditions alone or partner with others in the class. In the meetings that follow expeditions, we'll discuss what you observed, learned, or questioned at your expeditions. Our goal is to learn from each other's experiences and develop new answers and ideas for our future teaching.

Expeditions will allow participants to see first-hand the range of ways students learn to write and learn with writing at UW-Madison. Readings will focus on how writing is linked to critical thinking and how writing assignments can help students learn subject matter and teach them discipline-specific ways of writing. Course discussions will connect expeditions and readings to teaching practices, so you can learn from others about their diverse experiences and increase your knowledge of using writing to promote student learning in your discipline.

Course Texts and Materials

- Articles and book chapters (I'll provide copies)
- Online videos (I'll provide links)

Expeditions

As an Expeditions in Learning participant, you'll have "programmatic permission" to explore specific aspects of teaching on this campus. The following are expeditions that you'll be asked to attend or complete during the weeks that we don't have meetings. I really hope you find them interesting, inspiring, and thought-provoking! **Please be sure to plan your expeditions well in advance and be sure to talk to me about making arrangements.** Our class discussions will help you distill and synthesize what you observe and learn from these expeditions, so that you can connect them to your teaching, learn from colleagues about their diverse observations, and explore faculty and undergraduate experiences.

1. **Exploration of teaching with writing/teaching writing.** Your choice of:
    - attending a TA meeting for a Communication-B course
    - interviewing a Communication-B course coordinator or faculty member about their writing instruction philosophy and methods

    Please talk with me about your choice of course or instructor.

2. **A visit to the Writing Center.** Your choice of observing:
    - a Writing Center session in the main location
    - a Writing Center session in a satellite location
    - a Writing Center workshop for undergraduates

    Please talk with me about your preference, and be sure to plan for time to talk with the instructor you observe.

3. **Observation of one-one-one conferences between faculty and undergraduate writers.** Videos of conferences will be streamed online, and I'll provide you with the links.

4. **Undergraduate class session focused on writing instruction with a content course.** Options include observing:
    - peer review
    - a writing lesson
    - a writing activity
    - a group writing session

    Please talk with me about your choice of course and class session.

Schedule of Seminar Events (which is subject to change)

January 27:   Introductions, overview of main concepts and of expeditions
      Before next meeting: Read Chapters 1 and 2 of *Engaging Ideas*
February 3:   Discussion of reading, discussion and planning of expeditions
      Before next meeting: Read Chapters 3 and 6 of *Engaging Ideas*
February 10: Discussion of reading, Delta presentation

	Before next week: Confirm plans for first expedition
February 17:	Expedition #1 (no meeting)
	Before next meeting: Write down observations, reactions, and questions about expedition
February 24:	Discussion of expedition #1
	Before next week: Read "Responding to Student Writing" and watch *Beyond the Red Ink*, a short video found at http://pages.mail.bfwpub.com/hackerhandbooks/authors/videos/
March 3:	Discussion of reading and video, introduction to expedition #2 & #3
	Before next week: Confirm plans for second expedition
March 10:	Expedition # 2 (no meeting)
	Before March 31: Write down observations, reactions, and questions about expedition
March 17:	Expedition #3 (no meeting): *Videos of one-on-one conferences with students*
	Before March 31: Write down observations, reactions, and questions about conferencing videos
March 24:	Discussion of expeditions #2 and #3
March 31:	Spring Break
	Before next week: Read Chapter 15 of *Engaging Ideas*
April 7:	Discussion of reading
	Before next week: Confirm plans for fourth expedition
April 14:	Catch-up day: discussion/activity TBA
April 21:	Expedition #4 (no meeting)
	Before next meeting: Write down observations, reactions, and questions about expedition
April 28:	Workshopping Assignment Drafts
	Before next meeting: Write down observations, reactions, and questions about expedition and course overall
May 5:	Discussion of expedition #4 & Course Wrap-Up
	Turn in your revised assignment from last week's workshop

Appendix B: Survey of WAC Seminar Research Participants

[*Opening demographic questions omitted*]

Q1. What are three or four important things you've learned about teaching with writing through this course?

Q2. What are two or three concepts, practices, or theories from this course that you plan to implement in your future teaching?

Q3. Of our four expeditions (Expedition 1—interviewing a course coordinator or instructor; Expedition 2—observing a writing center session; Expedition 3—watching video of one-to-one conferences with course instructors; Expedition 4—observing a writing session in a course) which one(s) did you find most beneficial? Why?

Q4. In our course, we had a mix of graduate students, instructional staff, postdocs, and faculty from a variety of disciplines. In what ways do you think this range of participants influenced our learning?

Q5. In our next-to-last meeting, you had a chance to share a draft of an assignment. What advice did you receive that was most helpful?

Q6. What is your academic role [position on campus]?

Q7. Which [academic] division are you from [arts and humanities; STEM; social sciences]?

Q8. Of the various components of the course (in-class discussions of readings, viewing videos related to multilingual writers and other topics, going on expeditions, looking at sample assignments or other materials, workshopping assignment drafts, etc.), which components of the course were most useful to you? What made them useful?

Q9. Of the readings that we did, which did you find most beneficial? Why?

Q10. Which components of the course were least useful to you? Why? What would you suggest for future iterations of this course?

Q11. As you know, our course was designed to be a sustained learning experience with 10 meetings over the semester. What's your take on the importance of this sustained learning experience? [1=not important at all; 5=very important]

Q12. Is there anything else you'd like us to know? Feel free to offer more suggestions or reactions or comments.

Writing across College: Key Terms and Multiple Contexts as Factors Promoting Students' Transfer of Writing Knowledge and Practice

KATHLEEN BLAKE YANCEY, MATTHEW DAVIS, LIANE ROBERTSON, KARA TACZAK, AND ERIN WORKMAN

During the last fifteen years, researchers have studied how students transfer writing knowledge and practice into multiple contexts, including into many kinds of classes, among them in general education courses, in writing-intensive courses, and in writing-in-the-discipline courses. While some of these findings have been, as Joanna Wolfe, Barrie Olson, and Laura Wilder put it in 2014, "dismal" (42), other findings point toward consistent practices that can foster what we, here, define as a *writing-transfer-mindset*. For example, transfer researchers have documented multiple cases of students successfully repurposing, or transferring, writing knowledge and practice for use in many writing contexts, including within or between assignments in a writing course (e.g., VanKooten; DePalma) and between first-year composition (FYC) and disciplinary contexts (e.g., Yancey, Robertson, and Taczak). This latter study, which we build on for the research we report here, relies on a curricular design explicitly intended to promote writing transfer—the Teaching for Transfer (TFT) curriculum. As we explain more fully below, the TFT curriculum includes three integrated curricular components: a set of key rhetorical terms; a systematic reflective framework; and a culminating assignment, the Theory of Writing (ToW) assignment. Initially developed for use in a FYC course (Yancey, Robertson, and Taczak 2014), the TFT curriculum has since been adapted for use in upper-level writing courses and internships, and has been studied, in three iterations, at a range of eight institutions with diverse student demographics. Our aim in these expansions has been two-fold: (1) to understand the ways in which students transfer writing knowledge and practice from the TFT curriculum into other writing contexts, both in-and-out of school, and (2) to explore the efficacy of the TFT curriculum with a wider set of students, college courses, and institutions.

Across the three iterations of this research project and at all eight institutions, students consistently report and demonstrate—in surveys, interviews, and written documents--that TFT-based conceptual writing knowledge is key to their understanding about how, as they write across campus, writing works best in each individual context. This conceptual knowledge about writing, which goes beyond process-based writing or the practice of writing, is especially relevant to our understanding of how students fare in WAC contexts because of its potential to help students develop and employ a conceptual framework of writing knowledge and practice for approaching writing in diverse situations. In this article, then, we report on one dimension of this research, focusing in particular on a TFT-informed professional writing (PW) course and a TFT-informed writing-intensive internship; for both of these, we specifically address the role of TFT terms and multiple contexts as keys to fostering what we call a *writing-transfer-mindset*.

We begin by briefly outlining the signature features of the TFT curriculum and some of what we have learned in the three iterations of the study; we then introduce selected student writers, chosen as representative both of upper-level and internship TFT curricular adaptations and of our study's findings. These three students, including two from PW courses and one completing an internship, who successfully transferred their writing knowledge and practice into different writing contexts shared three characteristics facilitating this transfer: (1) a conceptual vocabulary, based in the TFT curriculum, for articulating writing knowledge; (2) an ability to draw on that knowledge to frame new writing tasks in multiple contexts; and (3) access to writing contexts. As important, they shared a fourth characteristic that seems an outcome of a writing-transfer-mindset: a sense of agency, indicated in part by their ownership of writing vocabulary and experiences, and in part by their developing understanding of writing as always and at once specific *and* contextual. Not least, we close with three recommendations helpful for fostering a writing transfer mindset.

The TFT Curriculum

The TFT curriculum, although adapted to each institutional type, includes three integral curricular components constituting an ensemble: (1) a shared set of writing concepts or key terms; (2) students' engagement in systematic reflection and the development of a reflective framework for thinking about writing concepts and practices; and (3) students' development of a theory of writing through completing a reiterative assignment, the ToW, in which students articulate their writing knowledge and practice based on learning about writing (e.g., through the key terms) and on analyses of the rhetorical choices made in responding to writing situations. Key terms provide a conceptual foundation for writing knowledge developed in the course, guiding the assigned readings, class activities, and major assignments, and serving as a focal point for students' reflective work throughout the course. Eight key terms that students need to think and write with are introduced, modeled, and reiterated within and across multiple assignments: rhetorical situation, purpose, context, audience, genre, reflection, knowledge, and discourse community. (Other key terms are added to these eight as appropriate for adaptations to upper division courses, such as the addition of "context of use" for a technical writing course.)

Reflection, one of the key words for the TFT course, is woven throughout the term at different deliberate points. As defined in a TFT course, reflection is a central and reiterative practice as well as a theoretical approach enabling students to develop the conceptual framework for transfer to occur (Yancey et al. 2014.; Taczak and Robertson, 2016). Reflection is deliberately designed into the course in three ways: students learn about reflective theory, complete a variety of writing-to-learn and formal reflective assignments, and engage in reflective activities. The culminating formal reflective assignment, the reflection-in-presentation (Yancey 1998) style "Theory of Writing" assignment, specifically asks students to identify the key terms they believe are most important to their writing processes—both their self-selected and TFT terms—and to theorize writing as articulated with their key terms in the context of their writing practices and the rhetorical choices they made while composing throughout the term. The students' ToW provides them with space to think about their relationship with writing—their writing processes, their understanding of the key terms they enact in their own writing, and their ability to create a knowledge-base of writing and its practices that can be repurposed for use in other contexts. The latter is of particular significance to WAC; in the ToW students reflect on the rhetorical decisions they have already made, and are planning to consider, in different writing contexts, across disciplines and elsewhere. Critical to this process, and to students' developing a writing-transfer-mindset, is students' understanding that writing transfer is possible, and appropriate transfer desirable.

Research Design and Methods

The research reported in *Writing Across Contexts*, which focused on students as they moved from three FYC classes into various WAC courses, provides a foundation for the current study. *Writing Across Contexts* began by comparing three versions of FYC in terms of their efficacy in supporting students' transfer during two semesters, the first when students completed an FYC course and the second when they engaged in several WAC courses. The study found that in the first two FYC courses—one an Expressivist course and the second focused on media and cultural studies—students did not transfer, in part because they did not have key terms identifying and articulating different writing tasks and practices, and in part because they were thus unable to read across different writing tasks for differences and similarities. Without key terms adequate to the task, students defaulted to terms they learned in high school; such terms (e.g., expression, mistake) did not help them address their college writing tasks. In contrast, the students in the TFT course—working with the key terms in writing assignments, accompanying analytical reflective tasks, and a culminating theory of writing (ToW) assignment—re-purposed, or transferred, what they had learned in the TFT course for new writing tasks in multiple kinds of courses across the curriculum, including in film, theatre, literature, biology, and chemistry.

The results of this first study demonstrated that the TFT curriculum helped students at one institution, a research institution in the southeast, successfully transfer writing knowledge and practice into new writing situations. In 2014–2015, the three original researchers were joined by two new researchers in a second iteration of this project, "The Transfer of Transfer Project: Extending the Teaching for Transfer Writing Curriculum into Four Sites and Multiple Courses," supported in part by a CCCC Research Initiative Grant. The aim of this second iteration was to trace the efficacy of the TFT curriculum in several ways, two of which were keyed to site and course: in four sites—one the research institution in the southeast; second, a private research institution in the west; third, a suburban Hispanic-serving institution (HSI) in the northeast; and fourth, a public urban institution in the northeast with the highest percentage of students of color in the region; and in two kinds of courses—introductory writing courses; and upper-level courses, technical writing and professional writing, whose outcomes include writing for multiple contexts.

This second iteration of the study demonstrated, generally, that TFT supported students' transfer of writing knowledge and practice in all four sites and in increasingly predictable ways. There are exceptions to this pattern, of course. Some students, typically students entering college with very strong writing skills and an impressive ability to read teachers, tend to parrot key terms without repurposing for new writing tasks; they do not transfer either TFT-based writing knowledge or practice, although they may nonetheless earn high grades in post-TFT classes requiring writing. Likewise, a very small percentage of students rely on their own key terms rather than adopting or adapting the TFT key terms; while these students may graft, or assemble, one or two TFT key terms onto their prior construct of writing, they rely on their earlier concept of writing and experience difficulty in repurposing writing knowledge and practice for new situations. Much like Reiff and Bawarshi's border guarders and Wardle's problem solvers, these students repeat old practices regardless of new rhetorical constraints and possibilities. At each of the study's sites, however, most students remixed their key terms with the TFT terms as part of repurposing knowledge and practice for new writing contexts. In addition, students articulated well the nature of the repurposing process for them. In other words, the TFT initial findings were repeated in the second iteration with students on very different kinds of campuses and courses. As important, findings included four observations qualifying or extending this general finding, among them that when students are cued that transfer is a course goal, they don't wait to transfer until a course is completed, but rather intentionally engage in more concurrent transfer than has previously been reported in the literature—using what they learn in a TFT course in a just-in-time fashion, for example, in workplace settings, internships, and, especially, in classes across the curriculum, both lower and upper levels.

The third iteration of this project, the eight-institution Writing Passport Project supported by CCCC and the Council of Writing Program Administrators (CWPA) grants, includes three community colleges and five four-year schools (including the four schools described above) collectively offering introductory and upper-level writing courses. The Writing Passport Project also includes a study of TAs teaching a TFT FYC course for the first time and a TFT-supported internship. Projects at all sites shared the fundamental integrative features of the TFT curriculum: (1) content as represented in key terms, (2) a reiterative set of reflective activities, and (3) a final TOW assignment. In addition, all students—ranging from a high of ten students at one campus to two at another—and three TAs were interviewed with the same set of document-based core questions (adapted appropriately for the teachers) at the same five points across the two terms: three during the TFT course and two in the post-TFT course. Students and TAs also completed two exit surveys with the same core questions at the same end-points of the two terms. (This pattern was adjusted for interns, with three interviews and one-exit survey occurring at the beginning, during, and at the conclusion of the internship, respectively.) All faculty kept teaching logs (e.g., detailing their emphases in class; ways that students are responding).

For each site at all three iterations of this study, IRB approval was obtained, and complete participant data sets were collected; data included the ToW assignments, five TFT and post-TFT interviews,[1] and two exit surveys. Student participants from the first iteration numbered fourteen, from the second iteration thirty-four, and from the third iteration fifty, for a total of nearly one hundred students. Materials were coded multiple times: they were (1) deductively coded by two researchers using the TFT key terms and synonyms (e.g., "reader" for audience); (2) inductively coded by two researchers using a grounded theory approach for emerging themes (e.g., use of TFT concepts to frame out-of-school writing situations); and (3) coded by software for students' self-identified key terms (e.g., expression, voice) that surfaced during the grounded theory readings.[2] Contextualizing the coding results were several data sources, including faculty teaching logs; maps of key terms that students created in some FYC classes; and students' texts composed in the term following the TFT course. Collectively, these data were analyzed to inquire into the efficacy of the TFT curriculum in supporting students' transfer of writing knowledge and practice as developed in two curricular sites—FYC and upper-level writing (ULW)—in TA preparation, and in writing internships.

The Role of Context as a Key Concept

The research on the three iterations of this project regarding the efficacy of the TFT curriculum has demonstrated that students' understanding of the contexts for their writing, and thus for successful transfer, occurs in different ways. One important practice that assists students in transferring writing knowledge and practice is the development of key terms. With appropriate writing vocabulary, students articulate the writing knowledge and practices they are developing, which supports the transfer, or repurposing, of such knowledge for different contexts of writing—both across the curriculum and out of school. These contexts, and students' *understanding* of context as a through-line for specific writing situations, provides students with a conceptual passport for developing a writing approach for each context. For students, who often perceive writing they do in a course as isolated both from other course work and from writing they do outside of school, context acts as a connector from one situation to another across multiple writing situations, including between courses in different disciplines. Such an understanding of context is crucial given the research on prior knowledge indicating that while students bring a variety of experiences, knowledge, and beliefs to their writing, they typically do not bring an understanding that writing is contextual and requires attention to rhetorical situation (Yancey et. al 2014). In the TFT curriculum, students learn the concept of context through multiple writing activities and especially in multi-genre projects, which encourage a conception of writing as contextually unique. This contextual understanding of writing, which disrupts students' prior knowledge that all "school writing" is the same and requires the same (or a similar) approach, provides a motive, a rationale, and a through-line for adaptation.

The Viability of Key Terms across Iterations: Providing a Vocabulary

In the first iteration of the research on TFT, we explored the ways students employed key terms as a mechanism for incorporating their prior knowledge of writing into a new understanding of writing. One participant, Rick, a first-year physics major, transferred quite successfully, but only after a series of setbacks helped him see the patterns across his writing. Struggling in the first-year TFT writing course, Rick couldn't understand the writing situation for an assignment, largely because he was more interested in expressing his perspective than in using the key terms to frame the writing assignment: the *rhetorical situation*, his *audience*, and the relationship of writing to *context*. When he received a poor grade, he didn't fully understand what he had done wrong, believing that as the writer of the assignment he should have complete freedom to say whatever he wanted. Several weeks later, when he was unsuccessful in writing his lab reports in a chemistry course—which were important to him given his identification with science—he looked at his writing in *both* contexts and found connections between the two that helped him understand the concepts of rhetorical situation and audience. As he reflected on why his writing and chemistry assignments hadn't been as successful as he'd hoped, Rick employed the TFT conceptual framework: "I ended up focusing a lot more on the topic than on the research, which is what mattered. I explained too much instead of making it matter to them (the audience)."

In the second iteration of the research on TFT, we witnessed the same phenomenon, but from another perspective when students, again, reported on the value of key terms, but in this case by linking an in-school context with one outside of school. For example, Teresa, a dual Business/English major taking an upper-level technical writing course and also writing as a marketing manager in her workplace, found the key terms essential, even plugging them into her cell phone for easy reference, as she explained: "I keep [the key terms] in my phone actually. That's what I use to reflect on and then to think about what to write when I have an assignment at work." As important, Teresa reported that drawing on her key terms contributed both to the quality of her texts and to her confidence in the business context of her job creating marketing and promotional materials: "I'm doing all sorts of things in marketing . . . that are relevant to what we learned in our class. Even just my emails to other people [at the workplace] are so much better. And I just feel better about my planning in all my writing, at work or school . . . I'm using my theory of writing . . . and my key terms audience and purpose." In other words, Teresa drew on her key terms to frame writing in new contexts, among them a marketing context; doing so, she observed, helped her "just [feel] better about my planning in all my writing, at work or school" and develop a kind of agency.

In the third iteration of this research, an upper-level student, Carrie, believed—just as Rick did—that writers should be able to exercise complete authority in a writing task regardless of rhetorical situation. Carrie experienced a setback when she earned a C grade on the first major assignment in her technical writing course. Through engaging in the TFT-based technical writing course, however, Carrie developed a vocabulary allowing her to conceptualize writing more rhetorically, as an interaction among writer, audience, and topic:

> Ever since I did badly on that [first assignment] I understand that it [successful writing] depends on the rhetorical situation, and that you have to know your audience, purpose, and the whole context to write something that will work in that situation . . . I do a lot of creative writing but that's different, and I just sort of shut off that side of me when I write in other classes. I think I can be creative with wording and that, but I'm not a creative writer in those situations.

Although students often write in different contexts, they don't always understand the different expectations accompanying those contexts. As suggested above, an important finding across these three research iterations is that an appropriate vocabulary and an understanding of the concept of context in writing are key, especially given how much contexts vary. These earlier findings also point to the ways the process of engaging with and using the terms can facilitate student agency as students transfer writing knowledge and practice to and from outside-school contexts. Such a process was articulated by Teresa, who, drawing on her key terms, read across the contexts of academic and workplace writing and adjusted accordingly. These potential adjustments, made between in-school and out-of-school contexts, give us insight into how students learn to understand contexts for writing as situated. Context as a conceptual through-line acts as a connector between situations that are like or unlike each other; context thus functions as a bridge for far transfer as defined by David Perkins and Gavriel Salomon (1992). Further, encouraging students to see context as simultaneously *a through-line and specific to the situation*, a perception contributing to a writing-transfer-mindset, may provide a means of effectively integrating writing into WAC courses more effectively. By providing students with the opportunity to develop a conceptual frame involving context with the idea that contexts are specific to situation, we as faculty can help students explore the similarities and differences from one writing situation to the next, especially writing situations they encounter upon entering a new discipline, a new sub-discipline, or even a new focus within a discipline. Such an exploration of similarity and difference, as recommended by the National Research Council's *How People Learn*, can help students develop a kind of intentionality about specific writing tasks as well as about what they can transfer from one writing situation to the next.

Adapting TFT to Upper-level Courses: Concepts, Vocabulary, and Agency

This connection between student agency and the development of rhetorical key terms was demonstrated by upper-level students in the third iteration of our study, where those in professional writing courses and internships often toggle between the conceptual impulse of TFT and the more immediate orientation of their in- and out-of-school writing. In making decisions about which of their diverse writing experiences and key terms were most relevant for a given situation, students developed a sense of writerly agency or authority over their own texts. Borrowing from Marilyn Cooper (2011), the definition of agency used here, as it emerges and is enacted in rhetorical situations, is

> the process through which [people] create meaning through acting into the world and changing their structure in response to the perceived

consequences of their actions. [This] enables writers to recognize their rhetorical acts, whether conscious or unconscious, as acts that make them who they are, that affect others, and that can contribute to the common good. (420)

As students draw on key terms to articulate their writing experiences, they "recognize their rhetorical acts," especially when writing in two very different contexts. In the TFT upper-level professional writing course, these contexts included the course itself and then another, student-selected context, ranging from workplace writing to self-sponsored and church-sponsored writing.

The TFT professional writing course studied here fits Sarah Read and Michael Michaud's model for a "multi-major professional writing course" designed to support transfer of writing knowledge and practice into, out of, and across course and workplace contexts (427–8). Although Read and Michaud argue for a Writing about Writing (WAW) professional writing pedagogy, and although Teaching for Transfer mirrors many of the same investments—writing as a diverse, study-able phenomenon; the importance of authentic genres; and a general orientation toward metacognition—the cases below, which have emerged in the third iteration of the TFT research, show that it is not a general rhetorical education (whether through genre or client-based approaches) through which students articulate their writing transfer. Instead, students articulate writing transfer as an agentive process at the confluence of key concepts; integrated, directed reflection; theorizing writing; and multiple contexts. That said, the students here exhibit a messier, though more self-directed, use of their prior knowledge than has previously been reported. Like students in Josephine Walwema and Dana Driscoll's study (2015), PW students Julie and Kyle engage in substantial theorizing of writing, but do so using both prior *and developing* knowledge across various domains of life. Instead of attending to documentation and source use as Walwema and Driscoll's students, however, the TFT students focus their attention on how a wide range of texts and contexts—such as those from religious and civic life—are transformed through varied and developing sets of key terms for various purposes: from identity formation to just-in-time transfer. More specifically, for Julie, the TFT curriculum provided the terminology for her to maintain and more deeply articulate a writerly identity, while also moving her from a "technically oriented" writing practice to a more elaborated set of writing practices, where she began to develop and articulate specific differences between school-sponsored and church-sponsored writing. For Kyle, the TFT course provided a space to transform his prior knowledge, which is heavily inflected by self-sponsored writing, and to begin articulating a set of values for a civic life he understands as closely connected to his university education.

Julie, a twenty-one-year-old woman from Brazil, is an English major and a Professional and New Media Writing minor; and her extracurricular writing—sponsored through her church—is integral to her changing understanding of writing and of ways different contexts call for different writing responses. As Julie began the TFT semester, her ToW was rudimentary, oriented to writing implements: "I have never been asked what I think writing is. In the time I was given to think about it, I decided that writing is just putting pen to paper. Or in the time we're currently living, it's putting fingers to keyboard." In other words, having never thought about a definition of writing, Julie identified it as inscription of a material kind. The TFT key terms were unfamiliar to her, but she found them helpful precisely because they could help her frame and navigate different writing contexts: "[the TFT terms are] useful—because it goes situation to situation. And it's not just ok, I have to follow this kind of format or set of rules. No, the exigence is different in every situation. The constraints are different in every situation. I feel like—I liked looking at it like that."

Moreover, in taking up different writing tasks for her church, Julie explains quite specifically how these terms are useful:

> So I work with kids and teenagers [at church] and I'm the communications person. With the teenagers, I'm the communications person, so whatever ideas or messages people need to convey to them . . . go through me. I have to kind of make it fit their teenager mind. I hear the idea, I say ok, here is what I need to say—I need to tell them this. But how am I going to make it in a way that going to make it appealing to them? So in that way there is a process, too. It's not just like 'oh, let's tell them right away'. If I'm texting them I'll start off like, we're called boss and metro, that's our name. I call them Metronians, I'm like 'Happy Friday, Metronians' or whatever. I'll start off with song lyrics and stuff to get their attention and then I'll do a who-what-where-when type of thing. Or I'll send them a video. I'll make them a video that displays the message. Or the graphic that I make; it usually has a picture: like if we're doing a secret Santa, I'll put a picture of Santa and him delivering presents. It's not usually—not always words that I use, but pictures—as little words [sic] as possible because they are teenagers and they don't want to read. If I send them a paragraph of stuff—of information—then they're not going to read it."

Drawing on a context she knows well, Julie interprets the key terms and concepts of the TFT in ways both appropriate and meaningful to her, and in describing her own experience, she demonstrates how she brings authority and agency to the task.

Kyle, the second PW student, is a twenty-four-year-old white man from Haverhill, Massachusetts, who worked his way through community college before transferring to the university, where he maintains a high GPA as a double major in English and Political Science. It was not always so rosy. Kyle identified his socio-economic background—"very poor, sometimes homeless"—as formative of both his personal and educational identities. The first draft of his Theory of Writing for the TFT course, posted to his blog, was in some ways more philosophy than definition, which is perhaps not surprising for a student whose interests include political philosophy:

> Outside the literal pen-on-paper definition, the answer can get very personal. [...] Personally, I find writing to be one of the most in-depth and differing modes of communication that human beings have at their disposal. [...] writing gives the opportunity to edit, revise and perfect what the author is trying to say. Due to this, the ideas are more fleshed out and focused, which can benefit all parties involved and thereby result in a more expansive and fulfilling form of communication.

Kyle sees context in another way: writing is larger than the classroom and there is the opportunity for agency, but he also understands that it's up to the writer to determine what's appropriate in "differing" situations. In addition, Kyle identifies some intellectual influences he draws from as a writer: "Reading Kurt Vonnegut has made me value humor in writing, Bob Dylan powerful imagery, and my left-leaning politics creates a lens as well. And so, the questions [about writing] don't *have* definitive answers, so I don't *know* they're accurate." He concludes by saying, "I have simply no idea what kind of a writer I am."

Kyle's first Theory of Writing assignment was preceded on the blog by his self-sponsored four-thousand-word review of Noam Chomsky's 2017 book *Who Rules the World?* with an epigraph from Kurt Vonnegut: "Do you realize that all great literature is all about what a bummer it is to be a human being?" He then explained the connection of these reviews to his general intellectual disposition, one in which citizens should be informed and engaged across disciplinary boundaries. Kyle developed and then felt called to pursue—by conversations with friends, in reading and music, and in particular by the political campaign of Bernie Sanders—an active political life connecting to his burgeoning "left-leaning politics." As the review suggests, Kyle as both citizen and political science major saw language, and metaphor especially, as a dimension of writing English and Political Science share. These two concurrent contexts shape his observations:

> You can be very effective with metaphors or something else when it comes to imagination and style. A lot of that is coming out of my Lincoln class, he's really good with metaphors and illuminating his political thought. But sometimes [metaphor is] like the whole point of creative writing. So if you're mixing them together, I guess creativity would be really important.

In other words, as a double major, Kyle routinely operates in two disciplinary contexts, and he is able to identify commonalities between them, like metaphor, that are also and at the same time employed differently. Moreover, in summarizing what he had learned about writing, Kyle read across the different assignments of the TFT course and provided a view of writing informed by key TFT terms he specifically connected and by his valuing of both the practical and the philosophical:

> Through our projects, especially projects 2 and 4, the practice of really focusing on a wide variety of audiences taught me how the term "purpose" is an extraordinarily important aspect of writing. Specifically, the second project made me imagine people I've never interacted with before, which helped me identify more with my audience, because I had to assume personalities, reactions, etc. Purpose helps a writer, no matter whether people are writing for form, problem solving, etc., which makes their writing more effective. This is not something I put much stock in before this class.

In addition, Kyle understands his Theory of Writing philosophically—as a living theory:

> In this way, taking what I've learned in this class, I can apply it alongside all the other knowledge I've accumulated so far. Also, in this way, my theory of writing changes for *every* class, because I've concluded that the "theory of writing" we discuss so much in this class is added to and changed throughout our entire academic and writing life. So, I will apply my theory of writing . . . to every class, because it is constantly changing and, obviously, affects how people write.

Given what seemed like an abundance of experiences defining this TFT upper-level course—including previous writing experiences, TFT, upper-level writing content, writing in other classes, and co-curricular and self-sponsored writing—Kyle and Julie illustrate how students tend to choose among these experiences and exercise authority when making decisions about the TFT content that seems most salient to them. Put another way, Julie and Kyle help us understand how students weave together an understanding of writing from sources they identify, including those from the classroom but not exclusive to it, and how engaging in such decision-making can foster a sense of writerly agency that allows students to navigate across WAC contexts with appropriate knowledge of writing that can be repurposed for those contexts.

Writing as Interns: Contexts, Key Terms, Learning, and Reciprocity

The role of context in writing transfer was also particularly important for upper-level students engaging concurrently in internships and in classes on campus, in the third iteration of our research. The internships and classes were thus inherently inter-contextual, providing an intersection of contexts that may be of special importance for transferring writing knowledge and practice. In addition, because the earlier TFT research had not included internships, an important focus of this part of the study was to ascertain if and how TFT might help students transfer from their school writing into their internship and from their internship into other sites of writing.

Three students participated: here we focus on one, Cassidy, a twenty-one-year-old white female college senior with multiple majors—one in Editing, Writing, and Media (EWM) with a minor in professional communication, and a second major in humanities, including a focus on art history. The first step in the study was to have Cassidy, like her peers, complete two individualized ninety-minute TFT-based workshops. The internship curricular approach to TFT thus differed considerably from classroom versions: rather than engage in a semester-long series of TFT reading and writing activities, the interns participated in two workshops distilling the TFT curriculum and engaging them in related transfer-oriented activities. The first TFT workshop focused on two areas: students' prior knowledge and beliefs about writing, and an introduction to the three signature components of the TFT curriculum, key terms, reflective practice, and a Theory of Writing (ToW). About half of this first workshop focused on key terms that the students brought with them into the study—Cassidy identified the writing key terms she used to define writing and mapped them—and the rest of the workshop introduced her to the three components of the TFT curriculum. The second workshop was also divided into two parts. The first half engaged Cassidy in responding to and then discussing a heuristic designed to help her consider how she might both learn from and contribute to the internship, as the image suggests; and the second part asked her to identify two very different writing situations she was currently in, and articulate what these two situations/tasks had in common and how they differed, a practice intended to encourage her to think, as an expert, about how writing situations can be both alike and different, as recommended by *How People Learn* (as noted above), and thus how reading across them could help her consider what might be successfully repurposed from one to another.

> **Using a heuristic to set the (learning) stage**
>
> - Who are you as a student?
> - Who are you as a student in this class/experience?
> - Who are you as a person in this class/experience?
> - What do you have to contribute?
> - What do you have to learn?
> - What key ideas can you draw on as you both contribute and learn?

The key terms students used to describe and define writing were especially important for the internship participants in the study given the literature on upper-level students and interns. Based on their study of interns, for example, Neil Baird and Bradley Dilger recommend that "Instructors need to be mindful of relationships between classroom practices and transfer" (708). Such practices, of course, can be expressed in the key terms crossing both classrooms and internships, especially when classes and internships are concurrent, as was the case for this study. And to assure that students' (prior) classroom conceptions and practices of writing were included, the study began, as explained above, by inviting both. In addition, for this study an even wider net was cast: participants were invited throughout the study to consider all contexts of writing as sources of writing knowledge and practice—past and present schooling experiences, workplace experiences, civic writing experiences, and personal writing experiences—and as Cassidy's experience will demonstrate, some of those non-school sources were especially informative for these participants. Key terms for interns are also especially important because, as Doug Brent's (2012) internship study demonstrates, without the vocabulary of key terms, interns can experience difficulty "explaining in detail on what prior experiences they might be drawing" (708), a finding echoing that of two other studies of upper-level students, the Hilgers, Hussey, and Stitt-Bergh's (1999) study and the Jarratt et al. (2005) study, both of which reported that while students had elaborate writing processes, they lacked a language useful for describing the writing concepts or practices they called upon. In this context, Cassidy's key terms, and the ways they shifted during her internship, provide evidence of the impact of introducing TFT key terms to interns, who can draw on them both to describe their experience and to facilitate writing transfer.

Three patterns in the development of Cassidy's key terms are worth observing. First, her key terms shift over time: the key terms she identified in fall 2017 were completely replaced by a new set as the spring 2018 term concluded, although as the internship progressed, some terms began to repeat, suggesting some stability to them.

Second, in explaining the sources for her key terms, Cassidy points to four contexts: classes current and past, the internship, the study itself, and her own experience, this last a function of her sense of agency. Third, Cassidy also transfers writing knowledge and practice from her internship into a co-curricular experience and is quite specific about the internship writing practices she employs in the co-curricular setting.

Cassidy's initial eight key terms for writing—paper, ink, inspiration, skill, language, ideas, vocabulary, and rhetoric—constructed writing as a material practice with *paper* and *ink*, bringing together *language* and *ideas* through *vocabulary* and *rhetoric*, with the help of writerly *inspiration*. As important, only one of the terms, rhetoric, was related to the eight TFT key terms, which, as mentioned above and borrowing from *How People Learn*, are conceptual in nature: rhetorical situation, purpose, audience, context, genre, reflection, discourse community, and knowledge.

Table 1
Cassidy's Key Terms Fall 2017-Spring 2018 (TFT terms in bold)

Fall 2017	January 2018	March 2018	April 2018
paper	rhetorical situation	media	media
ink	**audience**	**genre**	**genre**
inspiration	**exigence**	**exigence**	**exigence**
skill	Syntax	process	process
language	grammar	language	
ideas	Writer	writer	writer
vocabulary		revising	
rhetoric		reflection	reflection
		conventions/manipulation	

Cassidy's terms began changing, however, as her internship progressed. In January, having been introduced in the fall to the TFT terms, Cassidy shared a seven-word writing vocabulary that is more conceptual in nature, including both TFT terms—*rhetorical situation, audience, exigence*—and other terms—syntax, and grammar—while the terms for materiality and the author disappeared. In March, Cassidy listed nine terms, all of which continue to be conceptual in nature, with two terms repeated (in italics): *exigence, writer*, media, genre, process, revising, reflection, language, and conventions/manipulation; writer re-appears from the fall list and exigence from the

January list, while syntax and grammar, which could be included in language, drop out. The March list in that sense seems a function of a honing and consolidation process. By the end of April, Cassidy's key terms are largely a conceptual distillation of the March list, and this list, at six terms, is the shortest one: writer/composer, exigence, genre, media (through which the writing is created), process, and reflection. Half of the terms—exigence, genre, and reflection—are TFT terms. And not least, in identifying these terms, Cassidy also voluntarily defines three of them. Media, she says, is the platform or surface "through which the writing is created"; process is "the writer's creative process of putting their ideas into language and molding it into the media, not the mechanical process of editing and revising. Those things go under reflection, in my view"; and reflection "Encompasses editing, revising, etc., but also introspective reflection because writing is constrained by the composer's knowledge and abilities and is influenced by their world-view and beliefs." In sum, Cassidy's key terms shift over time; they include TFT terms but are not exclusive to them; they are consolidated and distilled; and as her definitions indicate, they are nuanced.

These progressive lists of key terms tell one story, but when in April, Cassidy was also asked about the sources for her key terms, she tells another story that both complicates and enriches the first. Three of the terms, she says—exigence, genre, and process—come from past or current classes and, sometimes, from other contexts as well, but not from TFT. *Exigence*, although a TFT term, has another source for Cassidy: it "certainly comes from my Rhetoric courses in college, though I'd like to qualify that I'm not simply regurgitating what I've learned. I believe the writer or composer must feel some kind of exigence to produce writing"; here Cassidy also asserts her agency in distinguishing between "simpl[e] regurgitate[ion]" and her belief. Genre, another TFT term, has multiple sources, though Cassidy does not cite TFT: it "is something we talked about in many of my courses, but it mostly comes from my Peer Tutoring in the [Reading Writing Center] RWC and [Digital Studio] DS class and my internship," both of which Cassidy was engaged in during the spring. Speaking specifically to her internship writing, Cassidy referred to the influence of genre on shaping writing even when the content is the "same": "In my internship, writing a social media post is vastly different than writing about the same topic for a blog post, which is very different from taking the same content and writing it in an opinion editorial." And the term process comes from a very specific class, the Peer Tutoring class. Interestingly, although Cassidy does not cite the TFT curriculum or the fall workshops as sources for exigence or genre, these two terms show up in multiple contexts: the TFT term exigence is a theoretical term from multiple courses, and the TFT term genre emerges from both a course and the internship.

Other terms have other sources. Writer/Composer, which was introduced in the March list, is, according to Cassidy, "a given because without a writer, writing could not come into existence on its own." Media, also introduced in the March list, comes from Cassidy's experience, as she explains: "Media comes from my experience because writing can take countless forms and doesn't necessarily have to be pen to paper. In my internship, I mostly write digitally." Here, we see Cassidy citing her own experience as a source and as a kind of agency, and we also see her consolidation of earlier terms: the paper and pen (ink) of her initial list have been consolidated into media, a term that also speaks to her internship writing. And like genre, above, reflection also has two sources. One is, again, Cassidy's experience: "from experience I knew that writing is constrained by the writer/composer's experiences, knowledge and world-view, and that editing and revising results from writers/composers reflecting upon their writing." A second source is the study itself: "I'd say the study helped me put a name to the concept and think critically about it, since I never really thought about it in terms of 'reflection' before"—a perception that has been articulated through all iterations of the larger TFT research project. Students report in their interviews that one of the benefits of the TFT curriculum is the vocabulary helping them describe and theorize writing knowledge and practices. Moreover, in this case, Cassidy cites multiple sources for her terms, and while half of the terms are TFT terms, she attributes only one of these, reflection, to the study. As important, Cassidy's final list of key terms, like those of other successful writers from the first iteration of the research (Yancey et al.), is a remix of terms, in her case including one from TFT; two appearing in TFT (and in other contexts for a useful kind of redundancy); and three from her own experience.

As Cassidy explains, her writing experiences are highly contextual and often complementary: a term like genre that appears in several contexts and is useable can be particularly salient. But multiple contexts also provide opportunities to see differences. Thus, when asked if she needed to adjust what she had learned in her coursework to write successfully in the internship, Cassidy drew on two terms from her earlier lists—language and audience—to explain that indeed she had:

> The analytical and academic language I'm used to using in school doesn't cut it in the communications field, because the goal of communications for a company or organization is accessibility. The audience must understand the messages we relay to them. Specifically, my clients' audiences are high schoolers, young adults, troubled youth, and lower-income families. However, because some of my clients rely on federal funding, some of our communications efforts have targeted policy-makers and legislators. In these instances, the language we used was closer to what I'm used to writing in school.

Here, Cassidy as an expert in these contexts explains how they are both similar and different: the content may be the same, but the *audience* will affect what *language* is used in communicating the content, and some audiences, like those providing *federal funding*, are closer to academics than to *young adults* and *troubled youth*. And when contexts are similar, Cassidy doesn't hesitate to draw on, or transfer, writing knowledge and practice that has been successful elsewhere. Thus, when asked if she had transferred writing knowledge and practice from the internship into other contexts, she responded affirmatively:

> My internship has mostly taught me about digital writing genres, so I've definitely used the skills I've learned in my role as public relations chair for the Skeet and Trap club. For example, I learned that the most effective way to write Instagram posts so they're seen is to include 30 hashtags, the maximum allowed by Instagram. I learned this through the social media guidelines at work. I've used this tip every time I've drafted Instagram posts for the club. I learned how to draft press releases, opinion editorials, blog posts, and newsletters, and I will certainly transfer these skills to future employment in the communications field.

We have much to learn from Cassidy. She, like her intern colleagues in this study, was a key-term reviser; and like her intern colleagues and other successful writers in all the iterations of the TFT project, was a key-term remixer, bringing together selected TFT terms with her own for a unique set of key terms. She drew from multiple contexts concurrently—classes, co-curriculars, the internship, and her own experience—finding in those contexts rich resources for transfer of writing knowledge and practice and for writerly agency based on articulated inter-contextual experience. Put simply, Cassidy has a writing-transfer-mindset.

Teaching for Transfer Across the Curriculum: Some Concluding Observations

Recent writing transfer research suggests, as we explain above, that what we do in our classrooms can influence students' transfer of writing practice and knowledge. That is what instructors hope for, but it also reminds us that curriculum design is fundamental to helping students in this effort. Of course, research has studied what such a curriculum might look like. For example, inquiring into the utility of two different curricula in supporting students' development of writing knowledge---one, a Writing about Writing (WAW) approach somewhat like the TFT approach and the second a rhetorically informed theme-based curriculum—Carol Hayes and her colleagues found that "different WAW curricula can produce different impacts" and that across all the curricula genre seemed to be a particularly different concept for students to theorize and apply: "It may . . . be that given the complexity of genre as a concept," they say, "an explicit writing studies curriculum might be necessary to teach it effectively" (80). Another study focused on how much course time and student engagement such topics might require to be successful. Thus, in identifying why a particular curricular approach with upper-level students didn't succeed, Walwema and Driscoll explain that what might seem like a reasonable commitment is in fact too little: "we are unconvinced that several in-class activities, one homework assignment, and one reflective piece were enough for meaningful change."

By way of contrast, focusing on a curricular approach for writing in chemistry, one with considerable success in helping students succeed in that context, Susan Green and her colleagues credit the TFT curricular approach as a major influence on its design:

> The assignment sequencing, in-class activities, peer review sessions, and teaching materials were all informed by Yancey, Robertson, and Taczak's (2014, 138–39) key suggestions for teaching transferable writing skills. Specifically, they encourage instructors to: (1) be explicit about the conventions of writing in a given discipline; (2) demonstrate, rather than explain, these conventions; (3) tap into students' existing knowledge; (4) teach writing as a composing process, rather than simply an end product; (5) teach reiteratively, reinforcing the concepts and practices of effective written communication across assignments and activities; and, finally, (6) help students develop metacognition, or thinking about their own learning, so that they recognize the role of strategies like sequencing assignments and peer review in their development as writers and learners. (112)

In part, that is the claim here: that the TFT curriculum, unique in bringing together a discreet set of key terms, systematic reflection, and students' Theory of Writing, asks students to engage in this set of interlocking concepts and practices as an *ensemble*. Moreover, the claim is also that in doing so, students develop a writing-transfer-mindset.

The value of the Teaching for Transfer curriculum for WAC courses is premised on what it can offer students: helping them develop a vocabulary of conceptual key terms with which to frame new writing situations. Helping students develop a writing-transfer-mindset, in other words, is possible. More specifically, if students are going to transfer writing knowledge and practices across the curriculum and into the disciplines of the university, as well as into external contexts, faculty across disciplines may want to consider the following key ideas and find appropriate ways to incorporate them into their own classrooms:

- *Identification and inclusion of key terms: Key terms give students a vocabulary by which they can begin to understand writing concepts and practices, create or strengthen a writing identity, and generate a theory of writing for use in future contexts*. Faculty may not be able to employ all eight of the TFT terms presented here, and, alternatively, they may want to include other writing terms, for instance, visual display of information. Such was the case in the TFT-influenced chemistry class, as Green et al. explain: "We regularly reinforced both the concepts of *chemistry* and of *communication*. Concepts such as *significant figures, readability, accuracy, genre, audience*, and *purpose* appeared across our handouts, and instructors used them repeatedly to explain and support the activities" (115). Here, then, the TFT key terms genre, audience, and purpose were remixed with the discourse community terms—specific chemistry terms significant figure, readability, and accuracy. As important, faculty will want to discuss and demonstrate the key terms in the context of writing in their discipline as well as asking students to do likewise.

- *Opportunities for students to revise and remix their set of key terms*. Asking students at various points throughout the semester to revisit their key terms helps them to create a structure for their thought process(es) as they connect learning about writing in different contexts—both in- and out-of-school writing contexts—and encourages students to identify relationships between and among their key terms as a way to understand what the writing situation is asking of them.

- *Opportunities for students to write in multiple contexts at the same time and for students to think of writing comparatively, with one writing situation compared to another for identification of similarity and difference as a tool for transfer*. As Thaiss and Zawacki observe, when students have double majors, as we saw with Kyle, those contexts often overlap and inform each other. What the TFT curriculum adds is the chance for students to trace similarities and differences across contexts by design. Moreover, as we saw with Cassidy, our students engage in multiple *kinds* of contexts, often concurrently, in courses and in co-curriculars, internships, and the workplace; tracing similar and differentiated practices across these contexts is every bit as important. In sum, when students explore their writing across contexts—like Rick learning about audience in English by understanding the concept of writing for an audience in chemistry, Kyle seeing metaphor as a similarity in political science and creative writing, and Cassidy reworking the same material for both troubled youth and federal grant makers—they have more opportunity to find meaningful and relevant connections across those contexts and to make their own knowledge about writing.

The potential of TFT for WAC, of course, is that students will become better writers and will write more effective texts. That potential also lies in its ability to help students create a greater sense of agency *as* writers, regardless of context. Key terms provide a stability by which students can articulate, and within that articulation recognize, how writing situations function, inside the classroom and outside of school as well. Students begin to understand that writing can, in fact, live outside the narrow context of writing a text for a grade and/or only within the institutionalized context of school. The potential of TFT for WAC, in other words, lies in helping students develop a writing-transfer-mindset. The future of writing across curriculum and across college, and thus the development of students as writers who can adapt and write in and among multiple contexts, includes, we believe, a more deliberate move towards teaching for transfer of writing knowledge and practice. Our hope is that the research and recommendations presented here will assist in such an effort.

Notes

1. The two institutions on a quarter system employed two (rather than three) interviews during the TFT term.

2. All of the double coding for the third iteration of the study is complete; we are currently creating an inductive coding scheme for this data set.

Works Cited

Baird, Neil, and Bradley Dilger. "How Students Perceive Transitions: Dispositions and Transfer in Internships." *College Composition and Communication*, vol. 68, no. 4, 2017, pp. 684–712.

Beaufort, Anne. *College Writing and Beyond: A New Framework for University Writing Instruction*. Utah State UP, 2007.

Bransford, John D., James W. Pellegrino, and M. Suzanne Donovan. *How People Learn: Brain, Mind, Experience, and School*. National Academy Press, 2000.

Brent, Doug. "Crossing Boundaries: Co-op Students Relearning to Write." *College Composition and Communication*, vol. 63, no. 4, 2012, pp. 558–92.

Cooper, Marilyn M. "Rhetorical Agency as Emergent and Enacted." *College Composition and Communication*, vol. 62, no. 3, 2011, pp. 420–49.

DePalma, Michael-John. "Tracing Transfer across Media: Investigating Writers' Perceptions of Cross-contextual and Rhetorical Reshaping in Processes of Remediation." *College Composition and Communication*, vol. 66, no. 4, 2015, pp. 615–42.

Driscoll, Dana L., and Josephine Walwema. "Activating the Uptake of Prior Knowledge Through Metacognitive Awareness: An Exploratory Study of Writing Transfer in Documentation and Source Use in Professional Writing Courses." *Programmatic Perspectives*, vol. 7, no. 1, 2015, pp. 21-42.

Green, Susan, Zornitsa Keremidchieva, Heidi Zimmerman, Amy Rice, Leah Witus, Marc Rodwogin, and Ruth Pardini. "Developing Students' Multi-Modal and Transferable

Writing Skills in Introductory General Chemistry." *The WAC Journal*, vol. 28, no. 1, 2017, pp 106–22.

Hayes, Carol, Ed Jones, Gwen Gorzelsky, and Dana Driscoll. "Adapting Writing about Writing: Curricular Implications of Cross-Institutional Data from the Writing Transfer Project." *WPA: Writing Program Administration*, vol. 41, no. 2, 2018, pp 65–88.

Hilgers, Thomas, Edna Hussey, and Monica Stitt-Bergh. "'As You're Writing, You Have These Epiphanies': What College Students Say about Writing and Learning in Their Majors." *Written Communication*, vol. 16, no. 3, 1999, pp. 317–53.

Jarratt, Susan, Katherine Mack, Alexandra Sartor, and Shevaun Watson. "Pedagogical Memory and the Transferability of Writing Knowledge." Writing Research Across Borders. 24 February 2008, Phelps Hall, UC Santa Barbara, CA. Presentation.

McCarthy, Lucille Parkinson. "A Stranger in Strange Lands: A College Student Writing Across the Curriculum." *Research in the Teaching of English*, vol. 21, no. 3, 1987, pp. 233–65.

Perkins, David N., and Gavriel Salomon. "Transfer of Learning." *International Encyclopedia of Education*, vol. 2, 1992, pp. 6452–57.

Read, Sarah, and Michael J. Michaud. "Writing about Writing and the Multimajor Professional Writing Course." *College Composition and Communication*, vol. 66, no.3, 2015, pp. 427–57.

Reiff, Mary Jo, and Anis Bawarshi. "Tracing Discursive Resources: How Students Use Prior Genre Knowledge to Negotiate New Writing Contexts in First-Year Composition." *Written Communication*, vol. 28, no.3, 2011, pp. 312–37.

Taczak, Kara, and Liane Robertson. "Reiterative Reflection in the 21st Century Writing Classroom: An Integrated Approach to Teaching for Transfer." *A Rhetoric of Reflection*, edited by Kathleen Blake Yancey, Utah State UP, 2016, pp. 42–63.

Thaiss, Chris and Terry Myers Zawacki. *Engaged Writers and Dynamic Disciplines: Research on the Academic Writing Life*. Boynton/Cook, 2006.

VanKooten, Crystal. "Identifying Components of Meta-Awareness about Composition: Toward a Theory and Methodology for Writing Studies." *Composition Forum*, vol. 33, 2016, compositionforum.com/issue/33/meta-awareness.php.

Wardle, Elizabeth. "Creative Repurposing for Expansive Learning: Considering 'Problem-Exploring' and 'Answer-Getting' Dispositions in Individuals and Fields." Introduction. *Composition Forum*, vol. 26, 2012, compositionforum.com/issue/26/creative-repurposing.php

Wolfe, Joanna, Barrie Olson, and Laura Wilder. "Knowing What We Know About Writing in the Disciplines: A New Approach to Teaching for Transfer in FYC." *The WAC Journal*, vol. 25, no. 1, 2014, pp. 42–77.

Yancey, Kathleen Blake. *Reflection in the Writing Classroom*. Utah State UP, 1998.

Yancey, Kathleen, Liane Robertson, and Kara Taczak. *Writing Across Contexts: Transfer, Composition, and Sites of Writing*. Utah State UP, 2014.

Building Sustainable WAC Programs: A Whole Systems Approach

MICHELLE COX, JEFFREY GALIN, AND DAN MELZER

From: Katherine T. Bridgman

Date: 02/19/2016

To: Jeffrey Galin

Subject: Question about WAC consultation

Hi Jeffrey,

I am currently the Writing Center Director at Texas A&M-San Antonio, and I have been tasked with helping our relatively new university start a WAC program. So far, we have established our WAC committee as a subcommittee through our Faculty Senate that includes representatives from our colleges as well as the WAC director (me).... We are also getting ready to downward expand this coming fall and admit our first classes of first and second year students. We currently serve only third and fourth year students as well as graduate students. A primary task of our WAC committee will be to begin outlining policies for faculty support, student support, and expectations for writing-intensive courses. Writing-intensive courses are one of the four high-impact practices that we are targeting with our downward expansion.

* * *

As I plan our first meetings – which will be condensed into two "retreats" this semester – I was thinking about the possibility of inviting a guest speaker to speak with my colleagues. While I have a small budget to work with, my budget would not allow us to bring someone to campus. Do you know of consultants who would be willing to Skype in for a session with our faculty?

Thank you for your time,
Katherine

We open with this message sent to Jeff because, as co-chairs of CCCC's WAC Standing Group, we continue to be impressed by the number of WAC programs just getting started. We often hear from those launching programs or re-starting dormant programs at the annual CCCC's WAC meeting or through requests for consultations, such as this one. In their 2008 national WAC/WID survey, Christopher Thaiss and

Tara Porter (2010) partly based their claim that the WAC movement is "alive and well" on this continued launching of new programs. In their survey, more than a third (36.3%, n = 206) of the institutions that identified as having a WAC program either have a program that is "just starting" or has existed for 1–5 years (p. 542). In addition, 152 institutions reported having plans to start a WAC program (p. 541).

We also open with Katherine's email because it represents the kinds of institutional challenges that WAC programs face, such as how to create institution-wide initiatives, plan for program growth, sustain program momentum, and prioritize strategic reforms over short-term fixes. These challenges often lead to program failure. Thaiss and Porter point out that "well over half of the 418 programs identified in [McLeod's] 1987 survey either no longer exist or have been 'restarted' in the years since" their 2008 survey (p. 558). Such a significant failure rate of WAC programs warrants serious attention.

In response to queries like Katherine's and out of concern for the writing programs we direct, we developed a systematic approach for building sustainable WAC programs. In this article, we provide an overview of our whole systems approach, offering a comprehensive theoretical model, which is derived from theories of complexity, systems, social network, resilience, and sustainable development. From these theories, we derive a set of principles and ground this theoretical framework in a WAC program-building methodology and corresponding set of strategies. Throughout this article, we return to the WAC program at Texas A&M-San Antonio (TAMUSA) to demonstrate how the theoretical framework works to develop a WAC program from the ground up. Although we present TAMUSA as a concrete application of our theoretical framework, our primary purpose is theory building: to lay out the broad strokes of the whole systems approach to initiate new ways of conceiving WAC program formation. More detailed applications of our theoretical framework to various WAC program contexts can be found in our monograph *Sustainable WAC: A Whole Systems Approach to Launching and Developing WAC Programs* (2018).

Why Theorize WAC Program Development?

In WAC literature, theory tends not to focus on the complexities of higher education or program administration, but rather on the writing pedagogies that are at the heart of WAC programs. This point is exemplified in "Theory in WAC: Where Have We Been, Where Are We Going?," in which Thaiss (2001) provides a comprehensive review of the writing theories that have informed WAC practice but does not touch upon theories related to WAC leadership or program development. This is not an oversight by Thaiss, but emblematic of a field that focuses more on theorizing WAC instruction than the administration of WAC programs. This focus on pedagogy may be inherent to the ways the field of WAC has developed and defined itself. Russell

(2002) attributes the success of the WAC movement to its focus on pedagogy, as faculty are asked to commit to a "radically different way of teaching" that offers "personal rather than institutional rewards" (p. 295).

When the literature does focus on WAC program administration, it tends to emphasize program description and advice rather than building a theory of administering and building WAC programs. The WAC literature describes individual programs (Fulwiler & Young, 1990; Segall & Smart, 2005; Thaiss et al., 2012); provides advice for developing specific program elements, such as faculty workshops or writing fellows initiatives (Mcleod, 1988; McLeod & Soven, 1991; McLeod et al. 2011; International Network of WAC Program, 2014); and describes challenges to WAC programs and steps WAC directors may take so that their programs persist (Townsend, 2008; Young & Fulwiler, 1990). All of these texts offer nuts-and-bolts advice for building and developing WAC programs rooted in experience, knowledge of the field, and writing theory and research—but not theories of writing program administration or methodologies for creating sustainable programs. Extending the focus on the features of enduring WAC programs, William Condon and Carol Rutz (2012) introduced a taxonomy for categorizing WAC programs according to their characteristics, identifying four types: foundational, established, integrated, and institutional change agent. However, like the earlier literature on enduring programs, Condon and Rutz do not attempt to explain the underlying reasons why WAC programs at higher levels in this taxonomy outlast programs at the lower levels. Even WAC surveys over the years that have looked at the issue of program longevity (McLeod, 1997; Thaiss & Porter, 2008) have identified representative program features that may be replicated rather than offering a systematic understanding of why these traits lead to program persistence.

Barbara Walvoord's (1996) "The Future of WAC" departs from this largely descriptive body of literature as the first attempt to theorize the vulnerability and endurance of WAC programs. Walvoord draws on social movement theory to analyze why WAC programs and the field at large have been vulnerable to such a wide range of challenges. Exploring program variability, for instance, Walvoord argues that WAC has been largely decentralized, realized through the development of programs on individual campuses and spread through conferences and a group of "traveling workshop leaders" (p. 61), but never becoming a national movement through the development of a national WAC organization. Walvoord sees this decentralization as strengthening individual WAC programs because it allows them to form their own goals in relation to their individual contexts, but also as leaving them "vulnerable to cooptation, becoming special interest groups, settling for narrow goals and limited visions, or simply being wiped out by the next budget crunch or the next change of deans" (p. 62). Indeed, the loss of so many WAC programs as indicated by Thaiss and Porter's 2008 survey is evidence of this continuing vulnerability.

Walvoord uses social movement theory to distinguish between micro-level actions (such as "changing personal behavior") and macro-level actions (such as "changing structures and organizations") (p. 60). For instance, she argues that faculty workshops, long the "backbone of the WAC movement," are effective at the micro-level as they "generate high energy and enthusiasm" for teaching writing among those that attend (p. 63), but do not lead to changes at the macro-level because they do not affect the wider campus culture or university structures. She then turns to the future of WAC, drawing on strategies used by social movements to suggest approaches for strengthening WAC programs, such as coming to a deeper understanding of the wider campus and societal contexts within which WAC programs live, connecting to other institutional and national movements, and connecting to university missions and accrediting bodies' standards. Though Walvoord's article has been widely cited, we do not see scholars taking on her larger claims or more pointed insights about WAC.

Our approach builds on Walvoord's germinal work. We start with her premise, using theory to better understand WAC program development within the complex and dynamic contexts of higher education. Like her, we theorize practice by providing WAC directors with strategies to develop enduring WAC programs. Like Walvoord, we keep our focus on program administration rather than pedagogy. As WAC program directors, we understand and value the power of WAC pedagogy on faculty and have ourselves led many workshops, but we believe that WAC directors need to do more than train individual faculty. They should aim to transform a campus culture to create lasting change by approaching the problem of program sustainability systematically. Departing from Walvoord, we find social movement theory inadequate. While it provides a useful lens for considering program vulnerability and suggesting strategies, social movement theory cannot provide WAC directors with a comprehensive theoretical framework, methodology, and set of strategies for launching, revitalizing, and reviving WAC programs, as does the whole systems approach we develop here.

To introduce this theoretical framework, we return to the email that opens this article. The newly appointed WAC director of TAMUSA, Katherine Bridgman, contacted Jeff to consult on their nascent program at a moment when we were drafting material on the planning stages of WAC program development for the whole systems approach. Jeff spoke with Katherine several times to learn more about the situation. He learned that TAMUSA is a branch campus with about 5,500 students. About 60% of their population are first generation college students, 70% are Hispanic or Latinx, and 64% of their students are first generation (Texas A&M). At the time Jeff met the director in January of 2016, TAMUSA was making plans to transition from an upper division two-year college to a four-year institution for fall 2016. Prior to starting these changes, the institution established a four-semester set of mandatory one-hour student support courses and a university-wide e-portfolio. Further, he learned that

TAMUSA planned to establish a WAC program that same fall, which would feature what the committee defined as a writing-intentional (W-I) program.

Like many new WAC directors, Katherine started by examining programs and practices at other universities as a way to conceptualize their own. She selected two WAC initiatives that proved effective on other campuses—student writing portfolios and writing-intensive requirements—and reached out to a WAC consultant for guidance on moving these initiatives forward. The primary problems with this approach are: (a) it looks outward, away from the institution, rather than inward to understand existing or previously existing writing initiatives; (b) it focuses primarily on isolated practices rather than a systematic process for integrating curricular change at a given institution; and (c) it concentrates on program initiation but not necessarily sustainability.

To address these problems, for TAMUSA and other new WAC programs, we need a theoretical model that can build from context and represent the complexity of large-scale reform. This model also needs to provide WAC directors and committees guidance on evaluating needs, setting goals, planning programs, implementing projects, assessing initiatives, and tracking sustainability. To create such a theoretical model, we turn to theories that provide tools for describing and introducing change to dynamic systems.

Theories That Inform Our Whole Systems Approach

Complexity theory, first used in computational and scientific fields to describe complex phenomena, provides an umbrella framework for our approach and offers ways to study the interactions among a large and diverse group of actors and organizations within a complex adaptive system. When scientists talk about such systems, they often refer to examples such as flocking birds, each of which makes minute adjustments in their flight in relationship only to the birds next to them. These decentralized decisions among individual birds are driven by feedback loops that either magnify a small action across the system or keep it in check. A flock of starlings, for example, can appear in such numbers that they seem to fill the sky. As one watches these large flocks, one sees how the micro-relationships among individuals can result in a flowing mass that sometimes splinters off but often forms amoebic shapes. Complex systems science works to understand the emergence of these coordinated macro-behaviors, the local rule-following activity that leads to these behaviors, how the system (flock) remains identifiable, and how the system maintains its relative internal stability (Leon, 2014).

Some scholars have argued that universities are complex systems (Leon, 2014) with multiple levels of stakeholders (students, faculty, administrators, board members). If we imagine the university as a social ecosystem, we can better understand how adding stresses within the system can lead to behavioral adaptations until the stresses become too great and lead to program failure. While a WAC program is not a complex system itself, it might lead to adaptive behaviors within the system that both increase its complexity and contribute to collective pattern-forming processes of the larger complex system. The greater the diversity and connectivity of the individuals at the lowest levels of the system, the more complex the system becomes and the more likely emergent and adaptive behaviors will be introduced. Perhaps this is the reason why WAC lore has often emphasized the need for WAC programs to start by gathering grassroots support and create an advisory board early in its development. According to complexity theory, the more top-down the program, the fewer interactions among individual actors in the system, the weaker the feedback loops, and the less likely emergent behaviors will spread across the system. It also stands to reason that systemic transformational change may have roots in top-down decisions or strategic plans but cannot be realized unless those goals resonate at all scales within the system.

While complexity science provides ways to understand how complex systems work, it does not offer strategies for intervening within the systems it studies. As scholars began to extend complexity theory from natural systems to social networks like corporations, they desired theoretical frameworks that were not just descriptive, but also predictive and focused on intervention.

Systems theory focuses primarily at the macro-level, mapping the system to better understand the relationships that govern it. Systems theory encourages us to approach complex systems by focusing on relationship patterns and by "using the concept of wholeness to order our thoughts" (Checkland, 1981, p. 4). Systems practice begins with stakeholder discussions of relationships among system structures and processes to paint a rich picture of the whole. These actors also create a conceptual model that exposes ideologies structuring the system and defines their ideal vision of it. This focus on system mapping to direct change requires moving beyond "parochial boundaries" (in the case of a university, individual courses, departments, and colleges) and finding the points of leverage where "actions and changes in structures" can lead to "significant, enduring improvements" across the system (Senge, 1990, p. 114). Points of leverage are highly connected places where even a small change might have significant ripple effects for the entire system (for example, linking a student writing portfolio to a graduation requirement rather than a first-year writing requirement). These ripple effects are what Senge refers to as reinforcing processes, where a single intervention can have a snowball effect on students, faculty, and the campus culture of writing.

A WAC director applying a systems approach might begin not by choosing WAC initiatives to implement, but by taking the time to study the campus system to create a rich picture of writing across the university. In fact, this is the first activity that Jeff encouraged the WAC committee at TAMUSA to undertake, work that they did in preparation for his second consultation. Their goal was to map the different writing activities happening on campus and then identify the stakeholders that impact or are impacted by these writing activities.

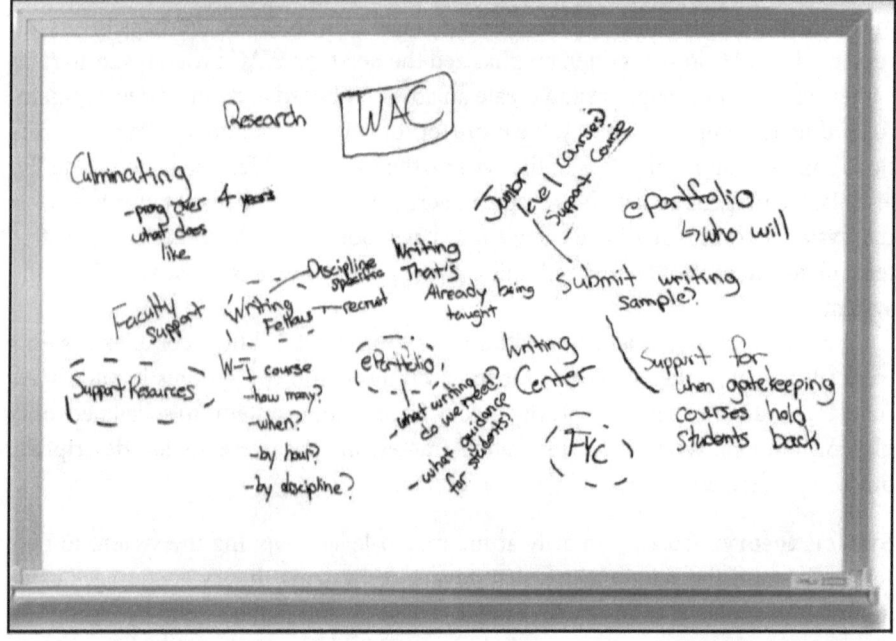

Figure 1: Photo of whiteboard program mapping completed by TAMUSA WAC committee.

This rough sketch provides a baseline understanding of a campus writing culture that stakeholders can use to consider their ideal goals for writing on campus and create alternative models of the system. The complexity of this rough sketch grows as the stakeholder group discusses lines of communication and interaction among each node, enabling them to identify points of leverage for introducing change to the university's curricular ecology.

Systems theory—and especially the more recent approach of "critical systems theory"—also recognizes that disparities of power exist in all human systems; changes to a system can affect different groups within the system differently; and when introducing change to a system we need to be particularly cognizant of those groups with less power, less of a voice, and less visibility in the system (see, for example, Flood, 1990; Jackson, 1985; Midgley, 1996). In the WAC literature, two groups of marginalized faculty and students have emerged as a focus: contingent labor and multilingual student writers (see, for example, Cox & Zawacki, 2011; LaFrance, 2015; Johns, 1991; Zawacki & Cox, 2014). Systems theory reminds us that it is important to consider potential unintended ripple effects in a system early in WAC program planning.

While systems theory provides a framework for considering the macro-level, to focus more on the micro-level, we draw on **social network theory**. This theory originated as a way to understand how ties among individuals impact social networks, beliefs, and behaviors, and it considers a group of people (e.g. faculty and staff) as an interconnected system of nodes with a wide range of ties, or links, to others. These connections can be visually mapped to examine the lines of communication, patterns of interaction, and distribution of knowledge within that system. Mapping communication pathways along a network of nodes can help to identify individuals who serve as conduits or bottlenecks. This theory prioritizes "the relationships and ties with other actors within the network" (Marsden, 2005, p. 8) rather than attributes of individual actors. For example, when considering the effectiveness of a WAC director, it is more important to examine the web of relationships that a WAC director establishes with others on campus than to focus on the director's personality traits.

Albert Lazlo Barabasi (2002) argues that interactivity with network hubs is key for innovative programs (such as WAC) since in complex networks, failures predominantly affect the smallest nodes first. Barabasi also points out that there is a critical threshold (the tipping point) where the number of links an innovation connects to begins to increase exponentially, and conversely, if an innovation fails to reach a threshold number of nodes, it is bound to fail. Finding points of interactivity in the university system is also key because of the network analysis concept of *preferential attachment*: actors are more likely to link to nodes that are already well connected and popular than to more isolated and less popular nodes.

The methodology that emerges from this theory is typically called social network analysis or organizational network analysis (ONA). Typically, ONA practitioners survey every member of the targeted group to uncover a specific set of organizational patterns within the group. Once the data is collected, the individual actors are visually mapped as a set of nodes in a three-dimensional network that provides links among actors in the form of lines connecting individuals, subsets, and larger groups. Such a detailed and comprehensive survey would not be practical or even necessary for most WAC programs. However, simply mapping the relationships among stakeholders could prove useful. At TAMUSA, this map would identify several sets of actors connecting the director to WAC committee members and each of those members to their respective departments. Katherine would also be connected to the writing center, which she directs, and the newly forming FYC program. Also included would be links to individuals in the library, faculty who will receive training, managers of e-portfolios, and curriculum committee members that will review course proposals across the institution.

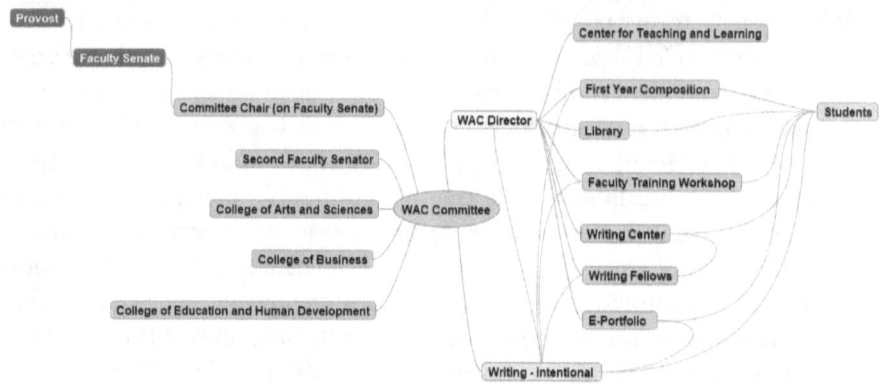

Figure 2: Early network map of TAMUSA's WAC program constructed by Jeff in consultation with Katherine Bridgman.

The more a stakeholder group can visualize the nodes, hubs, and links within the network, the easier it becomes to identify bottlenecks such as the "gatekeeping courses" mentioned in the institutional map, as well as conduits of change.

Complexity, systems, and social network theories offer approaches for describing, visualizing, and analyzing a complex system. To consider the effects of change on a system, we turn to resilience theory and sustainable development theory.

Resilience theory helps us understand how systems handle stresses yet maintain a relatively stable state. Resilience theory was first introduced to help understand the "capacity of ecosystems to handle challenges or changes to the system while maintaining a relative balanced state or to shift to an alternative, potentially transformative, state" (Folke et al., 2010, para. 3). For example, an ecosystem with an existing dam that has been in place for many years tends to reach a relatively stable state. As certain factors change over time, that same system can cross a threshold and reach an alternative stable state, which may or may not be as desirable as the previous state. For example, if the dam breaks and is not repaired, the system will settle into an alternative transformed state. The key to understanding these system changes are the feedback loops that "determine their overall dynamics" (Folke et al., 2010, para. 6). In the example of the dam, changes in the relatively stable state may be much less dramatic than a break, but lead nonetheless to equally significant shifts in the homeostatic state that the system reaches over time. Over-farming upstream could release enough phosphates into the lake to eventually result in a massive blue-green algae bloom that causes a mass fish kill. Resilience theory has implications for WAC program adaptation and longevity in relation to the curricular ecology—the relationship between social and curricular practices—of an institution. At TAMUSA, the introduction of downward expansion, e-portfolios, and a writing-intentional program all at once would put too much strain on faculty and curriculum committees to create a stable writing culture, so slowing down the development of the W-I initiative to ensure resilience became crucial. This shift enabled the WAC committee to propose a four-year timeframe for implementation so faculty could develop W-I courses and get them approved in sufficient numbers to avoid course bottlenecks for students taking these required courses.

Resilience theory reminds us that resilience and adaptability are dynamic processes that require constant monitoring and intervention. That initial stable state is going to shift over time as practices are tested and revised, as personnel come and go, and as program elements shift in purpose or function. To promote program resilience, the TAMUSA WAC committee established a system for re-certifying their W-I courses every three years and planned for the WAC committee to conduct an "annual program assessment using work that students include in their writing portfolios along with other documents from the program" (Texas A&M, 2017). Building in such monitoring is needed since interventions like the development of writing-intensive courses can easily shift away from their original intent with changes in the faculty who teach the course.

Compared to the other theories we've presented, **sustainable development theory** is significantly more project-focused and action-oriented, as it emerged to solve serious global challenges. Broadly defined, sustainable development is "development that meets the needs of the present without compromising the ability of future generations to meet their own needs" (United Nations World Commission, p. 43). This same UN report, referred to as the Brundtland Report, laid out the goal of building a future "that is more prosperous, more just, and more secure" (para. 3). This ambitious political agenda requires buy-in from stakeholders at every level of the system as well as clear guidelines for building consensus and introducing and assessing change. This theory thus provides a practical whole systems methodology for introducing change into a system by grounding program development in discrete projects that work through cycles of planning, doing, checking, and improving (Environment Canada, 2013) and for monitoring progress through sustainability indicators (Bell and Morse, 2008), further discussed below.

Sustainability serves as a core value and outcome of any significant curricular initiative, which is as important as the guiding vision of the curricular reform itself. No institution would undertake a potentially paradigmatic shift in its mission, with the time, money, and resources it takes to do so, without a desire for these changes to persist. Thus, in creating our whole systems approach for WAC program development, we've borrowed heavily from sustainable development theory. Inspired by a report on sustainability indicators that emerged from a sustainable development conference in 1996 in Bellagio, Italy (referred to as the Bellagio Report), we've developed a set of principles for sustainable WAC program development, while integrating insights from across the theories we introduce here. From sustainable development theory, we reconceptualized WAC programs and interventions (i.e. writing-intensive requirements, writing fellows programs, and faculty development institutes) as projects—each with their own cycles of development and assessment. And we've borrowed the idea of using sustainability indicators to guide program and project assessment. Below, we list the guiding principles we derived from the Bellagio Report and the five theoretical frameworks introduced above for developing WAC programs and then describe a methodology—also inspired by sustainable development theory—for putting these principles into action.

Principles for a Whole Systems Approach for WAC Program Development

The following principles represent a synthesis of our theoretical framework. They are interrelated and meant to be used as a full set, rather than piecemeal.

1. **Wholeness**: understanding a WAC program as a significant intervention within a complex system with competing ideologies and many levels, actors, and practices.
2. **Broad participation**: engaging stakeholders from all levels of the institution to help plan, approve, implement, and assess program goals, outcomes, and projects.
3. **Transformative change**: identifying points of leverage for introducing change to the university system at multiple levels, including changes in ideologies and practices as they relate to writing culture.
4. **Equity**: working to minimize disparities in current and future generations of WAC faculty and student writers.
5. **Resilience**: adapting to program challenges, maintaining self-organizing practices, and increasing the capacity for learning and adaptation to sustain desirable pathways for development.
6. **Leadership**: identifying leadership that can serve as the hub for the program, with the authority on campus to lead a cohesive effort of planning, launching, developing, and assessing WAC.
7. **Systematic development**: building a WAC program incrementally over time with a clear mission and prioritized goals.

8. **Integration**: building program components that synchronize with national and local mandates, integrate into existing structures and practices, and facilitate collaborative campus relationships.
9. **Visibility**: ensuring that program development, assessment, and change are transparent, regular, and public as well as promoting program events and successes through multiple means of reporting.
10. **Feedback:** identifying indicators and repeated measures to reveal trends, stimulate recursive and adaptive change, promote collective learning and feedback for decision-making, and determine whether a WAC program is in balance and whether individual WAC projects are sustainable and achieving their goal.

These principles underlie our methodology and strategies, which we describe below.

Whole Systems Methodology

Our whole systems methodology creates an iterative and participatory cycle to establish institutional change that integrates ongoing assessment of sustainability. It is designed for developing entire WAC programs as well as particular WAC projects (i.e. WI programs, faculty seminars, etc.) and tracks sustainability through the use of sustainability indicators (SIs) (see figure 3). We developed this methodology from two models used in sustainable development: Canada's Federal Sustainable Development Strategy (FSDS) (Environment Canada, 2013) and Bell and Morse's (2008) Imagine approach. The FSDS model was developed to implement a national strategy for sustainable development in Canada through a "plan, do, check, and improve" multi-stage approach. Like the FSDS model, Bell and Morse's Imagine model is project-based and cyclical, with stages of understanding context, imagining alternative scenarios, and publicizing projects. However, Bell and Morse's Imagine model places more focus on the participatory process of developing and using sustainability indicators to track and predict project sustainability.

SIs are the most significant distinguishing feature of sustainable development methodology. Emerging from the idea of indicator species, an SI may be understood as "a quantitative tool that analyzes changes, while measuring and communicating progress towards the sustainable use and management of economic, social, institutional, and environmental resources" (Olsson et al., 2004, p. 8). Rather than look at a single indicator, SIs "aim to develop a framework that tries to bring the economic, social and environmental aspects of society together, emphasizing the links between them" (Olsson et al., 2004, p. 9). For example, when considering the sustainability of a natural resource, one would not only focus on availability of the resource (say, coal), but also on environmental aspects (such as the impacts of extracting and burning coal on air and water quality and the release of toxic materials into the soil), economic aspects (such as the number of related jobs, impact on other industries in the area), and social aspects (such as the working conditions of coal miners and health risks to the local community). And each of these indicators must be clearly defined, reproducible, unambiguous, understandable, and practical. It should be possible to deduce from a set of chosen indicators the viability and sustainability of the given system being studied in comparison to alternate development paths, in this case, coal mining within a specific local ecology.

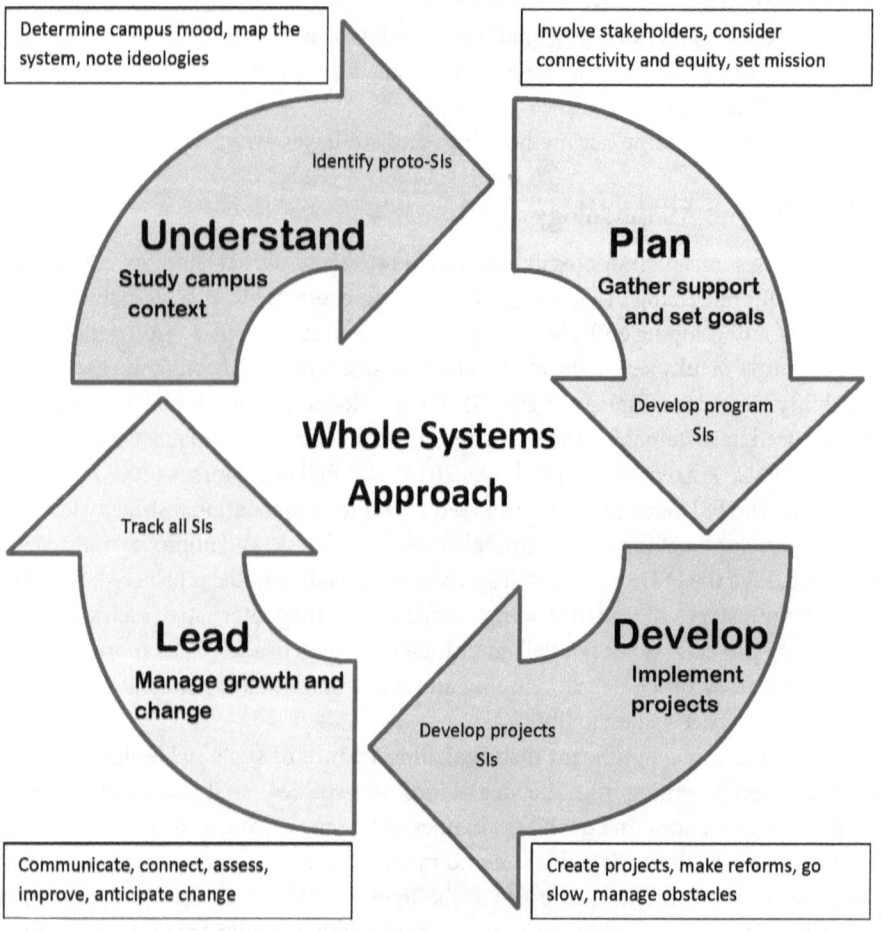

Figure 3. The whole systems methodology for transformative change.

To aid WAC directors in identifying SIs, we turn to a model introduced by Hardi and Zdan (1997) and extended by Bossel (1999). Their model focuses on three major systems, two of which include subsystems: the human system (comprised of individual development, the social system, and the government system); the support system (comprised of the economic system and infrastructure system); and natural system. These systems are outlined in figure 6, which Jeff adapted from Bossel (1999, p. 18) to reflect WAC concerns.

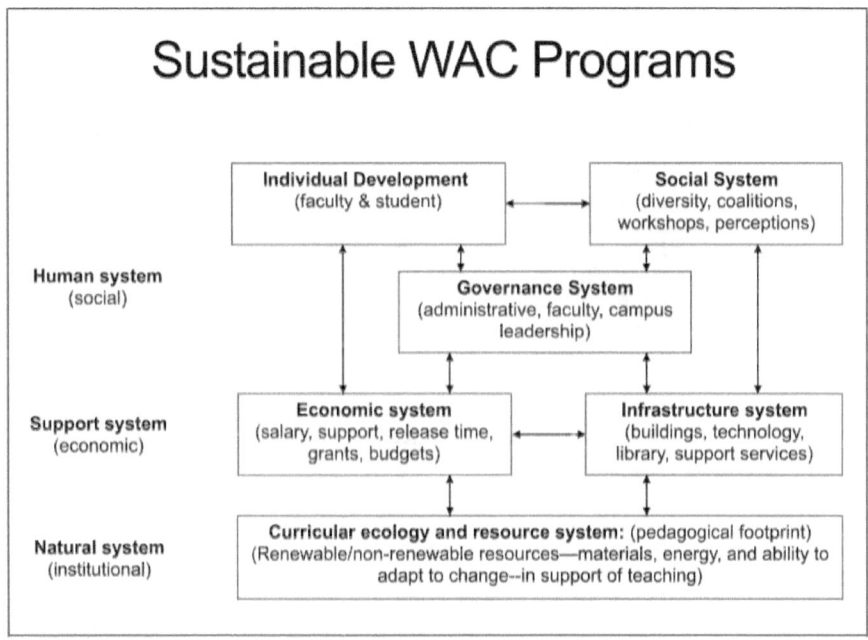

Figure 6: *The six major systems of the anthrosphere and their major relationships. Reprinted from Galin, Jeffrey R. (2010), Improving rather than proving: Self-administered sustainability mapping of WAC programs. Council of Writing Program Administrators Conference, Minneapolis, MN.*

These six systems of the WAC anthrosphere may serve as a heuristic for identifying SIs, particularly indicators of distress. Table 1 below demonstrates how TAMUSA might apply this heuristic to develop SIs for their W-I program:

Table 1

Example Indicators of Distress for TAMUSA

Level	Example indicators of distress
Individual	Director's time commitment increasing for WAC management without commensurate release time or compensation Compliance of W-I syllabi dropping significantly Student or faculty perceptions of WAC shifting negatively
Social	Membership of WAC committee decreasing or shifting so that it is no longer representative across campus Increase in administrative obstacles to program management or growth
Governance	Increasing class sizes resulting from university policy changes Dynamic program director leading too many faculty workshops to focus on other program development Decrease in writing quality in e-portfolios resulting from new statewide outcomes
Financial	Diminishing budget resulting from increased pressure from competing units Budget threshold overrun resulting from new costs and/or projects without commensurate budget increases
University Curricular Ecology	Fall in departmental participation resulting from merging or fracturing of college departments or divisions Insufficient classroom, office, or meeting space resulting from substantial changes in allocated space

Tracking SIs is so integral to sustainable development that we have included them in every stage of our methodology. The SIs themselves, however, are only the means of assessing the visibility and sustainability of a given program or project. Each of the four stages of the whole systems methodology—understanding, planning, developing, and leading—is scaffolded by a set of strategies that enable sustainable program development and growth.

Understanding, a stage we borrowed from the Imagine approach, involves examining the campus context, including the structures and network of relationships of the system.

Strategy 1: Determine the campus mood. "Campus mood" refers to the overall readiness of an institution for increased commitment to student writing. Determining the campus mood is a mix of collecting data, talking to stakeholders, reflecting on current writing practices across university contexts, identifying points of conflict and agreement about possible WAC program models, and identifying the current state of writing and teaching of writing on campus. This understanding will allow the WAC director to establish proto-SIs that mark the pre-implementation status of a WAC program. Determining the campus mood will also help program leaders facilitate an overall approach to program initiation, development, and timing. For example, if upper administration wants a WAC program but will not provide funds for a dedicated director, faculty support, or assessment processes, the mood for WAC might be judged somewhat hostile. Such a context would warrant a slower development, broader outreach, and possibly pilot projects that can be evaluated and then reported back to upper administration.

Strategy 2: Understand the system in order to focus on points of interactivity and leverage. Institutions of higher education are complex entities that not only foster connectivity through nodes and hubs (such as academic senates and centers for teaching), but also segregation and isolation (the siloed structure of departments and colleges). Creating rich visual maps of the places where writing occurs, the requirements involving writing, hubs of writing instruction, and the units and stakeholders impacting writing will help WAC directors choose interventions that will have leverage to make significant and sustainable change.

Strategy 3: Understand the ideologies that inform the campus culture of writing. The ideologies that define campus writing will inevitably shape the behavior of individual faculty and administrators. Understanding these ideologies helps to locate reinforcing processes that amplify problematic attitudes or behaviors. For example, an institution that is focused on timed writing tests is informed by a theory of writing as a product and creates an ideology and a process that reinforces that writing tasks can be completed and assessed in a single draft. Shifting from timed writing to portfolio assessment would not only change the theory of writing under which the system operates, but also could reinforce positive changes to students' conception of writing processes and teachers' writing pedagogies.

Planning involves gathering support, such as a WAC advisory board, and working with this group to determine program goals and the sustainability indicators that will guide program development.

Strategy 4: Involve multiple stakeholders in the system. Building WAC programs that have a high level of connectivity and influence requires the involvement of multiple stakeholders across the system and across scales, from individual faculty to department chairs to academic senate committees to deans and provosts. These stakeholders are crucial for building a WAC program through participatory processes, including collaborating to map the system, setting the mission and goals, determining and operationalizing program sustainability indicators, and setting the agenda for program development.

Strategy 5: Work towards positioning the WAC program so that it has greater interconnectivity and leverage in the institution. WAC programs that do not fully integrate into existing institutional structures and do not move beyond a small core group are rarely sustainable. From their inception, every WAC program should aim to be a hub within its institutional network and not just a node. Furthermore, it is more effective to locate a WAC program in existing hubs that are connected across disciplines preferentially, like writing centers, centers for teaching, and independent writing departments, than a less connected node like a traditional English department. WAC directors can also link to highly connected institutional structures such as the faculty senate, libraries, academic assessment, or the office of institutional diversity. Connecting the WAC program in these ways also increases program stability by not being perceived as marginal or temporary, but integral to the institution.

Strategy 6: Consider the impact of WAC on faculty and student equity. A whole systems approach acknowledges that disparities of power exist in all human systems, that changes to a system typically affect different groups unevenly, and that when systems change, particular attention should be paid to groups with less power and visibility. For instance, the creation of WAC curriculum such as first-year writing seminars could unintentionally increase reliance on non-tenure track faculty or workload for junior faculty (LaFrance, 2015). The creation of a timed writing assessment could lead to inequitable conditions for multilingual students (Janopoulos, 1995). How WAC affects the faculty it involves and the students it serves should be considered in the early stages of program development and tracked with one or two SIs.

Strategy 7: Set mission, goals, and sustainability indicators. While WAC programs often develop organically and even opportunistically, those that set a mission statement, goals, and sustainability indicators in the development phase are more likely to have a system-wide impact, since they will be more coherent and goal-driven. These goals and indicators should be shaped by a group of stakeholders from across the networked system, such as a WAC advisory board. The mission, goals, and program outcomes then serve as a foundation for systematic program development and assessment.

Developing uses a systematic approach to fulfil mission and goals through project development and assessment.

Strategy 8: Maximize program sustainability through project-based program development. Translating program outcomes into action requires an intentional project-based approach. WAC projects such as writing-intensive initiatives or faculty development retreats are self-contained to a large degree, each targeting a specific problem/outcome and moving through a full set of stages from inception to implementation and assessment. SIs are developed in the initial stages of the project and evaluated regularly to establish threshold boundaries within which each project can be expected to function successfully. Taken together, a set of projects is used systematically to fulfill the program mission and goals. Using a project-based approach enables

WAC leaders to prioritize which programs should be developed, in what order, and on what timeline to most impact the system.

Strategy 9: Make reforms at both the micro-level and the systems-level. In WAC programs, working at the micro-level (i.e. consulting with individual faculty, giving classroom presentations) and working at the systems-level (i.e. working with a department to create a departmental writing assessment plan, instituting a writing-intensive requirement) go hand in hand. Typically, when WAC programs start, the director focuses on the micro-level. This work is rewarding and can help the director establish relationships with faculty, create credibility, and build critical mass. However, if directors spend most of their time at the micro-level, then they can't spend much of their time at the systems-level, which is necessary for making enduring changes to the campus culture of writing.

Strategy 10: Plan for gradual rather than rapid reforms to the system. Academic institutions are complex organizations that do not change course easily. WAC programs seek to shift the culture of writing at the institution, and this kind of change happens incrementally. From established WAC programs, we know it can take many years to transform the writing culture a campus. Even specific projects can take years to develop fully. For example, a shift to building a writing-enriched curriculum model that involves departments making multi-year commitments to curriculum analysis and change might take several years to gain footing. Quick change can end in disaster, as quick changes do not allow time for cross-institutional buy-in or an understanding of the potential impact on other parts of the system.

Leading focuses on promoting program sustainability through program guidance and management.

Strategy 11: Deal with obstacles to program or project development systematically. The resiliency of a WAC program depends on its ability to overcome challenges and obstacles, which will inevitably arise throughout its development. A systems process for resolving conflicts necessitates a broad understanding of an obstacle, which includes collecting necessary data, considering the scope of its reach, coordinating with relevant stakeholders, balancing concerns that need to be considered, compromising, and proposing clear models or simulations to help predict the system's performance before the changes are implemented. For example, a dean who appeared supportive of WAC suddenly decides that a writing-intensive program cannot work because so many departments have large section courses. Rather than taking personal offense and confronting the dean, an approach might be to bring an external visitor to campus who made such a program work at another institution or encouraging use of breakout sections with TAs for the writing in these courses.

Strategy 12: Communicate regularly and at all levels of the system to keep the program visible. For WAC programs to be perceived as integral to the institution, they need to stay visible through good PR, partnering with popular campus hubs, and reminding other units of the program's relevance. This maintenance of visibility can take many forms—through WAC websites, newsletters, and event announcements—but also through such activities as preparing annual reports, attending campus meetings, joining university committees related to teaching and learning, and publishing results of WAC initiatives both locally and nationally. Creating visibility can also be about branding signature events like faculty retreats or student recognition ceremonies. Tracking visibility through SIs ensures that the program remains visible to faculty and administrators while not over inundating them with messages and events.

Strategy 13: Be aware of systems beyond your institution and connect to those that are beneficial to the WAC program. Changes in systems beyond your institution may affect the campus culture of writing. Some of these effects may be negative, such as a state government slashing funds for basic writing programs, and some may be positive, such as disciplinary accrediting bodies like IEEE, ABET, or CCNE increasing emphasis on written communication. Still other systems—such as the CCCC WAC Standing Group, the WAC Clearinghouse, IWAC conference, the WAC Summer Institute, NCTE, the Association for Writing Across the Curriculum, and the AACU—may provide a WAC leader with important resources, such as access to mentors, scholarship, and position statements. Tapping into such resources will assist WAC leaders as they seek to create change on their campuses.

Strategy 14: Assess and revise the WAC program. Systems tend toward segregation and stagnation, and comprehensive writing programs are susceptible to becoming static rather than dynamic if assessment feedback loops are not built into them. For example, a writing-intensive requirement without oversight or regular faculty development will most likely face dwindling enthusiasm and less coherence as a program. Ideally, WAC directors should identify a set of questions based on organizational and program maps (i.e. which departments are contributing WI courses?); identify the necessary but sufficient set of indicators to track program sustainability (i.e., what balance of WI course instructor rank would indicate a sustainable WI initiative?); develop an assessment model that keeps track of the full picture; and revisit the pool of questions and indicators as programs grow and change.

Strategy 15: Create a plan for sustainable leadership. There are many tales from WAC lore of vibrant WAC programs that crumbled when the leader stepped down or left for another institution. Distributed leadership models can help guard against this reliance on a single individual's energy or career choices. From a systems perspective, leadership that is located at only one point in the system and that comes from only one perspective is not as effective as leadership that is collective and disbursed throughout the system. Tactics include developing a critical mass of individual teacher-leaders across disciplines, working with a WAC advisory board or committee, creating graduation writing requirements that are overseen by cross-disciplinary committees, and developing an assistant director position.

The Whole Systems Approach at TAMUSA

When Katherine first reached out to Jeff, she described WAC as on the brink of the *developing* phase. Jeff convinced her and the WAC committee to take more time in the *understanding* and *planning* phases before moving forward. In his first meeting with the WAC committee, Jeff introduced four key points about program development, including the need to: (a) map visually how the program they were imagining would tie into existing initiatives on campus; (b) establish a clear mission statement and goals; (c) develop a set of sustainability indicators to track the emergence, growth, and sustainability of their WAC program; and (d) operationalize each SI by determining their bands of equilibrium with measurable thresholds of success and distress. This six-member committee had broad participation, with members from each college and the WAC director. It also had leverage to make change, since it was a subcommittee of the faculty senate and also had a direct line of communication to the provost.

Originally, the committee was going to propose only a single writing-intensive course requirement, but in an email to Katherine, Jeff prompted the committee to think about the larger goal of system-wide change:

> I would encourage you to think of WAC as the introduction of transformative change for the curriculum on your campus. If you can get [the committee] to think about more than just adding writing, but changing the way that writing is taught and perceived at the institution, then you have room to think of WAC as a shift in the whole curricular system, even if it is only starting with a few WI designated courses and some faculty support. If the committee can realize that a sustainable WAC program at most universities is much larger than a single WI initiative, they can set criteria for WI that situates it in this larger context. (Jeff Galin, personal communication, March 18, 2016)

The committee was persuaded by Jeff's argument that WAC should be thought of as a transformative intervention into the system, and they decided to aim for a more expansive four-course WI requirement. They slowed down the implementation process, established pilot courses to test out strategies, developed W-I criteria, extended the period for course development and faculty training to four years, and formulated an assessment plan.

During this process, the committee thought about project sustainability by considering the number of courses that need to be certified W-I (sufficient sections across the majors prevent bottlenecks for student progress), number of faculty trained (all faculty teaching W-I courses need to participate in WAC workshops), and sufficient funding (WAC director release time, faculty workshop stipends, assessment raters, departmental grants, additional faculty as course size drops). These parameters could all easily be translated into SIs. For example, they decided to cap W-I class sizes at twenty students. To establish an SI related to course size, they could set the band of equilibrium between fifteen students per course (a sign of distress, as it might indicate that students are putting off the requirement) and twenty-five students per course (another sign of distress, as it may mean that not enough sections are being offered). Indicating the band of equilibrium within which each SI remains sustainable can help WAC directors monitor initiatives and make arguments for appropriate funding and support.

When the new provost arrived mid-summer, he supported the committee's desire to slow down the implementation process from fall 2016 to fall of 2021. He also supported the committee's recommendation to shift from writing-intensive to "writing-intentional" courses and enabled one course to be piloted. The shift to W-I reflects a desire to focus on quality over quantity and an emphasis on high impact practices as defined by the AACU (Katherine Bridgeman, personal communication, April 18, 2017). A small group of instructors are now planning to pilot W-I courses in fall 2017 after participating in a six-week required training course and working with the WAC director. By 2021, all entering students will be required to take four W-I courses, thus increasing the chances for transforming the institutional culture of literacy.

The careful and strategic process that the WAC committee engaged in reflects a whole systems approach that values incremental but sustainable reform over quick and easy reforms that often fail due to lack of buy-in or lack of influence on and leverage within the system.

Building Sustainable WAC: From the Campus to the Field at Large

Our principles and methodology provide the coherent and theorized approach that has been missing from the WAC lore, while still taking into consideration the highly specific contexts of an institutional landscape, comprised of curricular histories and politics, changing faculty and student demographics, and evolving missions and goals. Furthermore, our approach provides justification for moving slowly and systematically, positioning WAC programs within institutional hubs, and supporting WAC leaders with adequate resources for making the kinds of transformative changes to campus writing culture that we know WAC can generate and sustain.

This focus on transformative change, and the theoretical and methodological sophistication needed to develop sustainable WAC programs, may seem intimidating at first. However, we feel that the typical process to starting a WAC program is more intimidating. Many new WAC directors jump right into program implementation and then become overwhelmed, as they have not laid the groundwork, coordinated with stakeholders, or created a strategic plan. This accelerated startup leads quickly to director burn-out. This may have been the path that TAMUSA took if they had not taken up Jeff's suggestions to slow down, think systematically and strategically, and pilot a program before full implementation. Furthermore, our approach provided justification to upper administration for a slower roll-out, more institutional resources, and more stakeholder collaboration, which may lead to more buy-in across campus.

WAC leaders have always stressed that WAC is not a quick fix to a "problem" with student writing but has the larger goal of transforming a campus culture of writing. Until now, WAC has not had a theoretically-based framework, methodology, principles, and strategies for enacting this goal. We hope our whole systems approach provides this. We are also hopeful that the whole systems approach can begin to address the larger concerns that Walvoord expressed about the sustainability of WAC as a field. Walvoord argued that the lack of a coherent theory for WAC, as well as the field's focus on how WAC plays out on individual campuses, has prevented WAC from achieving the status of a national movement. In our larger project, we explore the implications of this framework for better understanding the vulnerabilities of the field at large and creating structures that promote sustainability, such as an umbrella organization for WAC.

References

Barabasi, A. L. (2002). *Linked: The new science of networks*. Cambridge, MA: Perseus.

Bell, S., & Morse, S. (2008). *Sustainability indicators: Measuring the immeasurable?* 2nd ed. Sterling, VA: Earthscan. Retrieved from https://www.u-cursos.cl/ciencias/2015/2/CS06067/1/material_docente/bajar?id_material=1210909

Bossel, H. (1999). *Indicators for sustainable development: Theories, methods, applications*. Winnipeg, Canada: International Institute for Sustainable Development.

Checkland, P. (1981). *Systems thinking, systems practice*. New York: Wiley and Sons.

Condon, W., & Rutz, C. (2012). A taxonomy of writing across the curriculum programs: Evolving to serve broader agendas. *College Composition and Communication*, 64(2), 357–82.

Cox, M., Galin, J., & Melzer, D. (2018). Sustainable WAC: A whole systems approach to launching and developing WAC programs. Urbana, IL: NCTE.

Cox, M., & Zawacki, T. M. (Eds.). (2011). WAC and second language writing: Cross-field research, theory, and program development [Special Issue]. *Across the Disciplines*, 8(4).

Environment Canada. (2013). Planning for a sustainable future: A federal sustainable development strategy for Canada 2013–2016. Retrieved from https://www.ec.gc.ca/dd-sd/default.asp?lang=En&n=A22718BA-1

Flood, R. L. (1990). Liberating systems theory: Toward critical systems thinking. *Human Relations, 43*(1), 49–75.

Folke, C., Carpenter, S. R., Walker, B., Scheffer, M., Chapin, T., & Rockström, J. (2010). Resilience thinking: Integrating resilience, adaptability, and transformability. *Ecology and Society, 15*(4), art. 20.

Fulwiler, T., & Young, A. (Eds.). (1990). *Programs that work: Models and methods for writing across the curriculum*. Portsmouth, NH: Boynton/Cook.

Hardi, P., & Zdan, T. (1997). *Assessing sustainable development: Principles and Practice*. Canada: The International Institute for Sustainable Development. Retrieved from https://www.iisd.org/pdf/bellagio.pdf

International Network of WAC Programs. (2014). Statement of WAC principles and practices. The WAC Clearinghouse. Retrieved from wac.colostate.edu/principles/

Jackson, M. (1985). Social systems theory and practice: The need for a critical approach. *International Journal of General Systems, 10*(2), 135–51.

Janopoulos, M. (1995). Writing across the curriculum, writing proficiency exams, and the NNES college student. *Journal of Second Language Writing, 4* (1) 43–50.

Johns, A. M. (1991). Interpreting an English competency exam: The frustrations of an ESL science student. Written Communication, 8, 379–401.

LaFrance, M. (2015). Making visible labor issues in writing across the curriculum: A call for research. *Forum: Issues about Part-Time and Contingent Faculty, 18*(3), A13–A17.

Leon, J. (2014). *Complexity science 2: Complexity theory* [YouTube Video]. Retrieved from www.youtube.com/watch?v=P00A9IZ7Pog

Marsden, P. (2005). Recent developments in network measurement. In P. J. Carrington, J. Scott, & S. Wasserman (Eds.), *Models and methods in social network analysis* (pp. 8–30). New York, NY: Cambridge University Press.

McLeod, S. (Ed.). (1988). Strengthening programs for writing across the curriculum. San Francisco: Jossey-Bass, 1988. Reprinted by the WAC Clearinghouse, 2002. Retrieved from http://wac.colostate.edu/books/mcleod_programs/

McLeod, S., Miraglia, E., Soven, M., & Thaiss, C. (Eds.). (2011). *WAC for the new millennium: Strategies for continuing writing-across-the-curriculum programs*. Urbana, IL: NCTE, 2011.

McLeod, S., & Shirley, S. (1988). Appendix: National survey of writing across the curriculum programs. In S. McLeod (Ed.), *Strengthening programs for writing across the curriculum* (pp. 103–30). San Francisco: Jossey-Bass.

McLeod, S. & Soven, M. (1991). What do you need to start—and sustain—a writing-across-the-curriculum program? *WPA: Writing Program Administration, 15*(1–2), 25–33.

McLeod, S., & Soven, M. (Eds.). (1992). Writing across the curriculum: A guide to developing programs. Newbury Park, CA: Sage Publications. Reprinted by the WAC Clearinghouse, 2000. Retrieved from http://wac.colostate.edu/books/mcleod_soven/

Midgley, G. (1996). What is this thing called CST? In R. Flood & N. Romm (Eds.), *Critical systems thinking: Current research and practice* (pp. 11–24). New York: Plenum Press.

Miraglia, E. & McLeod, S. (1997). Whither WAC? Interpreting the stories /histories of enduring WAC programs. *WPA: Writing Program Administration, 20*(3) 46–65.

Monroe, J. (2006). *Local knowledges, Local practices: Writing in the disciplines at Cornell.* Pittsburgh, PA: University of Pittsburgh Press.

Olsson, J. A., Hilding-Rydevik, T., Aalbu, H., & Bradley, K. (2004). *European regional network on sustainable development: Indicators for sustainable development.* Cardiff: Nordic Centre for Spatial Development.

Russell, D. R. (2002). *Writing in the academic disciplines: A curricular history.* Carbondale, IL: Southern Illinois University Press.

Segall, M., & Smart, R. (2005). *Direct from the disciplines: Writing across the Curriculum.* Portsmouth, NH: Heinemann.

Senge, P. (1990). *The fifth discipline: The art and practice of the learning organization.* New York: Doubleday.

Texas A&M - San Antonio. (2017). Writing-Intentional Course Requirement Proposal.

Thaiss, C. (2001). Theory in WAC: Where are we going, where have we been? In S. McLeod, E. Miraglia, M. Soven, & C. Thaiss (Eds.), *WAC for the new millennium: Strategies for continuing writing-across-the-curriculum programs* (pp. 299–325). Urbana, IL: NCTE.

Thaiss, C., Bräuer, G., Carlino, P., Ganobcsik-Williams, L. & Sinha, A. (Eds.). (2012). *Writing programs worldwide: Profiles of academic writing in many places.* The WAC Clearinghouse and Parlor Press.

Thaiss, C. & Porter, T. (2010). The state of WAC/WID in 2010: Methods and results of the U.S. survey of the International WAC/WID Mapping Project. *College Composition and Communication, 61*(3), 534–70.

Townsend, M. (2008). WAC program vulnerability and what to do about it: An update and brief bibliographic essay. *The WAC Journal, 19,* 45–61.

United Nations World Commission on Environment and Development. Report of the world commission on environment and development: Our common future. Retrieved from www.un-documents.net/our-common-future.pdf

Walvoord, B. (1996). The future of WAC. *College English, 58*(1), 58–74.

Wasserman, S., & Faust, K. (1994). *Social network analysis: Methods and applications.* Cambridge, MA: Cambridge University Press.

Young, A., & Fulwiler, T. (1990). The enemies of writing across the curriculum. In T. Fulwiler & A. Young (Eds.), *Programs that work: Models and methods for writing across the curriculum* (pp. 287–94). Portsmouth, NH: Boynton/Cook.

Zawacki, T. M. & Cox, M. (Eds.). (2014). *WAC and second-language writers: Research towards linguistically and culturally inclusive programs and practices.* The WAC Clearinghouse and Parlor Press.

Inclusion Takes Effort:
What Writing Center Pedagogy Can
Bring to Writing in the Disciplines

SARAH PETERSON PITTOCK

Writing in 1996, Donna LeCourt influentially observed the ways writing across the curriculum (WAC) programs tended to initiate students into already normalized discourses, reproduce dominant ideologies associated with these discourses, and elide difference, particularly racial, class, and gender differences as well as non-academic literacies (390). Victor Villanueva has likewise expressed a deep skepticism about WAC. It's often "assimilationist, assimilation being a political state of mind more repressive than mere accommodation" (166). He called, instead, for a critical pedagogy, one that might show students how to subvert disciplinary conventions even as they are learning to imitate them (173). In response to these critiques, scholars have proposed new WAC frameworks and approaches that draw on critical composition pedagogies. For example, Chris Anson has observed the inattention to race and racialized assessment in WAC scholarship and called for new assessment practices that take into account students' complex, individual identities. Terry Zawacki and Michelle Cox have curated fresh research that investigates WAC programming in the context of global Englishes and translingualism, arguing for differentiated instruction for multilingual learners. Heidi Harris's and Jessie Blackburn's special edition of *Across The Disciplines* on rural, regional, and satellite campuses (Volume 11) attends to the variable of place and its intersection with non-traditional student demographics, describing WAC programming that works to increase access to digital literacies. And Juan Guerra has advocated the writing-across-communities approach, which develops students' existing literacies and anticipates their writing lives beyond the academy (145ff).

To further engage difference beyond disciplinarity and to contribute to critical WAC pedagogy, this essay suggests that WAC directors and practitioners look to writing center theory and research. For over four decades, WAC scholarship has aligned writing center and WAC pedagogy. Joan Mullin noted that both pedagogies value interdisciplinary conversation as well as one-to-one and small-group instruction, and both recognize the complexity of assessment as well as discipline-specific ways of knowing (184–5). Marc Waldo went farther, declaring the writing center to be "the last best place for WAC" because writing centers help the disciplines see "what they share as a common goal" (21): analysis, synthesis, argumentation, and effective writing processes. A separate special issue of *Across the Disciplines* (Volume 10) strengthens this connection, showing that anti-racism work can begin in the writing center and radiate out into classrooms and offices across campus. For example, a tutor who also teaches first-year composition might come to see writing as a vehicle for learning and activism, an idea he shares in the tutorial and in the classroom (Zhang). I here endorse the WAC-WC connection, arguing that together WAC/WID (writing across the curriculum/writing in the disciplines) programs and writing centers can support diversity and inclusion work on college campuses. More specifically, I suggest the premises and practices of writing center pedagogy can inform inclusive WAC/WID teaching approaches.

Writing center pedagogy has been deployed productively in the disciplines at Stanford University, where a new WAC/WID initiative places program-in-writing-and-rhetoric lecturers in departments as teaching partners. Writing specialists give in-class and faculty development workshops, support student publications, and prepare course materials—syllabi, in-class or on-line resources, or handbooks (for a summary of a Writing Fellow program quite similar to our own, see Soliday 24). In addition to teaching first- and second-year required courses, writing specialists tutor in the writing center and in their departments. At present, there are seven writing specialists in departments and programs including art history, human biology, and public policy working to develop robust cultures of writing and facilitate students' development as communicators, not just support them on an ad hoc basis.

The department of history was an early adopter of a writing specialist, eager to partner with the Program in Writing and Rhetoric to improve writing instruction. The department recognized the importance of writing to disciplinary knowledge and student success and sought new ways to teach history writing well, especially to less prepared students. I served as the history writing specialist for a year as I was interested in the chance to act as both a writing instructor and as an advocate for undergraduates within the department. In our writing center, I reach students, but the writing specialist position gave me the opportunity to interact regularly with teaching assistants and faculty, to share what I see and how I work in the writing center. In my experience as a writing specialist, I learned that inclusive writing pedagogy in the disciplines benefits from the radically student-centered perspective of the writing center that acknowledges the pre-existing strengths students bring to a department or program and focuses without wavering on what they want to learn, to say, to become. I wondered if my colleagues would agree, and asked other writing specialists how their tutoring practices and work in the departments are inclusive and how the two are related. Of the four respondents, two work in interdisciplinary science programs, one in the humanities, and one in the social sciences. I include my story in this case study because, as Wendy Bishop has argued, author-saturated texts should recognize their "constructedness," which includes the stance of the researcher, the questions asked, the investigative method, and the argument itself (152).

In reflecting on a set of conversations with my colleagues and on my own experiences, I see ways that inclusive tutoring practices can be adapted to work with students and faculty in the disciplines; I also see the ideological and structural factors that limit our impact. The writing specialists are able to influence curriculum and teaching practices and facilitate inter-program collaboration, but as of this writing, have less meaningfully influenced student writing assessment, even though assessment is an important dimension of much of the conversation on inclusion in writing studies and higher education. Nevertheless, this approach may be useful to universities that either do not have a freestanding WAC/WID program or, due to institutional barriers, quite separate writing centers and WAC/WID programs. In this approach, we leverage the portability of writing center pedagogy as well as the expertise of experienced writing center tutors to facilitate co-learning about writing pedagogy in the departments.

Recognizing that inclusion is an evolving pedagogy, I use our reflections on writing specialist work to illustrate what writing center practice can bring to writing in the disciplines to support student success and belonging: differentiated teaching, active reflection on the values and practices of a discourse community, a willingness to question if not test the rhetorical norms, and a commitment to engage campus partners in the work of inclusion. Working in tandem, writing centers and WAC/WID programs can support a campus-wide transformative praxis that recognizes the rhetorical affordances of social identities and linguistic variation. I begin by analyzing how writing center theory has addressed inclusion, describe how my colleagues and I practice inclusive tutoring, and then show how this teaching approach can be implemented in the disciplines.

Inclusion in Writing Center Scholarship

Today there is broad agreement about the value of diversity on college campuses (see for example, Page; Gurin; Bowman; and for a popular view, Hyman and Jacobs), leading to recruitment and admission of a diverse student body. Over half of Stanford's undergraduates are students of color and nine percent of undergraduates are international (Stanford University, "Common Data Set 2017–2018"); in addition to this, seventeen percent of a recently admitted class are the first in their families to attend college (Stanford University, "Applicant"). While all students may struggle to transition into college, those from less privileged or more marginalized backgrounds are more likely to perceive the campus climate and classroom cultures as unwelcoming or even hostile, impacting their learning negatively (Locks et al. 259; Dawn Johnson et al.). Inclusive teaching intentionally creates an equitable learning environment for all students, and through course content and design, both acknowledges students' social identities and works to redress the systemic inequalities that inhibit learning. As Dereca Blackmon, Stanford's assistant vice provost and executive director of the diversity and first-gen office put it, "diversity is a fact, inclusion is a practice, equity is a goal." A 2017 meta-review shows that inclusion in higher education takes effort, requiring inclusive curriculum design and delivery, inclusive assessment, and a "whole-of-institution" approach (Lawrie et al. 1). At the same time, the research shows that inclusion is "elusive," evolving definitionally and in praxis (Lawrie et al. 1).

In writing studies, the conversation about inclusion has returned repeatedly to the ways that curricula privilege or handicap students for their linguistic backgrounds. The touchstone text, the 1974 Conference on College Composition and Communication resolution the *Students' Right to Their Own Language*, recognizes that students "find their own identity and style" in "patterns and varieties of language," which may include the dialect of their nurture. The resolution also asserts that "The claim that any one dialect is unacceptable amounts to an attempt of one social group to exert its dominance over another. Such a claim leads to false advice for speakers and writers, and immoral advice for humans" (Conference). In spite of the strong, explicit language in the resolution, pedagogies and practices have been slow to change; Geneva Smitherman has called the fight to realize students' rights to their own languages an "historical struggle." "The game plan" in composition studies, Smitherman observes after over twenty years in the field, has always been "to reshape the outsiders into talking, acting, thinking and (to the extent possible) looking like the insiders" ("Retrospective" 25). For example, in pedagogies such as English for Academic Purposes (EAP) that rely heavily on genre and corpus analysis, both as a research method and as a pedagogy, students imitate the major rhetorical moves and style of the dominant writers and speakers in a field (Thompson and Diani). But when assimilation to the norms and protocols of academic literacy is mandatory, there are often costs for minoritized populations, especially when raced. Victor Villanueva, for instance, has narrated his loneliness, confusion, and loss of cultural identity as he became a successful academic (*Bootstraps*).

Drawing on the critical pedagogies of Paulo Freire and bell hooks among others, which recognize classed, raced, and gendered differences, compositionists have argued for students' integration with specialist discourse communities rather than their assimilation to these same communities (Benesch). Like Smitherman, Keith Gillyard draws on research that demonstrates the logic, systematicity, and linguistic adequacy of "nonstandard" dialects. Like Smitherman, he also argues for a pluralist approach to language teaching at the university (71). What Smitherman and Gillyard observe about many students of African descent applies to all those whose home languages and dialects are marked as "nonstandard"; they can feel diminished if not excluded in academic classes that insist on Standard Written English. When a student integrates with a disciplinary discourse community, however, they change the community as well as being changed by it: both parties gain. The writing center is one space on university campuses where integration of novices with the disciplinary discourse is negotiated.

Admittedly, for decades the writing center itself was a tool or site of assimilation. In its early incarnations, writing centers often taught writing through worksheets, and were known as drill and skill sites. In these centers, language was treated as a static, standardized thing, tutors and teachers made responsible for prescribing correctness. More progressive models of the writing center, which treat writing as a process, have also been critiqued for their "good intentions" because their emphasis on non-directive tutoring strategies would often withhold knowledge from the student populations that needed it most, maintaining the power structures (Grimm *Good Intentions*). And in Romeo García's estimation, "the new racism" is implicit in several decades of writing center scholarship that shows color blindness, a tacit disavowal of the privileged status of white-identified academic discourse, and ideologies that diminish the languages and traditions of people of color. But models of the writing center such as Andrea Lunsford's, which emphasize collaborative meaning making, argue that writers and speakers bring ideas and language to the center that contribute to new knowledge. More recently, the twenty-first-century writing center has been characterized as a site of polyglot meaning making as it recognizes global Englishes and multilingualism (Grimm "New Frameworks"; Jordan). The twenty-first-century writing center has also been conceived as a site of advocacy for diverse students, especially racial, cultural, and linguistic minorities. When positioned as a change maker within the university and beyond, writing centers work in equal measure to strengthen individuals' communication skills and to remove structural assumptions that interfere with student learning and thriving (Condon, "Beyond" 22; Grimm, "Retheorizing" 92).

A number of approaches have been formulated that can mitigate prejudice and increase feelings of belonging experienced by linguistic and racial minorities. In describing a "pedagogy of belonging," Julie Bokser emphasizes the importance of listening and argues that tutors need to feel comfortable talking with writers about their accents and style, noting how and to what extent students *want* to adopt an academic voice. We can't assume that they do (Bokser 58). Laura Greenfield's "The 'Standard English' Fairytale" asks us to reflect on how we talk about language. Specifically, "when 'Standard English' is imagined as a tool to participate in mainstream society, people of color are put in the oppressive position of having not to learn to speak a particular language . . . but of ridding themselves of all linguistic features that may identify them with communities of color" (47). Instead, writing centers and writing programs can "give all students as many language tools as possible" and develop a curriculum that helps them make choices about their language that "reflect their critical thinking, not the instructors' personal biases" (Greenfield 58). In other words, we can value all dialects and languages equally and then trust students to think about their grammar and language rhetorically, as a matter of choice given a particular situation and audience rather than as mere correctness. In demonstrating how African American Vernacular English can be communicative in an academic essay, Vershawn Ashanti Young further shows why writing programs and centers must disavow prescriptivism and instead teach grammar descriptively (65–66). Young highlights the possibility of multi-dialectalism, what he calls "code meshing," and co-learning across communities in the writing classroom and the writing center (67). Co-learning can extend to the cultivation of racial literacy, which enhances our ability to "challenge undemocratic practices" (Jane Bolgatz, qtd. in Michelle Johnson, 215). Michelle Johnson shows that engaged tutoring talk validates students' interest in race, their choice to use raced language, and their identities. When a tutor engages racial topics and languages humbly and with excitement, the student perceives that the tutor is an "ally in the difficult task of making meaning of race in writing and writing through race" (Johnson 223).

In addition to imagining new ways to work with students, writing center scholarship often strives to make change among staff and within the university, to evolve the idea of the writing center. A number of writing center directors are working to define a "transformative ethos" for the writing center (Blazer) in order to re-configure "a system of advantage" based on raced, classed, and linguistic privileges (Grimm "Retheorizing"). Frankie Condon and Bobbi Olson describe how, after blogs were published expressing linguistic bigotry on their campuses, they have "worked to construct a different kind of house altogether," a writing center that will not only make all feel welcome but that will also actively challenge linguistic supremacy (40). Nancy Grimm returns to the idea of "community of practice," which "offer[s] learners real opportunities to become active participants in the real work of the community and thus construct identities of participation" ("Retheorizing" 89). And Rasha Diab, Beth Godbee, Thomas Ferrel, and Neil Simpkins argue for the need for "self work" together with "work-with-others" to articulate both "the critique *against* racism" and "a critique *for* equity and justice." Their "pedagogy for racial justice" imagines the writing center as a site of activism (see also their "Making Racial Justice Actionable" in *Across the Disciplines*).

Writing center pedagogy thus made a number of important conceptual shifts. Writing was no longer a discrete skill but rather a way of knowing and being that requires students to develop a meta language that helps them think about writing as something complex and beyond grammar; disciplines were no longer closed, static domains that require privileged knowledge, but rather dynamic communities of practice. The space of the writing center itself became dedicated to developing diverse linguistic, racial, cultural, and social competencies. Students in these more progressive models were no longer deficient, dependent, or flawed but rather capable of making choices and partnering in meaning making. Their languages, backgrounds, and identities are welcomed and explored as assets that might contribute to new understanding. Finally, tutors and administrators become important partners in the quest for more inclusive, socially just university cultures. One-way assimilation is an ideal of the past, transformation of all the ideal of the present.

Not all share these conceptions of language and learning, however. In my work as a writing specialist and as a tutor, I have seen margins of papers annotated repeatedly by graders with NNE ("Non-native English") that contain, in addition to heavy line editing, responses to writing that suggest to students that there is a stable linguistic norm toward which we are all working and, more damaging potentially, that they are unequal to the task in spite of their fresh ideas and awesome research, which received less attention than their style. In Harry Denny's view, tutors and other academic staff can instead help writers and speakers understand the ways the dominant discourse is naturalized and their cultural capital dismissed by queering our pedagogy. Denny uses the term *queering* to help us dismantle the many binaries that structure our thinking about language and learning: "mentors ought to help students bridge the multiple literacies to which they have access and those dominant forms they require for academic success" ("Queering" 49). In this formulation, no one is excluded for their home literacies and the academic literacy they may potentially need to perform is made accessible through mentorship. What this mentorship looks like more specifically and why it contributes to an inclusive university learning environment is the subject of the next section.

From the Center to the Disciplines: Tutoring Talk that Supports Inclusion

In addition to working in departments and programs, writing specialists at our university continue to tutor undergraduates and graduate students from across the disciplines in our large generalist writing center. In the writing center, as in the departments, writing specialist tutoring demystifies writing conventions for writers new to disciplinary discourse communities. It also supports writers' relationships with their writings, taking into account all the social and cultural contexts that inform those relationships. This open stance communicates to students that their full humanity matters to the work of composing and vice versa, as Diab et al. recommend ("Multidimensional"). As one writing specialist explains, "My [tutoring] approach... is always gentle, curious, and interested not just in the writing assignment, but in the ways in which the writing assignment is connected to the tutee's life. This is at the heart for me of an 'inclusive' tutoring practice." At our center and many others across the country, inclusive tutoring practices emphasize four strategies: collaboration that honors student learning and writing goals for the session, a preference for non-directive tutoring to reinforce student ownership of their ideas and expression, instruction when students ask for it, and a process orientation that normalizes struggle.

Our tutoring sessions typically begin with the tutor asking: What brings you here today? What do you want to work on? In answering these questions, the student defines the major learning and writing goals for the tutoring session, and tutors may travel some distance conceptually or linguistically to be sure they are connecting with their students. As a writing specialist explained,

> A practice of inclusivity acknowledges that every human being is going to have a different reason for being in the writing center, even if they are from the same marginalized community and/or race, class background. I am leery of practices and theories that offer categorical suggestions for supporting belonging. I prefer to engage each individual as their own unique, powerful, complex person, connected to historical socio-cultural factors that have certainly informed their experiences, but often defined them in different ways.

A student-centered tutoring practice recognizes the idiosyncrasies as well as the community identities students bring with them to their writing. This response further suggests some of the ways students can feel and have been excluded from the writing center and by extension the university. When writing center practitioners make some reasons for visiting the center more legitimate than others or when they assume a potentially false link, often based in stereotype, between social identity and learning need, they diminish or deny dimensions of the student that may in fact be highly relevant and valuable to the task at hand. Instead, we can design learning opportunities that "meet students from all linguistic, class, and racial backgrounds *where they are* [emphasis mine]."

At the same time, tutors must help student writers consider genre and audience expectations. One specialist echoes Denny's use of the verb *bridge* as she specifies what the tutoring conversation with the writer might address ("Queering" 49):

> What becomes visible sometimes is that students may not understand what's being asked of them in a writing assignment. So being inclusive means finding a bridge for them from the way they're approaching something and the way they're being asked to approach it in the context of the assignment. Not in a way that sort of shuts down choices, but to help them understand the expectations that they need to be negotiating.

This writing specialist is careful to distinguish between exploring expectations as a set of prescriptions and expectations as a range of choices that students will need to "negotiate." Working with a tutor, students writing in the disciplines can investigate what ideas or practices from their cultural background or experience may be shaping their writing expectations and compare those with the writing expectations of the new audience. In the best circumstances, the tutor will be able to help students see how their knowledge, experience, and language can contribute to the new discourse community.

A tutoring practice that considers the social and cultural context of a student as well as their individual circumstances must be highly flexible, responsive, and expert. When asked what tutoring practices support student belonging, one writing specialist answered, "the foundation of inclusion that guides my work as a writing tutor is the art and skill of listening. Rather than asserting my perspective or interpretation prescriptively, I strive to instead create a listening space, wherein the student comes to his/her ideas and writing/speaking development by way of support and autonomy." Notably, we all agreed on the importance of listening to inclusive tutoring: listening that is open to the unexpected, that avoids anticipating a particular student response, and that creates "a space" for student thinking to emerge and develop.

Listening is a necessary but not sufficient condition for an inclusive learning environment. Varied, strategic tutor talk is also crucial. In an analysis of writing tutoring sessions led by experienced tutors and deemed successful, recent research describes tutoring strategies that support students to think more deeply than they could on their own as cognitive scaffolding (Mackiewicz and Thompson). This research also recognizes instruction as a valid and important tutoring strategy, disproving writing center lore that insists dogmatically on non-directiveness. In the writing specialists' reflections on inclusive tutoring, "part of the listening role is recognizing when that is wanted and knowing how much of it will support the students . . . many students do desire more direct instruction, too." In listening carefully and responding with a strategic and robust tutoring repertoire, tutors construct a teaching and learning environment that is broadly inclusive of diverse students and their varied learning styles. By contrast, tutoring that is exclusively non-directive may not meet the needs of students who have neither a clear understanding of academic conventions or rhetorical grammar; differentiated tutoring is what is required to support the learning of all, and especially of less privileged students (Salem 163–164). Inclusive tutoring also recognizes that in disciplinary contexts, the audience is very language or term sensitive. (For example, linguists will not use terms such as *second language learners* and *multilingual learners* interchangeably.) Tutors may need to give students the canonical or typical language they need to succeed, but there are a number of ways that can happen that protects student agency.

Lastly, an inclusive tutoring practice for the writing specialists helps students reflect on their writing process in a way that normalizes struggle. A specialist explains: "a lot of times people feel that their struggles to make sense of stuff or to get from draft to revision or from blank page to anything is somehow uniquely their problem." More specifically, they may have produced a draft, but the writer sees that "it's not there. And it's an inclination to see that as a failure." This "fixed mindset" can produce writing apprehension and distance novice writers from academic literacies (Dweck). In the inclusive writing tutorial, however, a tutor can help students see that "the draft is successful when it gets them to see what the next step is. And that is something that is normal. It's right. And it's writing when it works right. More advanced writers write more drafts. Have more flaws. Have more process. But they just don't have the self-criticism." I've helped students come to a more nuanced, forgiving understanding of the drafting process by describing my own, at times uneasy, experience with writing. I can also show writers what a topic sentence looks like in a particular genre and what it looks like in a first, highly imperfect draft. I assure novice writers that specialist writing won't always be difficult by emphasizing what's distinctive about learning to write in the disciplines: the content and genres are new. Our shared vulnerability in these moments builds trust and acknowledges the emotional labor of writing and learning.

What Writing Specialists Do: Toward an Inclusive Disciplinary Writing Pedagogy

As we have seen, writing center pedagogy has responded vigorously and productively to the racial and linguistic diversity of its tutors and students (Blazer; Condon, "Beyond"; Denny, *Facing*; Diab et al.; García; Greenfield; Greenfield and Rowan; Grimm, "New Conceptual" and "Re-theorizing"; Jordan; Johnson; Young). WAC scholarship has also contended with racial, socio-economic, and linguistic diversity. LeCourt called for WAC practitioners to recognize writers' "multiple discursive positions as a way of allowing for student difference and alternative literacies to find a space within disciplinary discourses" (399). WAC practitioners might "take courageous action," in the words of Diab et al, and find ways to "reshape [the] WAC curriculum to value linguistic diversity," exporting the social justice agenda of the writing center to the disciplines ("Multi-dimensional"). As writing specialists, we were able to apply many of the ideals and best practices of the writing center to our work with students and faculty in the programs and departments, but not all.

Writing specialist pedagogy emphasizes in equal measure students' identities as writers, their relationship with writing, and the disciplinary communication protocols they will need to succeed as writers in their fields. The pedagogy scaffolds rhetorical reading skills that help novice communicators identify the content and methods, the range of stylistic variation, and the writing opportunities of the discipline; in short, the chance to say something new and, in the best cases, a new way to say it. Writing specialist pedagogy thus emphasizes a version of what Graff and Bernstein have called in the title of their popular book, "They say, I say," an ability to recognize "the moves that matter in academic discourse" so that one can make a contribution. When practiced in the departments and programs with the goal of inclusion, however, writing specialist pedagogy takes Graff and Bernstein's approach one step further to cultivate what Sarah Vacek has called "meta multiliteracy," one's ability to explain strategies for communicating across diverse linguistic and cultural contexts. For example, writing specialist pedagogy supports the ability of students to articulate the affordances and limitations of colloquial versus professional language, the languages of literature versus history, or even, more specifically, those of specific sub-disciplines such as academic versus public history and the ability to then compare and integrate those academic discourses with the languages of the many communities to which they belong. Ultimately, writing specialist pedagogy seeks to empower and cultivate students' "critical agency as academic writers" (Hendrickson and deMueller 74).

The students I worked with in history are socioeconomically, linguistically, and racially diverse. They are often interested in the recovery work of figures or communities marginalized by dominant history—and of documenting the agency and historical contributions of these populations. Their sense of belonging in history varied according to their ability to explore their interests through existing coursework and with faculty as well as their success at reaching faculty readers and earning high grades. The belonging of these individual students matters, but so too does the vitality of the discipline. As Lisa Delpit has argued, discourses are not changed by conforming to them, but neither are they changed when students by design or by choice remain outside of them (292). Indeed, Jay Jordan observes that "discourses often thrive on the value novices add as well as on the disruptions they represent" (45). The task of the writing specialist is to convince the stakeholders of the merit of this point of view as well as to build a teaching infrastructure that will help students make transformative contributions to the disciplinary discourse communities. Writing specialists are called on to mentor not just the students but also the teaching assistants and faculty, helping them to make an important conceptual shift from difference as deficit to cultural and linguistic diversity as resource. In this shift, diversity is recognized as a fact, to return to Dereca Blackmon's formulation. Moreover, rather than working to get undergraduates to pass as experts, or asking everyone to sound the same, "language flexibility" becomes the learning goal (Blazer 22). This learning outcome includes audience and genre awareness plus the ability to adapt and mix languages and cultural traditions strategically, so that no one tradition, disciplinary or otherwise, is privileged to the exclusion of another.

An important step in this process is to help faculty make writing expectations explicit, which research has shown is one of the foundational requirements for writing assignments that promote deep learning (Anderson et al.). Transparent assignments further support student belonging, particularly among first-generation, low income, and underrepresented college students (Winkelmes et al). One writing specialist drew connections between her writing center experiences and her work with faculty: "Writing tutoring pedagogy comes into play in consultations with faculty.... They are also producing a piece of writing. It's an assignment. [I ask them] What are you trying to accomplish?" This respondent found herself modeling tutoring philosophy as she worked with faculty on assignment design: "It's important to be uncondescending and to approach it in a very collaborative and dialogic way ... At its core, [writing center philosophy] is about not coming in as someone who always already knows what the best way is." She notes that faculty often have unspoken expectations and goals: "There's a reason they're assigning it but it's unarticulated." The writing specialist helps faculty describe the goals of a writing assignment, its rationale, genre, and component parts, so that students have a clear target. In her conversations with faculty about assignment and syllabus design, the writing specialist approaches her work with the "same principle" that underlies her writing tutoring: "respect for their intentions and purposes and trying not to take over that." As this writing specialist elicits explicit writing expectations, she models a strategically non-directive teaching approach that has been championed in writing center literature (Corbett).

Of course, writing expectations can be conflicting, a byproduct of disciplines' "dynamism," to use a term that Ann Gere and her fellow researchers have recently used (245). As I sat in on history classes, I heard professors articulate very different premises for historical writing. Moving between classes, students may be confused by conflicting disciplinary expectations; they wonder, what sources do I need to engage, when, how, why? Another frequently asked question in the sciences: can a writer use the first-person? In tutoring, workshops, and assignment prompts, writing specialists can help novice writers understand that disciplinary norms such as personal voice shift by narrating a brief, relevant history of the discipline as well as by articulating the rewards and risks of a particular rhetorical strategy. To take the issue of the first person in science writing as an example: a writing specialist noted the tendency of scientists to "confuse" "the first person with a kind of subjectiveness ... [but in the] last decade or so, [the] tide has completely turned. Having a conversation about that shift can show that norms can shift and that people can play a role in the shift." In this approach, the writing specialist can show the student that practitioners change the discipline for reasons linked with the discourse community's "values":

> Norms about voice are connected to the values of this enterprise and so to the extent that these voices reflect values that people agree with or reflect them well, we can stick with them. That conversation has to speak to the domain of value of the discipline that they're working in.... There's nothing absolute.

In this answer, the writing specialist concurs with a phrase Andrea Lunsford invoked to locate control, power, and authority in the writing center, "the negotiating group"; the group determines what values are prioritized by the discipline and how those values are realized on the page (8). By including the novice communicator in this negotiation, the writing specialist makes the student a part of the group, the community of practice. In this frequent scenario, the writing specialist communicates writing expectations with the goal of empowering students to make rhetorical choices that are informed by their understanding of their professors' and the fields' expectations as well as their full linguistic and rhetorical repertoires.

One writing specialist explained why students must broadly understand the expectations of disciplinary writing:

> I think if you're talking to an audience that has a certain kind of expectation, it is going to be less effective to that audience if you are well outside that range, and you can make an informed choice about not delivering to people's expectations, but you can only make that choice if you really understand what that expectation is. . . .

For this writing specialist, communicating disciplinary writing expectations is crucial if students want to meet a new specialist audience. Yet, the writing specialist is careful to say students may work within "a range," and they must be aware of its non-negotiables and limits in order to make "an informed choice" about *how* and *to what extent* they adopt and adapt disciplinary language. The specialist continues: "It's a disservice to students to say *just be yourself in this new domain*. Because it also suggest there's nothing transformative about education. Learning stuff is going to transform you and that's going to be reflected in the kinds of voices you're able to have." While she doesn't elaborate on why students can't "just be themselves," she suggests that experimentation with new disciplinary language and logic is not only mandatory, but also a boon that promises transformation. Indeed, in her view, in entering a new discourse community, students are changed for the better as the range of voices they're able to deploy is expanded. That range is achievable only if the discourse community expectations are made explicit, their values articulated, and writers given the freedom to imitate, critique, and re-imagine.

That freedom can be engineered in in-class workshops given by the writing specialists. These workshops often begin by inviting students to rhetorically analyze discipline-specific examples, prompting identification of major components of argument as well as the disciplinary values that drive those components. There is often also an exploration of the benefits and limitations of particular rhetorical choices. For example, in a workshop I led on thesis statements in history arguments for an upper-division class, we looked at a number of different thesis paragraphs published in the undergraduate history journal. I asked students to rank the statements and defend their rankings. In this way, students were invited to describe what makes a thesis in the discipline more or less effective and to articulate their own values as readers of specialist discourse and to compare those values with the editorial board of the department's publication. Often a broad consensus emerges and the favorite theses are mined for disciplinary norms, such as use of the past tense, degree of certainty, and degree of specificity. In the variety of theses presented, however, students also come to see that writing in the disciplines is not a fixed target: there is no formula that will help a writer achieve a perfect thesis, and norms are determined through conversation much like the one in the workshop.

Writing specialists can also facilitate rhetorical analysis of published work, especially arguments that broke ground in the discipline in terms of content and style. For example, in a workshop lesson on topic sentences, I brought in representative paragraphs from George Chauncey's *Gay New York*, a crossover book that reached both academic and public audiences and was widely admired for its style and rich archival research. Students experienced the ways that a more inclusive history might be addressed to more than one audience and push the discipline in new directions. I asked them to tell me what made the topic sentences effective and if they might have written them differently. Encouraging students to name and assess rhetorical moves for themselves draws on their cognitive and cultural resources and passions, rather than reinforcing their deficits; it also helps to define their own writing goals.

As Helen Sword's recent research has shown, successful writers from across the disciplines both conform to and exceed conventions. For example, psychologist Alison Gopnik has worked out her writing style through email, conversations with family members, and careful attention to audience and style. In this way she is able to move from a first draft, "something that reads like a developmental psychological article" to "a spontaneous voice talking to you," many, many drafts later (Qtd. in Sword 69). Some of the faculty Sword interviewed encourage their graduate students to actively avoid reinforcing disciplinary conventions that diminish new knowledge; a professor reports asking his students, "'How do you write your research up in First Nation studies in ways that don't reproduce those 'othering' discourses that have plagued anthropology or sociology or other disciplines for so long?'" (Qtd. in Sword 82). Because not all academic experts aim to write to narrow disciplinary expectations and because in many fields those expectations may be contentious, Mary Soliday recommends that WAC/WID practitioners teach "typicality," which emphasizes the recurrence and context-specificity as well as negotiability of disciplinary conventions (39). (She also narrates a more optimistic model of student assimilation to specialist discourses, one that requires that students "creatively rework" others' words [39].) Instead of a rigid and deterministic insistence on imitation, in extended workshops, I would ask students: What is *your* model of greatness? What rhetorical moves can you adapt to your purposes?

Overall, writing specialist workshops in the departments and programs support a process orientation to writing, specifically the research and composition process in the disciplines. In one popular workshop I gave, we assessed how the outline of the same history project evolved over several weeks' work, culminating with a reverse outline of the published paper. Much like a tutoring session, I created a safe space to observe, question, discuss and invent. After assessing the change of an argument's structure over time and sharing a number of arrangement strategies, I invited students to begin to arrange their own arguments in a non-linear outline, using sticky notes. Other writing specialists similarly saw links between the writing tutoring pedagogy and their workshop design. For example, "I use listening skills quite often . . . when I deliver workshops. We usually start the workshop with a question and answer session with the professors to make sure that we keep the session directed on the student needs." Writing workshops that are informed by writing tutoring pedagogy demystify communication protocols and scaffold learning, but they do so in response to student concerns, questions, and goals, not according to an inflexible script.

One-to-one collaboration with students in their departments similarly begins with the writer and their relationship to writing rather than with the target writing, the disciplinary conventions. One respondent explained: "Conceptually, writing center pedagogy has informed so much of my one-on-one tutoring. In both [the writing center and the department], I always start the same way. I want to know who the person is first, what brought them there, how do they feel about writing in general? What are their writing habits? Strengths? Fears? Needs?" She notes that the needs are very diverse, from translating technical knowledge into a grant proposal, to fine tuning sentences for clarity, to working on writing productivity. She respects the diverse reasons writers come to see her, never presuming that she knows what's at issue, but rather allowing the writer to represent their needs and goals to her first. To assess the writing task, she uses the same rhetorical approach as in the writing center, asking the writer: "Who is the audience? What is the purpose? How do [the answers to] these questions inform the structure, tone, style, length, organization?" Again, this approach draws on the writer's strengths and knowledge. She further notes, "it always amazes me how much students want to talk about these things, how much they just need somebody to listen to them and with some gentle guidance help them to move forward." Here the writing specialist positions herself as a trusted and wise coach. She recognizes that writers in the disciplines need encouragement and confidence "to finish their work." In the one-to-one work with students, writing specialists toggle back and forth between discussing the rhetorical issues on the page and what may be playing out in the writer's head and heart.

Recognizing the emotional labor of integrating prior languages and identities with a new academic language and identity is part of an inclusive writing pedagogy. Michelle Iten explains, "This [integration] is hard work: sorting through dissonant value sets; surmounting regular waves of feeling deeply out of place; dealing with fears that adding an academic identity requires losing or betraying one's home identity..." (38). Some students can become discouraged or resistant, especially those whose style specialist readers consistently find problematic. In one-to-one meetings, writing specialists can help students negotiate this feedback, to understand that a lot of line edits are not a poor reflection on their character or effort, to help them see patterns, and to learn revision strategies to avoid the style issues that trouble their readers most consistently. At the same time, a writing specialist might talk about ways to highlight students' contributions to the scholarly conversation, whether through a new comparison, fresh archival evidence, or a neologism that brings the languages of their research and home communities together. Other students are eager to become disciplined. To these students, I offered instruction when requested, but also encouraged reflection at the end of conferences. I often asked students to reflect on their experiences writing in history to compare and contrast them with writing in other discourse communities. These conversations give students the chance to own their growing expertise in History and their research and writing choices.

The Affordances and Limitations of Writing Center Pedagogy in the Disciplines

As a program that bridges the writing program, writing center, and departments, the writing specialist initiative contributes meaningfully to a "whole-of-institution" approach to inclusion. And most writing specialists felt that by modeling alternative approaches, they were able to influence more inclusive writing curriculum design and delivery in the departments or programs. Many assignment sheets and syllabi improved: skills were more strategically scaffolded, writing expectations made explicit, success accessible. One specialist also noticed a subtle but foundational change in attitude to writing per se. For a writing specialist who largely works with scientists, her work validates writing as a skill and set of habits that can be cultivated, as something that needs to be taught:

> Faculty and students know that writing well is important, but it is always the act that comes after the truly important work—which is the science experiment or the data collection or the project design or the problem set. So my goal has always been to get them to see writing as included IN these processes, as part of the skill set, not the aftermath.

Without an institutional commitment to explicitly teach advanced writing in the disciplines, it can be easy for students and faculty alike to fall back on deficit discourse, the idea that some people are too unprepared or just plain unable to produce discipline-specific prose. But like the writing center, which maintains that all writers can benefit from working with skilled readers and tutors, some departments and programs with writing specialists have been able to center writing in their conversations about curricula and student learning to move beyond conceptions of writing pedagogy as remediation. The result is that help-seeking is no longer stigmatized. One specialist shared that she believed her presence in a program had encouraged "a willingness to admit to not being a strong writer and to seek help and support because their ego is not attached to it as a skill they should have. So in terms of inclusivity—I think... they are ok with being 'included' as people who need writing support."

However, progress has been uneven, dependent on the goodwill and interest of the individual departments and professors as well as the conceptualization of writing and the writing teacher. In some spaces, some professors continue to cherish a narrow view of writing as surface style, largely a matter of correctness. In these cases it can be difficult to advocate institutionally for the idea of linguistic diversity as resource we saw so prominently in the writing center scholarship. That kind of advocacy may be contained within the one-to-one dynamic of tutor and student. As a writing specialist reported: "I make sure that students who are dealing with minor, yet challenging, grammar issues still feel engaged as thinkers and writers and never reduced to a comma error." They further remarked that one writing specialist alone in a department—untenured, part-time, temporary—

> is not enough to really counteract dominant faculty narratives on student deficit.... Much of the faculty imagines my role in the department to be one of helping "bad" writers. In this capacity, I get sent struggling writers and am listed on many syllabuses as this kind of resource. Conceptualizing the [writing specialists] in this way may actually work against the cultivation of inclusive learning environments.

In this scenario, the presence of a writing specialist in a department or program potentially reinforces deficit constructions of less-experienced students and the impression that some students are more welcome or able to participate in specialist discourse than others. These caveats indicate that a writing center approach alone will not create a more inclusive approach to teaching writing in the disciplines. Other significant factors that support an inclusive writing pedagogy in the disciplines include the perception of the writing teacher as a professional identity, the status and security of the writing and WAC programs on any given campus, and the centering of traditionally underrepresented voices on syllabi and in the classroom, ideas that are well supported by the research on inclusion (see for example, Lee, et al.).

Two other growth opportunities in our program are worth noting. I heard little reflection on grading practices, even though our original definition of inclusion isolated assessment as a major feature of inclusive learning environments. While I worked to eliminate linguistic and racial bias from my assessment of and feedback on student work-in-progress in my one-to-one work in the history department, I had limited opportunities as a writing specialist to intervene in grading practices. I was able occasionally to draft rubrics and give teaching assistants relatively brief, one-off workshops on commenting on writing. In drafts of rubrics I could downplay an emphasis on correctness and instead reward process, but I was not involved in applying it to student writing. At our university, it may be that grading is still felt to be the purview and prerogative of the faculty, or it may be that our WAC/WID initiative has not yet made writing assessment a priority. In either case, this area reveals one of the salient limitations of writing center pedagogy. Tutors are often counseled to motivate writers with moderate praise, but not to predict or comment on grades (see for example, Fitzgerald and Ianetta, 50 and 61–63). Further, writing center philosophy has generally been agnostic about what makes writing "good" in order to center student writing goals and acknowledge diverse, community-specific, and evolving writing standards. Inspiration for inclusive writing assessment practices in WAC/WID programs may thus need to come from other sources than the writing center literature. Asao Inoue's *Antiracist Writing Assessment Ecologies: Teaching and Assessing Writing for a Socially Just Future* would be a good place to start. And even though much of the scholarly conversation on inclusion in the writing center uses the rhetoric of social justice, I do not hear this rhetoric made explicit in the reflections I gathered from my colleagues, though I think the logic is there implicitly. I see this as an opportunity, and as an example of the ways writing center pedagogy might advance WAC/WID diversity and inclusion initiatives. Mya Poe has already argued that WAC/WID programs can teach race and writing together to support more effective assignment design, assessment, and classroom culture ("Re-Framing"). I am hopeful the anti-racist agenda of recent writing center scholarship can find new energy and approaches in WAC/WID programs, including mine.

Conclusion

I have argued that inclusion is the work of WAC/WID practitioners and that seeing their work through the lens of writing center philosophy and practice highlights why. Writing center pedagogy can be exported to the departments to help practitioners reframe conversations about student deficit as an opportunity for shared growth and for approaches to teaching that emphasize linguistic variation as resource. Research suggests this is already happening. Zawacki and Cox note that recent research on second-language readers' adaptive strategies to heavy college reading loads shows faculty encouraging students to draw on their own experiences and cultural resources to succeed (24). With its emphasis on collaboration, writing center theory and practice can also help WAC/WID practitioners plumb faculty expertise on inclusion (Lunsford; Ede). For example, social scientists will likely be familiar with sociologist Dorothy Smith's "institutional ethnography," which values the standpoint of diverse lived experience in order to demystify ruling relations and promote social justice. And scientists may reference Londa Schiebinger's research that has recently argued that diversity in research teams leads to better science because new questions and methods are considered (Nielsen et al.); or they may remember physicist Evelyn Fox Keller's biography of Barbara McClintock, which revealed that McClintock's "feeling for the organism," an alternative way of knowing and naming the enterprise of biology, led to breakthroughs in genetics and eventually a Nobel Prize. Through conversations with faculty about inclusion in their particular fields, WAC/WID practitioners gain insight into discipline-specific learning challenges and opportunities, faculty teaching expertise is leveraged, and new teaching approaches emerge.

While the writing center has been theorized as a place where writers and tutors develop, less frequently it's recognized as a space of professional development for all who teach writing at the university. Patti Hanlon-Baker's and Clyde Moneyhun's article "Tutoring Teachers" is one article that describes the writing center as a place where teachers become expert at radically student-centered writing pedagogy. I extend their argument to observe the ways WAC/WID professionals can bring their writing center work into the disciplines and departments. WAC/WID programs might consider requiring all of their staff as well as their faculty partners to tutor in the generalist campus writing center. In the generalist center, differences other than disciplinary difference remain salient as tutors work to support students' academic literacies while recognizing and affirming linguistic variation. One-to-one writing center work with writers from across the disciplines reminds instructors and writing pedagogy professionals what it's like to read a writing assignment sheet for the first time, how novices respond to new writing tasks, and why the varied identities writers bring with them to their writing practice matter; in other words, we are reminded how and why we center student writing goals as we work to make meaning and progress together with students. As a result of her work, a writing specialist sees changes in the writer and the discipline: "Helping people to own their written voices is a big part of helping them to own their expertise. That's a part of the transformation. You authentically own a voice you craft for yourself in your writing.... When you develop a voice for yourself, you're impacting the range of voices that other people can do .. the way you do it is going to be yours." Inclusion in this model is not just about the student being heard, though that's important, it's also about encouraging and cultivating diverse points of view, diverse expression, and diverse voices, on campus and in the field. Writing center and WAC pedagogies and programming can and should continue to inform each other, even in, perhaps especially in, WID initiatives. The writing center is often presented as an alternative to the classroom—and it is commonly set apart—but if we imagine the university as one big writing center, we might devise more equitable, inclusive pedagogies.

Works Cited

Anderson, Paul, et al. "The Contributions of Writing to Learning and Development: Results from a Large-Scale Multi-Institutional Study." *Research in the Teaching of English*, vol. 50, no. 2, 2015, pp. 199–235.

Anson, Chris. "Black Holes: Writing Across the Curriculum, Assessment, and the Gravitational Invisibility of Race." *Race and Writing Assessment*, edited by Asao Inoue and Mya Poe, Peter Lang, 2012, pp. 15–28.

Benesch, Sarah. *Critical English for Academic Purposes: Theory, Politics and Practice*. Lawrence Erlbaum, 2001.

Bishop, Wendy. "I-Witnessing in Composition: Turning Ethnographic Data into Narratives." *Rhetoric Review*, vol. 11, no. 1, 1992, pp. 147–58.

Blackmon, Dereca. "Exploring Biases: Unpacking Microaggressions." Presentation to the Program in Writing and Rhetoric Program Meeting, Stanford University, May 15, 2015.

Blazer, Sarah. "Twenty-first Century Writing Center Staff Education: Teaching and Learning towards Inclusive and Productive Everyday Practice." *The Writing Center Journal*, vol. 35, no. 1, 2015, pp. 17–55.

Bokser, Julie A. "Pedagogies of Belonging: Listening to Students and Peers." *The Writing Center Journal*, vol. 25, 2005, pp. 43–60.

Bowman, Nicholas A. "Promoting Participation in a Diverse Democracy: A Meta-Analysis of College Diversity Experiences and Civic Engagement." *Review of Educational Research*, vol. 81, no. 1, 2011, pp. 29–68.

Chauncey, George. *Gay New York: Gender, Urban Culture, and the Making of the Gay Male World, 1890–1940*. Hachette UK, 2008.

Condon, Frankie. "Beyond the Known: Writing Centers and the Work of Anti-Racism." *The Writing Center Journal*, vol. 27, no. 2, 2007, pp. 19–38.

Condon, Frankie, and Bobbi Olson. "Building a House for Linguistic Diversity: Writing Centers, English-Language Teaching and Learning, and Social Justice," *Tutoring Second Language Writers*, edited by Shanti Bruce and Ben Rafoth, UP of Colorado, 2016, pp. 27–52.

Conference on College Composition and Communication. *Students' Right to Their Own Language*, 1974, reaffirmed Nov. 2003, annotated bibliography added Aug.

2006, reaffirmed Nov. 2014, www.ncte.org/library/NCTEFiles/Groups/CCCC/NewSRTOL.pdf.

Corbett, Steven J. "Tutoring Style, Tutoring Ethics: The Continuing Relevance of the Directive/Nondirective Instructional Debate." *Praxis: A Writing Center Journal*, vol. 5, no. 2, 2008, www.praxisuwc.com/corbett-52.

Delpit, Lisa. "The Silenced Dialogue: Power and Pedagogy in Educating other People's Children." *Harvard Educational Review*, vol. 58, no. 3, 1988, pp. 280–99.

Denny, Harry. *Facing the Center: Toward an Identity Politics of One-to-One Mentoring*. Utah State UP, 2010.

—. "Queering the Writing Center." *The Writing Center Journal*, vol. 25, no. 2, 2005, pp. 39–62.

Diab, Rasha, et al. "A multi-dimensional pedagogy for racial justice in writing centers." *Praxis: A Writing Center Journal*, vol. 10, no. 1, 2012, www.praxisuwc.com/diab-godbee-ferrell-simpkins-101.

—. "Making Commitments to Racial Justice Actionable." *Anti-Racist Activism: Teaching Rhetoric and Writing*, edited by Frankie Condon and Vershawn Ashanti Young, special issue of *Across the Disciplines*, vol. 10, 2013, wac.colostate.edu/atd/race/diabetal.cfm.

Dweck, Carol S. *Mindset: The New Psychology of Success*. Random House Digital, Inc., 2008.

Ede, Lisa. "Writing as a Social Practice: A Theoretical Foundation for Writing Centers?" *The Writing Center Journal*, vol. 9, no. 2, 1989, pp. 3–13.

Fitzgerald, Lauren, and Melissa Ianetta. *The Oxford Guide for Writing Tutors: Practice and Research*. Oxford UP, 2016.

Freire, Paulo. *Pedagogy of the Oppressed*. New York: Continuum, 2007.

García, Romeo. "Unmaking Gringo-Centers." *The Writing Center Journal*, vol. 36, no. 1, 2017, pp. 29–60.

Gere, Anne Ruggles et al. "Interrogating Disciplines/Disciplinarity in WAC/WID: An Institutional Study." *College Composition and Communication*, vol. 67, 2015, pp. 243–266.

Gilyard, Keith. *Let's Flip the Script : An African American Discourse on Language, Literature, and Learning*. Wayne State UP, 1996.

Graff, Gerald, and Kathy Bernstein. *They Say / I Say: The Moves that Matter in Academic Writing*. 3rd ed., Norton, 2016.

Greenfield, Laura, and Karen Rowan, editors. *Writing centers and the New Racism: A Call for Sustainable Dialogue and Change*. UP of Colorado, 2011.

Greenfield, Laura. "The 'Standard English' Fairy Tale: A Rhetorical Analysis of Racist Pedagogies and Commonplace Assumptions about Language Diversity." *Writing Centers and the New Racism : A Call for Sustainable Dialogue and Change*, edited by Laura Greenfield and Karen Rowan, Utah State UP, 2011, pp. 33–60.

Grimm, Nancy M. *Good Intentions: Writing Center Work for Postmodern Times*. Boynton/Cook, 1999.

—. "New Conceptual Frameworks for Writing Center Work." *The Writing Center Journal*, vol. 29, no. 2, 2009, pp. 11–27.

—. "Retheorizing Writing Center Work to Transform a System of Advantage Based on Race." *Writing Centers and the New Racism: A Call for Sustainable Dialogue and Change*, edited by Laura Greenfield and Karen Rowan, Utah State UP, 2011, pp. 33–60.

Gurin, Patricia, et al. "The Benefits of Diversity in Education for Democratic Citizenship." *Journal of Social Issues*, vol. 60, no. 1, 2004, pp. 17–34.

Harris, Heidi, and Jessie Blackburn, editors. WAC/WID Program Administration at Rural, Regional, and Satellite Campuses [Special Issue]. *Across the Disciplines*, vol. 11, 2014, wac.colostate.edu/atd/rural

hooks, bell. *Teaching to Transgress: Education as the Practice of Freedom*. New York: Routledge, 1994.

Hyman, Jeremy S., and Lynn F. Jacobs. "Why Does Diversity Matter at College Anyway?" *U.S. News & World Report*. August 12, 2009, www.usnews.com/education/blogs/professors-guide/2009/08/12/why-does-diversity-matter-at-college-anyway. Accessed August 16, 2018.

Inoue, Asao. *Antiracist Writing Assessment Ecologies: Teaching and Assessing Writing for a Socially Just Future*. Parlor Press, 2015.

Iten, Michelle. "The First Discipline is Class: Aiming at Inclusion in Argument across the Curriculum." *WAC Journal*, vol. 28, 2017, pp. 34–51.

Johnson, Dawn R., et al. "Examining Sense of Belonging among First-Year Undergraduates from Different Racial/Ethnic Groups." *Journal of College Student Development*, vol. 48, no. 5, 2007, pp. 525–42.

Johnson, Michelle T. "Racial Literacy and the Writing Center." *Writing Centers and the New Racism: A Call for Sustainable Dialogue and Change*, edited by Laura Greenfield and Karen Rowan, UP of Colorado, 2011, pp. 211–27.

Jordan, Jay. *Redesigning Composition for Multilingual Realities*. NCTE, 2012.

Keller, Evelyn Fox. *A Feeling for the Organism: The Life and Work of Barbara McClintock*, 10th Anniversary edition. Macmillan, 1984.

Lawrie, Gwen, et al. "Moving Towards Inclusive Learning and Teaching: A Synthesis of Recent Literature." *Teaching & Learning Inquiry*, vol. 5, no.1, 2017, pp. 1–13.

LeCourt, Donna. "WAC as Critical Pedagogy: The Third Stage?" *Journal of Advanced Composition*, vol. 16, 1996, pp. 389–405.

Lee, Amy, et al. *Engaging Diversity in Undergraduate Classrooms: A Pedagogy for Developing Intercultural Competence: ASHE Higher Education Report*, vol. 38, no. 2. John Wiley & Sons, 2012.

Locks, Angela M, et al. "Extending Notions of Campus Climate and Diversity to the transition to College: Experiences with Diverse Peers and College Sense of Belonging." *The Review of Higher Education*, vol. 31, no. 3, 2008, pp. 257–85.

Lunsford, Andrea. "Collaboration, Control, and the Idea of a Writing Center." *The Writing Center Journal*, vol. 12, no. 1, 1991, pp. 3–10.

Mackiewicz, Jo, and Isabelle Thompson. *Talk about Writing: The Tutoring Strategies of Experienced Writing Center Tutors*. Routledge, 2018.

Moneyhun, Clyde, and Patti Hanlon-Baker. "Tutoring Teachers." *The Writing Lab Newsletter*, vol. 36, nos. 9–10, 2012.

Mullin, Joan. "Writing Centers and WAC." *WAC for the New Millennium: Strategies for Continuing Writing-Across-the-Curriculum Programs*, edited by Susan H. McLeod et al., NCTE, 2001, pp. 179–99.

Nielsen, Mathias Wullum et al. "Making gender diversity work for scientific discovery and innovation." *Nature Hume Behavior*, vol. 2, 2018, pp. 726–34.

Page, Scott E. *The Difference: How the Power of Diversity Creates Better Groups, Firms, Schools, and Societies*. 2nd ed., Princeton UP, 2008.

Poe, Mya. "Re-Framing Race in Teaching Writing Across the Curriculum." *Anti-Racist Activism: Teaching Writing and Rhetoric*, edited by Frankie Condon and Vershawn Ashanti Young, special issue of *Across the Disciplines*, vol. 10, 2013, wac.colostate.edu/docs/atd/race/poe.pdf.

Salem, Lori. "Decisions . . . Decisions: Who Chooses to Use the Writing Center?" *The Writing Center Journal*, vol. 35, no. 2, 2016, pp. 147–71.

Smith, Dorothy E. *Institutional Ethnography: A Sociology for People*. Rowman Altamira, 2005.

Smitherman, Geneva. "'Students' Right to Their Own Language': A Retrospective." *The English Journal*, vol. 84, no. 1, 1995, pp. 21–27.

—. "The Historical Struggle for Language Rights in CCCC." *Language Diversity in the Classroom: From Intention to Practice*, edited by Geneva Smitherman, Victor Villanueva, and Suresh Canagarajah, Southern Illinois U P, 2003, pp. 7–39.

Soliday, Mary. *Everyday Genres: Writing Assignments across the Disciplines*. Southern Illinois UP, 2011.

Stanford University. "Applicant Profile." *Stanford University*. https://admission.stanford.edu/apply/selection/profile.html

Stanford University. "Stanford University Common Data Set: 2017–2018." ucomm.stanford.edu/wp-content/uploads/sites/15/2018/06/stanford-cds-2017.pdf

Sword, Helen. *Air & Light & Time & Space: How Successful Academics Write*. Harvard UP, 2017.

Thompson, Paul, and Giuliana Diani. *English for Academic Purposes: Approaches and Implications*. Cambridge Scholars Publishing, 2015.

Vacek, Kathleen. "Developing Tutors' Meta-Multiliteracies Through Poetry." *Praxis: A Writing Center Journal*, vol. 9, no. 2, 2012, www.praxisuwc.com/meta-multiliteracies.

Villanueva, Victor. *Bootstraps: From an American Academic of Color*. NCTE, 1993.

—. "The Politics of Literacy Across the Curriculum." *WAC for the New Millennium: Strategies for Continuing Writing-Across-the-Curriculum Programs*, edited by Susan H. McLeod et al., NCTE, 2001, pp. 165–78.

Waldo, Mark. "Last Best Place for WAC: The Writing Center." *WPA: Writing Program Administration*, vol. 16, no. 3, 1993, pp. 15–26.

Winkelmes, Mary-Ann, et al. "A Teaching Intervention that Increases Underserved College Students' Success." *Peer Review*, vol. 18, nos. 1–2, 2016, pp. 31–36.

Young, Vershawn Ashanti. "Should Writers Use They Own English?" *Writing Centers and the New Racism: A Call for Sustainable Dialogue and Change*, edited by Laura Greenfield and Karen Rowan, Utah State UP, 2011, pp. 61–72.

Zawacki, Terry Myers, and Michelle Cox, editors. *WAC and Second Language Writers: Research Towards Linguistically and Culturally Inclusive Programs and Practices*. Parlor Press and the WAC Clearinghouse, 2014.

Zhang, Phil, et al. "'Going there': Peer Writing Consultants' Perspectives on the New Racism and Peer Writing Pedagogies." *Anti-Racist Activism: Teaching Writing and Rhetoric*, edited by Frankie Condon and Vershawn Ashanti Young, special issue of *Across the Disciplines*, vol. 10, 2013, wac.colostate.edu/docs/atd/race/oziasetal/.

WAC Journal Interview of Asao B. Inoue

NEAL LERNER

Those of us teaching in writing across the curriculum/writing in the disciplines (WAC/WID) are often caught between a rock and a hard place: While we see writing as a means of helping students become agentive, the forms of that writing are usually dictated by disciplinary faculty or university "standards" or the fields themselves in which status quo is rarely questioned. While writing is, indeed, a tool of discovery, it can also be a tool of oppression when the ideas of what counts as "good" writing are regulatory and prescriptive.

This tension is not only present in WAC/WID, of course, as research and theory in basic writing and first-year writing have long focused on this dilemma and the ways that writing can be both a cudgel of status quo values (read: narrow and elitist) and a challenge to those values. In WAC/WID, however, these conversations only seem to happen in the backchannels, if at all, and the status quo is rarely challenged. Further contributing to the problem is the highly visible lack of teachers and scholars of color in WAC/WID research and practice.

A prominent voice that has challenged these ideas, particularly through the lens of writing assessment, is Asao B. Inoue, Ph.D., who is a Professor in the School of Interdisciplinary Arts and Sciences and director of university writing at the University of Tacoma. Through his award-winning publications, including the co-edited collection *Race and Writing Assessment* (Peter Lang, 2012) and the monograph *Antiracist Writing Assessment Ecologies: Teaching and Assessing Writing for a Socially Just Future* (Parlor 2015), and his leadership as past chair of the Conference on College Composition and Communication, Asao Inoue guides us to the future of WAC/WID, a future in which social justice is at the forefront.

Neal Lerner: What's your origin story about coming to teaching writing, particularly in terms of key moments or people that had a major influence?

Asao Inoue: I took a summer class near the end of my undergraduate degree (BA in English Literature with a minor in Writing Studies) at Oregon State University. This was in the early 90s. The course was an advanced writing class that focused on teaching writing. It was taught by Chris Anderson, who is still there. He was the Director of Composition at the time. I'd taken several other courses from him and admired him and found his style of teaching inviting. His feedback on my writing was always encouraging, and I wanted to write for a male teacher, which was rare for me up to that point. Chris would write with us in class and read some of his writing to us. His words always sounded poetic, musing, tentative, humble. I love this about him as a teacher. In the summer class, we read and discussed composition studies articles and rhetoric as an ancient Hellenic practice of citizenship. I was introduced to the idea of pedagogy, that teaching writing was a thoughtful and planned practice, something scholars thought deeply about. While it wasn't until a bit later that I began to study rhetoric, I got some of my first lessons about rhetoric in that class by reading Berlin, Faulkerson, Faigley, Hairston, Ede (who happened to teach in our department), and Lunsford.

In fact, my first substantive and meaningful lesson that influenced me as a teacher and writer in those early years was Peter Elbow's book, *Writing Without Teachers*. During that summer, I was getting married, and I worked the graveyard shift at a gas station. I had some time on my hands. The class finished in late June, but I had all of July and August before the wedding and grad school began. I asked Chris: What can I read over the summer to prepare me for my work in grad school and as a teacher of writing? He suggested that I read Elbow's book and do the activities in it as best I could. So, during the long graveyard hours at a deserted gas station in Corvallis, I read slowly and carefully that book. I would read a section or chapter, then write oil-stained page after page, in the garage, the smell of gas and oil thick in the air, with one eye on the page and one on the pumps. That book and my writing was deeply satisfying. I can remember being eager to go to work at 9 pm so that I could get started on my reading and writing. While today for most writing teachers, perhaps, Elbow's book is too simplistic, not political enough, or simply an anachronism, I still find much in it worth sharing with my students, like chapter 4, "The Teacherless Writing Classroom." It's still one of the better places I know to help early writers read each others' drafts and find practices and confidence in those practices.

The book also planted a metaphorical seed in me as a teacher and researcher, which I've carried with me to this day. In chapter 2, "The Process of Writing—Growing," Elbow opens with a parable of sorts about a land where the people couldn't touch the floor no matter how much they tried because their process was to reach up to the sky. What I love about that parable is how in hyperbole we can see the paradigm in which people often get trapped, and this is Elbow's point about the parable. Writing teachers and students often think that the best way to write is the same old ways that haven't worked in the past for most people. Now, Elbow has his answer, which I like, but I see this parable having a much wider application. In my own work in writing assessment, I've taken (often unconsciously or subconsciously) this parable to heart. Why must we assess students writing in the ways we have? Maybe there is more to an assessment than the tool or rubric or assignment or feedback practice, maybe its an ecology? Why do teachers not think first about what, how, why, and in what ways assessment happens in their classrooms before they think about curricula, texts, assignments, lessons? Why do we think that using standards help students to write better, maybe they are actually white supremacist, racist?

One more moment that has been important to me as a teacher. Years later, I was in a tenure-track job at Chemeketa Community College in Salem, Oregon, a year from tenure. My wife had just given birth to our second son. We were in bed. I was reading Victor Villanueva's *Bootstraps*. The book was like a thunderstorm that was both frightening and exhilarating. Every page spoke to me, about me, was about me. Victor and I are similar in many ways, how we grew up, what happened, why. That book showed me a way out of my self-blame and shame of my failings in school, and my deep insecurities about myself as a writer and thinker. It was the Marxian critique, Gramsci, and Freire that Victor's book introduced me to. But I realized right then, in that bed, next to my wife, how much I still needed a good, male mentor, one who was more like me, who was a scholar-teacher of color. Chris was wonderful, and very important. He opened the door for me to see that there is this beautiful life of teaching writing to others, but he is white and from a middle-class upbringing in Spokane. Victor gave me purpose and confidence. Victor showed me how I could be, and in a multitude of ways that seemed attainable, even as he was such an academic rockstar. In that bed, I realized I had to leave my job and go back to school. It was a frightening decision, but one I could not turn away from. When I told my wife that I needed to do this, to go to WSU and work with Victor to get a PhD, it was the first time I'd cried in front of her. It could have gone wrong, but because I followed Victor, it didn't.

Neal Lerner: What do you see as the present state of WAC/WID? What would you like WAC/WID to look like in the future?

Asao Inoue: This is a hard question for me because I don't really consider myself a WAC/WID scholar. I've directed several WAC programs (I currently direct one), and I've read in the literature, but I don't contribute directly to it. So, what I say here is really from the perspective of an outsider who looks in, and likely is missing critical works and perspectives that I just don't know about. What I see now, is a lack of any substantive theorizing or use of theories of race and racism, intersectional or not, in how teaching or learning writing across disciplines happens or could happen. I'd like to see more of that. Vicki Tolar Burton voiced a version of this problem in her 2010 *CCC* review of WAC literature. More recently, Frankie Condon and Vershawn Ashanti Young published a co-edited collection, *Performing Antiracist Pedagogy*, that offers a much needed set of discussions around racism in WAC contexts. Mya Poe also has done some good work in this area. I'm thinking in particular of her 2013 article in *Across the Disciplines*, "Re-Framing Race in Teaching Writing Across the

Curriculum." But very little scholarship directly addresses the ways in which the discourses expected of nurses, business majors, engineers, and others across all fields and professions are quite simply white supremacist. It's harsh sounding language, language that makes many uncomfortable, but it's language needed if we want real structural changes. We gotta call it like it is. This kettle ain't black. It's white. White supremacist. And we gotta find ways to help our colleagues in compassionate ways to deal with this structural problem around the sole use and assessment of white language norms. I'm getting really tired of hearing colleagues in Nursing or Business or Engineering tell me, or imply, that their students must use a white standard of English if they are going to be communicative and effective in their fields or professions. That's just bullshit. And it hurts students, Black, Latino/a, Asian, Native/Tribal, and White alike. We all lose. Our disciplines lose. I'd like to see more projects that do this larger, harder work that stretches outside of the Humanities. It's harder than similar work in the Humanities because we in the Humanities generally have accepted the structural critique of racism and whiteness, and when we hear it applied to language standards in classrooms, we generally are sympathetic, even if we don't always know what to do about it.

Neal Lerner: A common critique of WAC/WID is that it doesn't challenge the status quo, but instead merely enables status quo discursive forms, hierarchies, imbedded racism, etc. to perpetuate. Do you agree?

Asao Inoue: Given what I've said about what I hope to see in WAC/WID scholarship in the future, yes, I do. When I work with faculty from across disciplines, revealing this problem is one major thing I try to accomplish. I start by explaining the way in which language can exist and work, which is among people. It travels with people. People communicate, so people make and prepetuate standards, which are deeply about those people. If this is true, then the discourses in any discipline are directly influenced by those who have used and controlled those discourses. That's mostly white males of middle- and upper-class standing in the US. No surprises. We all know the histories of our disciplines and of the academy generally. For most of its global history, higher education and the research and discourse communities that make up those institutions have been White, Western, male, heteronormative, and Christian. This kind of *habitus* is the status quo. And because race is so taboo, few can imagine that what they do when they communicate in their fields or professions, or expect from their students, is anything but trying to communicate, honestly, ethically, and clearly. It is difficult for many to see outside of their own *habitus*, their own dispositions and embodied habits of language. What seems communicative, honest, ethical, and clear to someone trained in the discourse of nursing can be very difficult to see as harmful and white supremacist. It's how you save lives. And this is true, but what is also true is that it harms many students of color and multilingual students. When disciplines and teachers use their idiosyncratic versions of their white disciplinary discourses as the standard by which to judge all students, they perpetuate white language supremacy. When they see their Black or Latino/a or multilingual students failing or doing poorly, they think, "ah, I just need better ways to respond to writing—I need new strategies to help students master the standard." And that is the conscientious teacher. But that response is deeply misguided because it naturalizes the standard, keeps invisible the nature of the status quo as anything but one historical group's language norms, at the expense of many others.

Neal Lerner: Is there such a thing as an "activist" WAC/WID? If so, what might that look like?

Asao Inoue: I wish I could say that I've given this deep and long thought. I haven't, but right now, what I think would be activist WAC/WID work would be to cultivate an antiracist and anti-white language supremacist project on two fronts simultaneously. The project's goal would be to change societal structures that shape the way we judge language and make decisions about it and from it. The first front, of course, is cultivating more discussions and curricular changes around white language supremacy in the academy, which start with changes in assessment ecologies across the disciplines. I think this is done in small ways already, but could be—maybe given the violence and problems we see in our world today—should be the main aim of all WAC/WID faculty development programs. Why help faculty maintain racist systems? Racist systems hurt people. I ain't into aiding and abetting injustice. The second front, the more difficult one (as if the first wasn't difficult), is to reach out into the community and business sectors, cultivating changes there in language judgment practices.

What makes our society's white supremacy so durable and malleable, so ever-changing, is its overdetermined nature. Structures upon structures that structure more structures. This is also the nature of our own *habitus* and why it is hard to not be white supremacist. We can change our hearts and our intentions, but that doesn't change our standards, or the dispositions we've cultivated over many years about what is clear, what is valuable, what is good or bad in language practices, or what we think our students will need in their futures because others are not as enlightened as us—the delaying of activism and social justice for the sake of our students! Can you hear how foolish and counterproductive that sounds?

So, successful activist work starts in at least these two fronts simultaneously, so that a critical mass can happen before the overdetermined nature of our language judgment systems co opt our in-the-moment tactics that are meant to prevent racism or white supremacist outcomes. In the final chapter of Michelle Alexander's *The New Jim Crow*, in which she offers some ways to change the problem of Black and Brown mass incarceration in the US, which is the epitome of racism and white supremacy from top to bottom, she draws on Martin Luther King, Jr.'s later strategies for civil rights work in the country. Alexander explains that King understood that the best strategy for true structural changes in the US that would liberate everyone meant that the movement couldn't be about civil rights, but must be about broader human rights. Thomas F. Jackson makes this argument in his 2007 book, *From Civil Rights to Human Rights: Martin Luther King, Jr. and the Struggle for Economic Justice*. The point is, human rights was for King an intersectional and wider, even global, set of structures that overdetermined the racism and civil rights problems he started trying to tackle. It was about poverty, labor, health care, the environment. Pull the thread of how to address white language supremacy in your classroom and you find that the garment is made of many threads that stretch to other places outside the university and your discipline, many of which seemingly have nothing to do with writing well in your discipline. I think successful activist work that looks to address antiracism and white supremacy in language judgment practices must deal with, must find allies in other fields that do this work already, other problems too, showing the ways, for instance, food scarcity, poverty, the criminalization of Black and Brown men that begins at a young age, health issues and environmental issues that harm people and are attached to where some must live, are just as much about writing in the disciplines or writing across the curriculum, or writing in the professions as some idiosyncratic notion of "good writing."

Neal Lerner: Are current movements towards inclusive teaching practices for diverse student learners at odds with teaching writing in WAC/WID contexts?

Asao Inoue: No, I don't think so, for all the reasons I've been mentioning already. Inclusive practices for assessing writing (assessment is the engine of learning to write—that's my primary term for pedagogy, learning, not teaching), are fundamentally about the human right to language in the ways one can. As our national organization has endorsed, all people have the right to the language of their nurture. And this right should not equate to exclusion from fields of study, professions, or anything else. It may mean that we as a complex society need to work differently as listeners and readers, form new *habitus*—why should we expect everyone to language to us in ways that we language.

Perhaps one practice I have promoted over the last few years, labor-based grading contracts, which eliminates the use of a dominant white standard to determine grades in classrooms, and instead uses quantifiable labor to determine progress and grades, could be seen as at odds with many w-courses or writing in the major courses. [NL: See Inoue, Asao B. (2005). Community-based assessment pedagogy. *Assessing Writing 09.3*, 208–38; and Inoue, Asao B. (2012). "Grading Contracts: Assessing their Effectiveness on Different Racial Formations." In Inoue, Asao B. and Mya Poe (Eds.), *Race and Writing Assessment*; New York: Peter Lang.] Those courses often have content that needs covering, and so for many teachers, students need to be assessed on how well they know that material. A labor-based system seemingly ignores what a student has learned or displays in writing or other activities, but this is a misunderstanding. Without getting into the weeds of the kind of assessment ecology and pedagogy I'm calling for, I'll say this about inclusive assessment practices for diverse learners in WAC/WID contexts, and we should be clear here with our euphemisms, "diverse student learners" means primarily students of color and multilingual students. All students come to school to learn and have fun, and paradoxically, these conditions contribute to another aspect of the human condition, suffering. Because of this, we should hope that our students are willing to freely reveal their weaknesses and failures to us, and we should be willing, as teachers who read their writing, to reveal our own weaknesses and failures at making meaning out of their words. If this is the way in which we learn to language, then inclusive practices should be universal in school, and they cannot be at odds with diverse learners. In fact, most conventional ways of judging students language practices, grading and assessing them, are at odds with diverse students' language practices. This is exactly why we have WAC/WID programs, because teachers from all disciplines see and feel that their "students cannot write," and they do not know how to teach to them or read their writing productively. The difficulty is that, like Elbow's parable, too many teachers keep trying to reach the floor of inclusive assessment writing practices by stretching up to the sky, then complaining about how the floor cannot reach their fingertips.

Getting Specific about Critical Thinking: Implications for Writing Across the Curriculum

JUSTIN K. RADEMAEKERS

Introduction

The development of students' critical thinking abilities has long been an omnipresent concept in composition theory, in writing pedagogy, and, indeed, in many of our writing classrooms. Perhaps some readers have even listed critical thinking as a learning outcome on one of your course syllabi? As a writing across the curriculum (WAC) director and composition instructor at my own institution, I've found that the phrase "critical thinking" has a great deal of import across the curriculum, more so than other phrases I've tried to share with faculty teaching writing across the curriculum—phrases like *genre awareness, knowledge transfer,* or even . . . *rhetoric.*

Recent articles in *The WAC Journal* have noted critical thinking as a liberal learning concept that is at work activating the key features of threshold concepts (Basgier, 2016); and as an outcome of the revision process (Bryant, Lape, & Schaeffer, 2014). Other landmark works in WAC draw deliberate connections between critical thinking and faculty workshops (Fulwiler, 1981); the sequencing of composition courses (Beaufort, 2008); and the integration of critical thinking with disciplinary writing assignments (Bean, 2011). We might take as further evidence of critical thinking's omnipresence in composition pedagogy its appearance in the 2014 Council of Writing Program Administrators (WPA) "Outcomes Statement for First-Year Composition" as well as within CCCC's own 2015 position statement, "Principles for the Postsecondary Teaching of Writing." In fact—writing aside—faculty, staff, *and* administrators in higher education might be hard-pressed to find a concept more widely shared and agreed upon across the curriculum than the expectation that students should develop *critical* and analytical thinking skills during their pursuit of a higher education.

Yet, despite the prominence of critical thinking in composition courses and higher education curricula, a widely shared and agreed upon definition of this term proves elusive, which complicates its import into WAC conversations. The present study builds from existing scholarship on critical thinking and language in an attempt to delineate a clear and nuanced view of critical thinking in the context of writing across the curriculum.

The lack of a widely agreed upon definition of critical thinking in academic discourse isn't for lack of trying. Forty-six critical thinking experts once assembled (in 1990) on behalf of the American Philosophical Association to develop what became known as the *Delphi Report* (Facione). Since that 111-page report in 1990, the Association of American Colleges & Universities (AAC&U) has made serious contributions toward articulating critical thinking, which their "VALUE" rubric defines as "a habit of mind characterized by the comprehensive exploration of issues, ideas, artifacts, and events before accepting or formulating an opinion or conclusion." While this definition helps universities move toward a universally agreed upon definition of critical thinking, the AAC&U's definition evades complicated disciplinary questions through the generous interpretability of what constitutes "comprehensive exploration," or what indicates whether a student's "habit of mind" has achieved a critical character. Those readers who study writing in the disciplines, undoubtedly read this AAC&U definition and begin to ask: does comprehensive exploration look different in history than it does in communication studies or physics?

We might expect definitions from organizations like the AAC&U to be intentionally vague so as to apply to many diverse academic disciplines and programs, but our own composition research also ubiquitously generalizes what it means to "think critically" and to utilize that thinking in writing processes. The 2014 iteration of the *WPA* "Outcomes Statement for First-Year Composition" provides the following definition:

> *Critical thinking* is the ability to analyze, synthesize, interpret, and evaluate ideas, information, situations, and texts. When writers think critically about the materials they use—whether print texts, photographs, data sets, videos, or other materials—they separate assertion from evidence, evaluate sources and evidence, recognize and evaluate underlying assumptions, read across texts for connections and patterns, identify and evaluate chains of reasoning, and compose appropriately qualified and developed claims and generalizations. These practices are foundational for advanced academic writing.

This definition offers more specificity than the AAC&U's definition in that particular "habits of mind" are understood to be analytic habits, synthetic habits, interpretive habits, and evaluative habits, and to be "comprehensive" is more specifically to "separate assertion from evidence, evaluate sources and evidence, recognize and evaluate underlying assumptions, read…for connections and patterns" etc. As worded, it's clear that these specific habits and traits of comprehensiveness are indeed "foundational for advanced academic writing"; but, when synthesized, these habits and traits also amount to tasks that look a lot like something very specific—*rhetorical analysis* of text. But is this the kind of critical-thinking-through-writing my social work students in first-year-writing courses will need most? Considering first-year writing's unique role of educating all incoming students and in preparing all students to think critically through academic writing, it's worth asking whether rhetorical analyses of "printed texts . . . or other materials" prepare students for the habits and traits expected of them in other coursework. This is not to say that close rhetorical reading of text is not a valuable skill for all students to learn; rather, in the same way that Howard Tinberg explains that "metacognition is not cognition" (*Naming What we Know*, 75), we might come to see that generally valuable academic thinking skills are not the same as skills for thinking critically in one's discipline.

Principle eight of CCCC's 2015 "Principles for the Postsecondary Teaching of Writing" reads: "Sound writing instruction supports learning, engagement, and critical thinking in courses across the curriculum" and provides the following explanation:

> Instructors emphasize that writing development is continuous and supports learning, engagement, and critical thinking by using activities and assignments to help students learn and engage with information, ideas, and arguments within specific courses. Beyond specific writing courses, instructors emphasize this purpose when they create opportunities for students to recognize expectations for writing within their disciplines and use writing to help them prepare to participate in their intended disciplines. Institutions and programs emphasize this purpose by providing faculty in other disciplines opportunities to learn about and incorporate writing strategies in their pedagogy.

Here, we see that an instructor's emphasis on writing development is "continuous" and supports critical thinking through "activities and assignments" that "help students learn and engage with information, ideas, and arguments within specific courses." The lack of specificity here might lead some to conclude that if instructors just continue assigning writing, students will begin engaging with discipline-specific information, ideas, and arguments critically; that all assignments and activities that are continuously developing writing are simultaneously teaching students to critically engage with the thinking and content required by specific courses. CCCC's explanation provides more specificity by asserting a principle that instructors should "create opportunities for students to recognize expectations for writing within their disciplines and use writing to help them prepare to participate in their intended disciplines." As with the 2014 *WPA* "Outcomes Statement for First-Year Composition", we see the CCCC's explanation of critical thinking narrow to the point of prescribing something very specific; in this case, what we might see as disciplinary discourse analysis and/or genre awareness, which is aspirational content in first-year writing.

The definitions provided by the AAC&U, CWPA, and CCCC statements are all useful steps toward an explicit understanding of what it means to think critically and the role of writing in the work of critical thinking habits of mind. Yet, these statements on critical thinking also take on a character that is at once vaguely general—*critical thinking is a habit of mind*—and then explicitly narrow in first-year composition—*critical thinking is rhetorical analysis; critical thinking is genre awareness*. What emerges in the space left between these two positions is a debate as to whether critical thinking is a general skill (a view associated with Robert Ennis's 1987 work), a variety of discipline-specific skills (associated with John McPeck in 1990), or an array of general skills that can be privileged in different orientations by different disciplines.

A More Nuanced Definition of Critical Thinking

Tim John Moore's 2011 study *Critical Thinking and Language* is the most recent and comprehensive examination of opposing disciplinary distinctions for critical thinking as a learning objective in higher education. Conducted over the course of one year (2005 to 2006), Moore utilizes spoken data—from seventeen in-person interviews—and textual data (i.e. teaching documents collected from participants) to parse out disciplinary meanings of critical thinking in history, philosophy, and literary/cultural studies. Moore concludes that all disciplines in his study loosely understand critical thinking as "an extra edge of consciousness" (234) while seven distinct "dimensions of difference" in critical thinking emerged among interview participants. Though only a single study, such distinctions offer profound implications for higher education pedagogy, especially for teachers, scholars, and administrators of WAC programs.

One potential use of a more nuanced definition of critical thinking for WAC teacher-scholars is that critical thinking can become a neutral ground for starting conversations across campus about what writing moves are valued by different disciplines. Since writing is required for advanced thinking, conversations about writing in the disciplines can begin with conversations about what kind of critical thinking is important in a particular discipline/course. Once faculty (in workshops or conversations with a WAC director) determine the kind of critical thinking they value from students (e.g., awareness of subjectivity), those faculty can begin to discuss how those expectations become imbedded in writing conventions (e.g., the use of first person). As WAC scholars begin to talk about critical thinking in more specific terms, fruitful conversations about how expectations for student writing are embedded in expectations for student thinking can begin to take place.

Another benefit of a more nuanced definition of critical thinking for WAC teacher-scholars is that as faculty and WAC directors get specific about the kind of critical thinking a course is seeking from students, informal and writing-to-learn assignments can be discussed as important tools for helping students practice the kind of thinking their instructors want to encourage in their writing. For example, if a professor speaks with a WAC director about the importance of objectivity as a form of critical thinking, then writing-to-learn assignments that help students revise away subjective language can be employed in that classroom. In cases such as this, conversations about specific uses of critical thinking can become the backdrop for planning informal and writing-to-learn assignments.

Finally, a more nuanced definition of critical thinking for WAC teacher-scholars can help propel conversations about discipline-specific writing conventions, traditionally unearthed by content and disciplinary discourse analyses in WID scholarship. Examination of disciplinary privileges for specific modes of critical thinking offers a new lens for understanding disciplinary writing conventions. Is there a particular kind of critical thinking that history students are being asked to hone as they mature in their academic programs? And if so, what kind of disciplinary writing assignments promote such thinking? Would rhetorical analysis and genre awareness approaches in first-year writing courses sufficiently prepare students for the kind of thinking expected of them in history courses? If there are specific arrays of critical thinking skills that different disciplines privilege, could programs be creating composition-learning communities of students from disciplines not typically associated with one another (say history and physics) based on the kind of critical thinking privileged by their disciplines?

Such questions could be a fruitful line of inquiry for composition research were the field to explore disciplinary perspectives on critical thinking in more detail. The present article aims to contribute toward this detail by furthering Moore's 2011 investigation of critical thinking in a way that has been framed for composition and writing researchers.

Moore's study offers important implications for university curricula, writing instruction, and for better understanding the disciplinary nuances in conceptualizing *critical thinking* as a learning outcome, but the study is not without critique. Martin Davies' 2013 article "Critical Thinking and the Disciplines Reconsidered" takes Moore to task for what Davies describes as a "relativist attitude" that is "dangerous and wrong-headed" in its "specifist approach" (15). A key concern for Davies is that Moore constructs a false dilemma that critical thinking is either a "universal category" that would apply to all disciplines, or a "catch all" concept and therefore really only has a plurality of discipline-specific meanings when examined more closely (6). In partial agreement with Davies' contention, this study explores a third position: that there may be discipline-specific privileges for particular critical-thinking skills, but these skills remain general critical-thinking skills available and valuable to all.

There are other key ways to build on Moore's study. First, the disciplines studied by Moore—history, philosophy, and literary/cultural studies—are all traditionally understood as humanities disciplines. Would the loose understanding of critical thinking as "an extra edge of consciousness" with the seven distinct "dimensions of difference" revealed by Moore hold true if we extend such questions to disciplines in natural science, social science, business, and art? Secondly, his study takes place at an urban research institution in Australia. Are these disciplinary distinctions for critical thinking present at a public university in the US? Thirdly, does the low sample size of Moore's study (n=17) offer the possibility that he captured an anomaly or institutional group-think that may not hold true among a larger population of participants? With an eye toward writing research and these critiques of Moore's study in mind, the present study explores critical thinking across the curriculum at a large public university in the Mid-Atlantic United States with more than double the participants of Moore's and with a much more diverse representation of academic disciplines.

Study Methodology

Participants

This study involved 45–60 minute individual interviews with thirty-seven faculty members, as stated, at a large public university in the Mid-Atlantic United States. Faculty were selected at random by a research assistant who invited participants via university email. Invitations were made with an explicit goal to achieve diverse representations across five of the university's six academic Colleges. This resulted in interviews with the following faculty:

- Accounting (1)
- Anthropology (1)
- Athletic training (1)
- Biology (1)
- Chemistry (1)
- Communication sciences & disorders (2)
- Communication studies (2)
- Counselor education (1)
- Criminal justice (1)
- Early & middle grades education (1)
- Economics (1)
- English (2)
- Geography & planning (1)
- Health (1)
- History (1)
- Human resources (1)
- Kinesiology (1)
- Literacy (1)

- Management (3)
- Marketing (1)
- Music (1)
- Philosophy (1)
- Physics (3)
- Psychology (1)
- Public health (1)
- Social work (2)
- Special education (2)
- Women's & gender studies (1)

The greatest number of interviews were held with faculty in the College of Business and Public Management (9), followed by the College of Arts and Humanities (8). The College of Sciences and Mathematics (7) and the College of Education and Social Work (7) had equal participation, while the College of Health Sciences (6) had the least participation among faculty. All interview participants signed written consent forms prior to participation.

Data Collection

This study collected three types of data for analysis: interviews recorded through a typed transcript, assignment sheets and descriptions from faculty, and faculty suggestions of works (articles, books, film, etc.) that each participant saw as exemplifying critical thought in their discipline. The typed transcript was produced by a research assistant who attended all in-person interviews. To ensure proper meaning was understood, a short-hand transcript was also taken by the interviewer and could be used to clarify meaning in the written transcripts. Interviewees agreed to provide any follow-up clarification if needed following the interviews.

There were an estimated thirty-two hours of interview data collected among the thirty-seven participants. Thirty-two of these interviews took place in the offices of participants, three interviews were held over the phone, and two interviews took place in the office of the lead researcher. The interviews were organized around ten questions asked of participants after they had consented to participation and transcription of their responses. The questions asked of participants are based on questions outlined in Moore's study of critical thinking with some variation. Those questions are as follows:

1. How would you define your discipline, and what kind of thinking and inquiry it emphasizes?
2. Is being critical valued in your discipline?
3. When, if ever, does your discipline use the term "critical"?

4. What does it mean to be "critical" in your discipline?
5. Can you point us to a strong example of a critical work in your field?
6. How do you define "critical thinking"?
7. How do you teach critical thinking in your discipline?
8. Do you see this kind of critical thinking as general or specific/unique to your discipline?
9. Which assignments in your courses require the greatest deal of critical thinking?
10. Would you be willing to share some assignments, readings, etc. that you think are examples of critical work in your discipline?

Deviation from this question list occurred at times in order to clarify questions for participants or to follow-up on interesting answers that could be further articulated in the transcript. For example, some faculty didn't have a clear sense of how to answer question one (How would you define your discipline and what kind of thinking and inquiry it emphasizes?). In these situations, I would ask: "Is there maybe a grand question your discipline is ultimately exploring or trying to address?"

Additionally, after asking question five (Can you point us to a strong example of a critical work in your field?) I recapitulated participant answers for participants so I could be sure I had a full understanding of their sense of what it means to be critical in their discipline before moving on to questions about critical thinking itself (questions six through ten). Question seven (How/do you teach critical thinking in your discipline?) often led to multiple assignment descriptions from interviewees, in which case I often honed in on ways that writing is used to think critically or to capture critical thought.

There were fifteen participants, or 40.5% of interviewees, that provided assignment sheets and descriptions of assignments that highlight critical thinking in respective disciplines. There were twenty-three participants, or 62% of interviewees, who were able to point toward an "exemplary work" of critical thinking during the interview. In Moore's study, this data took the form of collecting discipline-specific study guides, but no such culture of study guides existed at this specific university. Instead, faculty were asked what they would point students toward as demonstrating strong critical thinking in the discipline.

Data Analysis

The thirty-seven transcripts of faculty interviews and supplemental documents (assignment sheets and readings when provided) were uploaded and stored in a cloud-based file management system where they were placed in individual folders labeled based on disciplinary identification (e.g. Social Work 2). The transcripts were then analyzed in two separate phases: the first phase analyzed participant transcripts and any available supplemental documents on individual terms, and the second phase analyzed patterns across participant transcripts.

The first phase of this analysis consisted of a process that began by rereading the entire transcript and drafting an approximately 100-word summary of how the interviewee conceptualized critical thinking in the interview. This summary helped condense interviewee responses into a manageable unit of analysis. Summaries took note of what the interviewee sees as the goal, or epistemological function, of the discipline, and what kind of critical thinking is needed to perform well within that disciplinary epistemology. Here is an example summary derived from an analysis of data from an anthropology interview:

> For this [anthropology] interviewee, part of thinking critically is making sure what you're doing is always situated in response to a larger (social?) issue. The goal of anthropology is to "shed light on how different people in different contexts confront those (death, suffering, betrayal, love, hate) issues." Critical thinking is about seeing relationships among things that you at first don't see or recognize. This comes from moving between the micro and the macro which requires accepting complexity and making connections between things that seem disconnected (Anthropology 1).

Next, summaries were analyzed with attention to which "dimensions of difference" in critical thinking, identified by Moore, were indicated by interviewees as essential to critical thinking in the interviewee's academic discipline. Transcripts were reread for direct and indirect indications that a particular dimension of critical thought was privileged by the academic discipline. Those dimensions of difference exist as pairs on spectrums (see Table 1).

Table 1
Dimensions of Difference Definitions

Text-internal critical thinking (object-oriented) Texts are the principal object of inquiry in the work of critical thought.	**Text-external critical thinking (object-oriented)** Texts are a basis for critical thinking about an external "real-world" object.
Objectivist critical thinking (object-oriented) An objective meaning and understanding of an object can be derived if approached critically.	**Subjectivist critical thinking (object-oriented)** Meanings and understandings of objects are always influenced by the interpreter, and we must be critically aware of how our realities inform understanding.

Heuristic critical thinking (process-oriented) The process or procedure for being critical is stipulated or outlined in advance.	**Hermeneutic critical thinking (process-oriented)** The process of being critical is left open and processes are informed by the object/material being considered.
Theory-implicit critical thinking A prevailing (doxic) theory (such as empiricism) is *implied* in the doing of critical work, not made explicit.	**Theory-explicit critical thinking** A defined theory is made *explicit* as a framework for doing critical work (such as a Marxist critique).
Evaluative critical thinking (object-oriented) Critical thought is used to make a *judgment* about the *value* of material or an object.	**Interpretive critical thinking (object-oriented)** Critical thought is used to make *commentary* about the *nature* of material or an object.
Epistemic critical thinking Critical thought is oriented toward *reflection* on the truth or falsity of a claim about the object (is it true that…?)	**Deontic critical thinking** Critical thought is oriented toward possible *actions* to be taken in regard to an object (what should be done in this case…?)
Neutralist critical thinking Critical thought is directed toward pure understanding without ulterior motive.	**Activist critical thinking** Critical thought is directed toward an ultimate or ulterior goal of social or environmental change.

In the majority of transcripts, interviewees described critical thinking in their academic discipline in a way that would privilege one dimension of a pairing over another (e.g., would privilege text-external critical thinking over text-internal critical thinking). In some cases, however, neither dimension was evident in a given dimension pairing and therefore neither was noted. In other cases, both dimensions in a given pairing were given emphasis, and in these cases, both dimensions were noted (e.g., some interviewees emphasized both objectivist critical thinking *and* subjectivist critical thinking as essential).

The term *privilege* was adopted in this analysis to address Davies' critique of Moore that discipline-specific emphasis on a dimension does not *reject* a view of critical thinking as generalized, nor *affirm* a view of critical thinking as specialized. The presumption in the present study is that all academic disciplines value all dimensions of critical thinking in one way or another, but that different academic disciplines may lean more heavily toward certain dimensions; for example, literature may privilege text-internal thinking, but still value critical thought that applies a text to a concept outside of the text (text-external).

Once dimensions had been noted, the responses to question eight were examined in the transcript, and a determination was made as to whether the interviewee saw the kind of critical thinking sought from students as a *general thinking skill* or as a skill *specific* to the interviewee's academic discipline. This question was added to the interview protocol to further address Davies' critiques of Moore.

A next step of analysis was noting from the interview transcript the method through which the interviewee attempts to teach students to think critically; this included the reading of supplemental documents such as assignment sheets (when provided) to generate further understanding of the interviewee's perspective on critical thinking. Data for this step of analysis stemmed from questions seven and nine. Question seven (How do you teach critical thinking in your discipline?) captured process-related assignments that faculty used to try and generate a particular way of thinking, including formal writings and informal in-class exercises. Question nine (Which assignments in your courses require the greatest deal of critical thinking?) captured product-related assignments that faculty used to test whether students were thinking critically or not. Assignment sheets (when supplied) were analyzed to validate or challenge the conclusions of interview transcript analysis, not as a form of evidence detached from its user/designer. For example, here's an example of a 100-word transcript summary from an interviewee with an instructor of counselor education:

> For this [counselor education] interviewee critical thinking requires [counseling students] bringing in as much information as [they] can in order to have a broad enough perspective to reflect on it. Much information has to do with the self; being reflective about who [the student is] as a counselor, including as a person, as a practitioner, and [reflecting on their personal] ethics and values. [Counselors] must continue to analyze [themselves] so as not to be a different person than practitioner—the two must align toward a genuine self (from Psychology). [This interviewee explains that] critical thinking is a "higher level thinking" that involves analysis and synthesis through reflection so you can know your own weaknesses and strengths, biases and judgments, why are judgments being made, what are my triggers[?] This is so integral that a debate in the discipline is whether counselors should recuse themselves from counseling those with different value systems. To be critical is to be aware of all of this as you engage in counseling. Ultimately you become a critical thinker when you can be intentional about the questions you ask because you see the broad perspective (Counselor Education 1).

This interviewee provided a supplemental assignment sheet for a "Case Analysis" assignment. In this example, the assignment sheet was analyzed with respect to the interviewee's view of critical thinking as described in the transcript, particularly the interviewee's sentiment that critical thinking is a matter of being "aware" and able to "reflect" in the work of counseling others. The assignment sheet (Figure 1) validates this view of critical thinking in the assessment rubric for the "Case Analysis" as indicated by the highlighted language. In cases where supplemental assignment sheets challenged or refuted an interviewee's account of critical thinking, such language was highlighted in red (though no such observations were made). In total, fifteen participants (40.5%), provided supplemental assignment sheets during or after their interview for analysis.

Name_____   Points_____

EDC 576 Case Analysis Evaluation Rubric

Successful completion of the assignment indicates mastery of: Objectives: 1, 2, 3, 4, 5, and CACREP SLOs A.3, E.3, I.3, M.3; and PDE SLOs I.C.7, IV.A.5.

Evaluation Item	Met	Not Met
Demographics are included		
Shows thoroughness and sophistication when discussing influencing factors and interventions, including teacher/consultee characteristics, student/client characteristics and environmental characteristics		
Includes other data, such as observations, as appropriate		
Analysis and hypotheses are evident		
Mode of consultation and rationale is included		
Student creates interventions that reflect and are sensitive to unique system factors		
Student creates interventions that are sensitive to unique consultee characteristics		
Student develops interventions using the appropriate sources		
Student includes the family in the intervention to the degree that is appropriate		
Student identifies unique consultant-consultee variables that can facilitate or inhibit the creation of a collaborative relationship and indicates consultation mode most appropriate		
Student gives a self-reflection showing understanding and application of how this project impacts counselor identity.		
Student presents an organized paper, which includes all required information and is free of spelling and grammatical errors.		
Includes at least 5 citations in the body of the paper and paper is written in APA style		

Figure 1. Excerpt of Counselor Education 1 Supplemental Assignment (highlights added)

A third piece of information informing the analysis of interview transcripts was the analysis of any works (text, film, model) that interviewees pointed to as exemplary critical thinking in their academic discipline or field. A total of twenty-three faculty (62%) offered what they saw to be an example of strong critical thinking, but among those twenty-three faculty only ten participants, or 27% of interviewees, pointed to a specific textual example (author and title of a work) that could be analyzed (see Table 2). In these cases, works were accessed and surveyed to see how/if the interviewees' views of critical thinking were revealed in the exemplary texts. Other participants pointed to exemplary works that could not be analyzed for a variety of reasons: some interviewees said they "modeled" this kind of thinking to the class; others pointed to general theorists but no specific works. Further, others pointed to general types of texts, like "research articles with a linear train of thought" (Physics 3), and others could not think of exemplary models of critical thinking at all. Moore's study relied on "subject outlines" used by professors to show students what they are "expected to adopt in the subject" (57). "Subject outlines" as described by Moore resemble "subject guides" in a North American context, but as far as was made evident, only one interview participant's department had developed such a document.

Table 2.

List of Faculty Participants Supplementing Interview with Exemplary Document

Interview Name	Is this view of critical thinking validated by exemplary text, example?	Included in Analysis?
Biology	Darwin	No
Communication Disorders 2	Yes, author's own textbook	Yes
Economics	Samuelson, Paul Anthony. Foundations of Economic Analysis." (1983).	Yes
Education	Robert Marzano's educational theories.	No
English 2	Bernstein, Robin. *Racial innocence: Performing American childhood and race from slavery to civil rights.* nyu Press, 2011.	Yes
Geography 1	Massey, Douglas S., and Nancy A. Denton. *American apartheid: Segregation and the making of the underclass.* Harvard University Press, 1993.	Yes
Health 1	Hacking, Ian. Rewriting the soul: Multiple personality and the sciences of memory. Princeton University Press, 1998.	Yes
History 1	Ammon, Francesca Russello. *Bulldozer: Demolition and Clearance of the Postwar Landscape.* Yale University Press, 2016.	Yes
Kinesiology 1	Professor acts as a role model interpreting cases to demonstrate critical thinking.	No
Literacy 1	Michael Pressley's work on Reading Comprehension	No

Interview Name	Is this view of critical thinking validated by exemplary text, example?	Included in Analysis?
Management 1	Trevino, Linda K., and Katherine A. Nelson. *Managing business ethics: Straight talk about how to do it right.* John Wiley & Sons, 2016.	Yes
Management 2	Good companies are managed critically, such as Netflix and Underarmour	No
Management 3	Validated by venture capital rounds modeled after "Shark Tank"	No
Management 4	Case studies	No
Music 1	Performances of work in the baroque era must have very specific embellishments.	No
Physics 2	Examples of good and bad science; Newton, Einstein, Climate Change	No
Physics 3	Any research article in physics that shows a linear train of thought.	No
Public Health 1	Validated by case studies.	No
Social Work 1	Tatum, Beverly Daniel. *Why are all the Black kids sitting together in the cafeteria?: And other conversations about race.* Basic Books, 2017.	Yes
Social Work 2	O'Connor, Alice. *Poverty knowledge: Social science, social policy, and the poor in twentieth-century US history.* Princeton University Press, 2009.	Yes
Special Education 1	Guest presenters and the professor's own modeling of critical reflection	No
Special Education 2	By videos and teachers own modeling	No
Women's and Gender Studies	Crenshaw, Kimberlé. "Mapping the Margins: Intersectionality, Identity Politics, and Violence against Women of Color." *Stanford Law Review*, vol. 43, no. 6, 1991, pp. 1241–1299.	Yes

A second phase of analysis was the identification of noteworthy patterns, hereafter referred to as "critical thinking dimensional strains" that emerged (e.g., a text- external/objectivist/hermeneutic/theory-implicit/interpretive/epistemic/neutralist dimensional strain). While a pure view of academic disciplines would expect certain disciplines to be clearly aligned with similar sets of dimensions (e.g., expect sciences to be mostly objectivist, heuristic, theory-implicit, epistemic, and neutralist), these neat categories did not bear out in interviews, as will be discussed in the results section of this study. Instead, analysis revealed what this study labels "dimensional strains" that exist among disciplines not typically associated in pure views of academic disciplines. Patterns that appeared at least three times across different disciplines were labeled as "significant dimensional strains" in this analysis, while scenarios with at least two pattern appearances were noted for discussion and further investigation. An example of a dimensional strain would be multiple academic disciplines valuing the critical thinking dimensions that are text-external, subjectivist, hermeneutic, theory-explicit, interpretive, deontic, and activist.

A third and final step in the second phase of analysis was the identification of academic disciplines that were coded in the first phase of analysis as emphasizing both ends of a paired critical thinking dimension (e.g., disciplines that describe *both* text-internal critical thinking and text-external critical thinking). This information was analyzed because dual dimension use may imply greater critical-thinking complexity for these disciplines, and hence a pedagogical challenge narrowing the expected critical thinking skills for students studying in that academic discipline and the expectations for writing in those disciplines.

Results

The General vs. Specific Debate in Critical Thinking

As discussed earlier, Davies' key critique of Moore is that he constructs a false dilemma that critical thinking is either a "universal category" that would apply to all disciplines, or a "catch all" concept and therefore really only has a plurality of discipline-specific meanings when examined more closely (6). As a result, this study explored a third position, that there may be discipline-specific emphasis on particular critical-thinking skills, but these skills remain general critical-thinking skills available and valuable to all disciplines. This study explicitly asked participants whether the critical thinking skills they valued from students were general skills or skills specific to their discipline. Of the critical-thinking skills they were describing, 73% (n=27) of participants viewed them as general skills, 21.6% (n=8) of participants viewed them as specific or unique to their academic discipline, while 5.4% (n=2) could not definitively answer or considered it might be both. In sum, while many different critical thinking skills were privileged by faculty and competing definitions were offered, the vast majority (73%) maintained the critical-thinking skills they described as universal or general skills not specific to their own academic discipline. This suggests that while faculty may privilege certain critical-thinking dimensions in their academic discipline, they maintain a view of these dimensions as general critical-thinking skills.

Dimensions of Critical Thinking Emphasized by Interviewees

As detailed previously (Table 1), Moore identifies seven "dimensions of difference in critical thinking beliefs and practices" (212). Table 3 shows data relating to dimensions of difference privileged by different disciplines, including the frequency with which a given critical thinking dimension was privileged among all thirty-seven interviews, as well as the disciplines that revealed privilege for each dimension. As shown below, epistemic critical thinking was the least privileged of any dimension among these thirty-seven interviews, while text-external critical thinking was privileged the most.

Table 3

Frequency and Disciplinary Privileges of Critical Thinking Dimensions. Ordered by frequency in left column.

Text-external critical thinking (object-oriented): *Texts are a basis for critical thinking about an external "real-world" object.* Frequency: 83.8% (n=31) Privileged by: Accounting, Anthropology, Athletic Training, Biology, Chemistry, Communication Disorders, Counselor Education, Criminal Justice, Economics, Health, History, Kinesiology, Literacy, Management, Marketing, Education, Music, Physics, Public Health, Social Work, Special Education	**Text-internal critical thinking (object-oriented):** *Texts are the principal object of inquiry in the work of critical thought.* Frequency: 35.1% (n=13) Privileged by: Communication Studies, English, Women's & Gender Studies, Geography & Planning, History, Management, Philosophy, Physics, Psychology, Public Health
Subjectivist critical thinking (object-oriented): *Meanings and understandings of objects are always influenced by the interpreter, and we must be critically aware of how our realities inform understanding.* Frequency: 75.7% (n=28) Privileged by: Anthropology, Athletic Training, Chemistry, Communication Disorders, Counselor Education, Criminal Justice, English, Women's & Gender Studies, Geography & Planning, Health, History, Literacy, Management, Marketing, Education, Music, Physics, Public Health, Social Work, Special Education	**Objectivist critical thinking (object-oriented):** *An objective meaning and understanding of an object can be derived if approached critically.* Frequency of Privilege: 37.8% (n=14) Privileged by: Accounting, Anthropology, Athletic Training, Biology, Chemistry, Communication Disorders, Economics, Kinesiology, Management, Philosophy, Physics, Psychology, Special Education

Deontic critical thinking: *Critical thought is oriented toward possible actions to be taken in regard to an object (what should be done in this case ...?).* Frequency: 70.3% (n=26) Privileged by: Athletic Training, Communication Disorders, Counselor Education, Criminal Justice, Economics, English, Geography & Planning, Health, Women's & Gender Studies, Literacy, Management, Kinesiology, Marketing, Education, Music, Public Health, Social Work, Special Education	**Epistemic critical thinking**: *Critical thought is oriented toward reflection on truth and falsity of a claim about the object (is it true that...?).* Frequency: 32.4% (n=12) Privileged by: Accounting, Anthropology, Biology, Chemistry, English, Philosophy, History, Physics, Psychology
Theory-explicit critical thinking: *A defined theory is made explicit as a framework for doing critical work (such as a Marxist critique).* Frequency: 67.6% (n=25) Privileged by: Communication Disorders, Counselor Education, Criminal Justice, English, Economics, Women's & Gender Studies, Geography & Planning, Health, History, Literacy, Management, Marketing, Education, Philosophy, Physics, Psychology, Social Work, Special Education	**Theory-implicit critical thinking**: *A prevailing (doxic) theory (such as empiricism) is implied in the doing of critical work, not made explicit.* Frequency: 35.1% (n=13) Privileged by: Accounting, Anthropology, Athletic Training, Biology, Chemistry, Communication Disorders, Kinesiology, Management, Management, Music, Public Health, Women's & Gender Studies.
Neutralist critical thinking: *Critical thought is directed toward pure understanding without ulterior motive.* Frequency: 67.6% (n=25) Privileged by: Accounting, Anthropology, Biology, Chemistry, English, Economics, History, Management, Marketing, Music, Philosophy, Physics, Psychology, Special Education	**Activist critical thinking**: *Critical thought is directed toward an ultimate or ulterior goal of social or environmental change.* Frequency: 37.8% (n=14) Privileged by: Counselor Education, Criminal Justice, English, Geography & Planning, Health, Women's & Gender Studies, Literacy, Management, Physics, Education, Public Health, Social Work, Special Education
Hermeneutic critical thinking (process-oriented): *The process of being critical is left open and processes are informed by the object/material being considered.* Frequency: 64.9% (n=24) Privileged by: Accounting, Anthropology, Biology, Chemistry, Counselor Education, Criminal Justice, English, Economics, Women's & Gender Studies, Geography & Planning, Health, History, Management, Marketing, Education, Music, Physics, Psychology, Special Education	**Heuristic critical thinking (process-oriented)**: *The process or procedure for being critical is stipulated or outlined in advance.* Frequency: 37.8% (n=14) Privileged by: Athletic Training, Biology, Communication Disorders, Kinesiology, Literacy, Management, Public Health, Social Work

Interpretive critical thinking (object-oriented): Critical thought is used to make commentary about the nature of material or an object. Frequency: 59.5% (n=22) Privileged by: Anthropology, Biology, Communication Disorders, Counselor Education, Criminal Justice, English, Women's & Gender Studies, Health, History, Literacy, Management, Marketing, Education, Music, Physics, Public Health	Evaluative critical thinking (object-oriented): Critical thought is used to make a judgment about the value of material or an object. Frequency: 56.8% (n=21) Privileged by: Accounting, Athletic Training, Chemistry, Communication Disorders, Economics, English, Geography & Planning, Health, Kinesiology, Women's & Gender Studies, Management, Philosophy, Psychology, Social Work, Special Education

Emergence of Dimensional Strains

Dimensional strains, as described in the data analysis section of this study, are patterns of critical thinking dimensions that emerged after analysis. There are forty-nine possible dimensional strains because there are seven dimensions of difference and two possibilities in each dimension. The probability of each dimensional strain appearing equally is 2.04%. As a result, dimensional strains that appeared more than twice (6.3%) in different academic disciplines are highlighted here as significant.

In analyzing dimensions of difference across disciplines, three dimensional strains (three or more occurrences) emerged within the data of this study; eight dimensional strains were found in only pairs, and twelve dimensional strains were unique, having no other interview transcripts replicating that dimensional strain. In total, 67.5% (n=25) of interview transcripts belong to a dimensional strain that appeared in other interviews and 32.5% (n=12) of interview transcripts were unique, reflecting a straining of critical-thinking dimensions not articulated by any other interviewee.

The most significant dimensional strains are those that were revealed in at least three separate instances as shown in Table 4.

Table 4

Significant Dimensional Strains of Critical Thinking

Strain A: English, History, Physics (n=4)	Text-internal/Subjectivist/Hermeneutic/Theory-explicit/Interpretive /Epistemic /Neutralist
Strain B: Counselor Education, Criminal Justice, Early & Middle Grades Education, Health (n=4)	Text-external/Subjectivist/Hermeneutic/Theory-explicit/Interpretive/Deontic/Activist
Strain C: Gender Studies, Geography & Planning, Special Education (n=3)	Text-external/Subjectivist/Hermeneutic/Theory-explicit/Evaluative/Deontic/Activist

Taking Strain A (Table 3) as an example we see that this exact dimensional strain appeared in 10.8% of interviews (n=4) among the academic disciplines of English (n=2), history, and physics. This study reveals that these four academic disciplines privilege skills that involve thinking critically (1) within the discrete confines of a text, (2) through an awareness of one's biases and assumptions, (3) in a way that is open-ended/non-guided,(4) in a way that names a theory used in the interpretation of an object of inquiry, (5) in order to understand the nature or essential meaning of that text, (6) with a goal of understanding whether or not those claims are true, and (7) without regard to a ulterior agenda of societal or environmental change. While English, history, and physics all deal with objects of inquiry external to text (context, artifacts, physical phenomena), in this study, these disciplines located critical thinking as largely a matter of critical *reading*. For English, this critical reading may be applied to a variety of texts; in history, this critical reading may be applied to interpretations of original source materials; and in physics, this critical reading may be applied to experimental articles. As one physics interviewee explains: "Being critical in physics is about looking at results and saying: Ok, what are the conditions for what these results hold, and can we broaden it? With what conditions? . . . It's about being critical with the results and questioning if the method was right in obtaining the results" (Physics 3). For this professor, those skills come from asking students to carefully read experimental articles and scrutinize methods and results.

Strains B and C are very similar, with the exception that evaluative critical thinking is privileged over interpretative critical thinking. Though only one dimension differs among these two strains, the difference between interpretive critical thinking and evaluative critical thinking might mean an entirely different set of genres, assignments, and expectations on student writers.

The three significant dimensional strains of critical thinking marked above accounted for 29.8% of interview transcripts. That is, about 30% of faculty reported an approach to critical thinking that (unbeknownst to the interviewer or interviewees) was part of a significant pattern of critical thinking among other faculty from different academic disciplines.

An additional seven dimensional strains emerged as paired strains of critical thinking (Table 5); however, only three of these pairings occurred among different academic disciplines (four pairings emerged among responses from the same academic disciplines).

Table 5

Pairs of Dimensional Strains

Biology & anthropology	Text-external/objectivist/hermeneutic/theory-implicit/interpretive/epistemic/neutralist
Economics & special education	Text-external/objectivist/hermeneutic/theory-explicit/evaluative/deontic/neutralist
Philosophy & psychology	Text-internal/objectivist/hermeneutic/theory-explicit/evaluative/epistemic/neutralist

In total, of the interview transcripts analyzed, 32.4% (n=12) reveal unique dimensional strains not reflected in any other interviews, 21.6% (n=8) reveal pairings among the same academic disciplines, 16.2% (n=6) reveal pairings of different academic disciplines, and 29.8% (n=11) reveal significant dimensional strains among three or more different academic disciplines.

Disciplines with Dual Dimension Use

In nineteen instances, both of the two available dimensions of difference were marked because analysis showed evidence that both were privileged in a given academic discipline (i.e., an interview showed privilege for text-internal *and* text-external critical thinking, or objectivist *and* subjectivist critical thinking, etc.). For example, one physics professor articulated an expectation that students can critically read experimental articles and interrogate methodology (a text-internal skill) and also be able to design their own experiments that can help model physical phenomena (a text-external skill). While no academic discipline ever squarely locks into only a single dimension of critical thinking (e.g., critical readers in literature are still considering context and application of knowledge; objectivists in anthropology are still shading their understanding of ritual with their own cultural experience), the instances in which interviewees explicitly expressed both dimensions are noteworthy. These instances are noteworthy because they may indicate highly complex expectations for student critical thinking (expectations of multiple complex mental tasks at once) that could bear further articulation. These instances occurred as follows:

Instances of Text-internal and Text-External Privileging

- A women's and gender studies professor privileged text-external and text-internal critical thinking because in an academic discipline concerned with how gender stereotypes become normalized, text may be a primary device of normalization. This professor also privileged theory-implicit

critical thinking in that postmodern power relations are the implied backdrop of understanding gender normalizations, but theory-explicit critical thinking is privileged by identifying intersectionality, Marxism, etc. This professor also privileged evaluative critical thinking in that students are asked to determine how power relations are being reproduced in, say, an advertisement, but also interpretive critical thinking is privileged in that students can determine the nature of society as normalizing particular gender stereotypes.
- A geography and planning professor privileged mostly text-external critical thinking, as students examined non-textual concepts like *access to food in areas of urban poverty*, but the public policy and law policy aspect of this discipline requires students to do critical interpretations of text in and of itself as they are asked to read, write, and evaluate the impact of written public policies.
- A history professor privileged mostly text-external critical thinking in interpreting the past, but text-internal critical thinking is highly valued when text (especially original source evidence) is the object of historical study.
- Two different management professors privileged primarily text-external critical thinking with ethical decision making in case study scenarios as the object of inquiry, but text-internal critical thinking was privileged in that students must also think critically about the ethics of a source and the implications of a theory, which comes from close reading of those texts.
- A public health professor privileged text-internal critical thinking in the case of scientific literacy, and emphasized the importance of students doing close readings of health research articles; however, this professor also privileged text-external critical thinking, as students must learn to make connections between culture and disease.

Instances of Objectivist and Subjectivist Privileging

- An anthropology professor privileged both objectivism and subjectivism because culture can be objectively known, but we must also know ourselves and our own cultural influences and be attuned to them in anthropological work.
- An athletic training professor privileged objectivist and subjectivist critical thinking because diagnosis of injury is objective, but there must also be an intense awareness of how trainer bias influences diagnoses, making "metacognition" a central premise of critical thinking for athletic trainers.

- A chemistry professor privileged objectivist and subjectivist critical thinking because while objectivity is needed to control a chemical experiment, the interviewee also sees being critical as partially recognizing one's own subjectivity without "devolving" into relativism
- A music professor privileged objective critical thinking in that the past is knowable and should inform a performance of historical music, but subjectivist critical thinking was privileged in that part of a musical performance, however much it may be historical, is always original in some way to the performing musician.
- A physics professor privileged objectivist critical thinking as a matter of controlling experimentation of physical phenomena, but also privileged subjectivist critical thinking in explaining that students' thinking and the "length-scale" of humans in general always informs an experimental design and the creation of predictive models; humans are always subjected to interpreted physical phenomena from the length-scale perspective of the human being. A second physics professor mostly privileged text-external critical thinking about physical phenomena under experimentation, but also privileged text-internal critical thinking to the extent that critically reading other scientists' work is paramount to developing critical thinking skills in science.

Instances of Heuristic and Hermeneutic Privileging

- A biology professor privileged heuristic critical thinking as a matter of "the deductive reasoning process," but also privileged a hermeneutic process of open-ended questioning that forms the biological research question or object of inquiry at its outset.

Instances of Evaluative and Interpretive Privileging

- A communication disorders professor privileged evaluative critical thinking in the determination of a final clinical decision (how a client should be treated), but interpretative critical thinking as vital to the initial assessment of the situation or case.
- A communication studies professor privileged evaluative critical-thinking skills as essential to determining the effectiveness of a work of communication, but interpretative critical thinking as a means of invention in determining how to act in a given scenario.
- An English professor privileged interpretive critical thinking in cases in which English students may be determining an ultimate or important meaning of a text, but evaluative critical thinking was privileged in

scenarios where students were critiquing a work and valuing that work as strong, weak, etc. This professor also privileged neutralist critical thinking in situations where texts are reading for pleasure or interest alone, and activist critical thinking in situations where critical readings of text are linked to a broader agenda.
- A health professor privileged evaluative critical thinking and interpretive critical thinking. While evaluative critical thinking seems to dominate as students are asked to determine whether a way of thinking about health conditions is valuable and healthy, interpretive critical thinking is also privileged in that students use the science of psychology to make claims about the nature of humans and human health.

As this analysis reveals, critical thinking dimensions are not clear-cut lines. While many disciplines clearly privilege one dimension over another, there are also clear cases where interviewees explicitly described an expectation of dual dimensions in critical thinking, especially the cases of text-internal close readings and text-external application of knowledge; cases of objectivist and subjectivist thinking expectations; and cases of evaluative and interpretive thinking.

Limitations

While this work does validate many of Moore's initial findings in a different institutional and geographical setting, further research is required to determine how critical thinking may be approached differently at differently classified institutions. Both the present study and Moore's study involved faculty teaching at large public universities (>15,000 students) both of which are located in suburbs of major metropolitan areas (>4 million people). Repetition of this study at institutions such as two-year and community colleges, small liberal arts colleges, rural universities, and technical colleges may yield different conceptions of critical thinking across the curriculum.

An additional limitation of this study is its emphasis on academic conceptions of critical thinking alone. In many instances interviewees in this study implied that the critical-thinking skills they emphasize in the classroom are essential for professional success, but this is not the same as an examination of the critical-thinking skills that private, public, and non-governmental organizations look for among their employees. Future research examining employer conceptions of critical thinking in their profession would be an important step in examining to what extent academic valuing of critical thinking maps on to professional valuing of critical thinking.

Finally, further research might examine the degrees of variation in privileging dimensions of critical thinking within a single discipline. It's unclear how much diversity in views about critical thinking might emerge in, say, twenty interviews with faculty from a single academic discipline.

Discussion

The results of this study have significant implications for writing across the curriculum pedagogy and writing studies research.

Some Implications for WAC/WID

Re-casting writing instruction for fellow faculty not as a matter of teaching students to mimic a general academic style, but as a matter of teaching students to be critical, disciplinary thinkers is one of the greatest challenges I've faced in my time as a WAC director and coordinator of faculty workshops. But despite decades of scholarship and grassroots work by writing program administrators, many faculty don't automatically correlate writing and thinking, preferring instead an antiquated notion that writing is merely sharing or transmitting critical thoughts that happen (somehow) outside of language. Another great challenge that many WAC directors face is guiding faculty away from a view that their expectations for student writing are general expectations for all writing, and toward an understanding that their expectations for student writing are quite specific to both their discipline and their personal taste as a reader. Debates about grammar and style expectations during faculty workshops—like the oft cursed split infinitive—muddy workshop leaders' attempts to get to the heart of the matter, which is that these stylistic preferences are more deeply rooted in preferences, expectations, and epistemological nuances of the disciplines, activity systems, and genres at work. That is, the more immediate stylistic concerns that get emphasized in so many of our conversations with faculty about student writing, are really representative of much deeper disciplinary expectations for thinking within a discipline that go unarticulated. A faculty members' frustration with student use of first-person in a research essay, for example, might be better understood as an indication of that faculty member's privileging of *objectivist critical thought* over *subjectivist thought*. The dimensions of critical thinking detailed in this study, I find, offer a compelling vocabulary for WAC directors seeking to address both of these common challenges.

During the time that I've undertaken the research in the present study, I've subsequently begun talking more with faculty across the curriculum about what they value in student thinking and writing in terms of how they want students to engage with texts, their preferences for objectivism or subjectivism, whether they dictate hermeneutic or heuristic inventive process, how they expect students to engage with theory, etc. These are conversations about the kind of thinking faculty value from students in their disciplines, but those values also get presupposed (deliberately or not) into expectations for student writing and into student assessment and assignment design. I've found that enthusiasm to discuss critical thinking among faculty far exceeded the enthusiasm I've witnessed in discussions about writing conventions alone. Yet, we see from landmark works like John C. Bean's *Engaging Ideas* (2011) that writing is as much about advanced and critical thought as it is about effective communication of those thoughts; indeed, we know that clarity is often a result of advanced thinking about an issue. The results of this study affirm that beneath a general notion of critical thinking lies a set of critical-thinking dimensions that become privileged across disciplines, courses, and faculty preferences. These dimensions of critical thinking are important to understand because in many cases they may subtend disciplinary writing conventions and the rhetorical features that faculty privilege in assessing student writing.

Implications for Writing Curriculum Development

This study affirms the value of viewing critical thinking as a set of general skills in which different academic disciplines may privilege different dimensions, while all dimensions remain valued by those disciplines generally. What this means for writing curriculum development is that a closer assessment of the critical thinking dimensions that are privileged by students' academic disciplines could powerfully inform pedagogy in first-year and writing-emphasis/intensive courses.

For example, in a first-year writing course in which many education majors are enrolled, what assignments might best prepare those students for the critical thinking expected of them in future work? If a dimensional strain among educators (1) privileges the use of text (2) as the basis to think about non-textual scenarios (3) through an awareness of one's biases and assumptions (4) in a way that is open-ended/non-guided (5) that names a theory used in the interpretation of an object of inquiry (6) in order to determine what should be done about an issue and (7) in order to improve a defined societal or environmental issue—might that lead to different kinds of rhetorical analysis, genre awareness, and composition techniques for these future writers in the field of education?

First-year writing programs are often limited in regard to disciplinary writing instruction because students are commonly in their first year of studies and have little knowledge of their own discipline from which to draw, even if these students are grouped in learning communities. More often, first-year writing courses are populated with students from very different majors and/or undecided/undeclared programs. First-year writing courses could instead introduce students to all fourteen dimensions of critical thinking and practice composing in genres that embody specific strains of these dimensions. This might powerfully prepare students to transfer knowledge of critical thinking moves that writers make into the genres of their future disciplines.

In writing-emphasis courses or writing-enriched curricula, a better understanding of the dimensional strains privileged by different academic disciplines might become an excellent starting point for suggesting writing-to-learn assignments to faculty across the curriculum. If faculty in, say, counselor education, privilege subjectivist critical thinking, might some writing-to-learn assignment focus on a reflection of student biases and assumptions? If faculty in geography and planning privilege deontic critical thinking, might some writing-to-learn assignments focus on explaining how an essay conclusion in that discipline should inform public policies? If faculty in physics value critical thinking as linear trains of thought in research writing, might some writing-to-learn assignments introduce syllogistic exercises?

Implications for General Education Assessment

The implications of critical-thinking dimensional strains don't just apply to composition courses. A deeper understanding of critical thinking's dimensional strains should encourage general education programs at universities to think more specifically about how the general education curriculum educates students on different dimensions of critical thinking. Such a model would look far different than merely stipulating "critical and analytical thinking" as a general education goal, which consequently gets attached to most general education syllabi without attention to which critical thinking skills are being emphasized. Furthermore, general education programs attaching specific student-learning outcomes (SLOs) to general education goals might use these critical-thinking dimensions as outcomes further articulating a general goal of critical and analytical thinking. These are the very goals writing courses so often have as attributes, but so rarely get articulated in specific ways.

This study is a mere continuation of a growing conversation in WAC/WID and writing studies research that examines more specifically how assumptions about critical thinking in disciplines get embedded into the genres and exercises we ask our students to write. Composition researchers in WAC/WID have long fought for acknowledgment across higher education that writing, invention, and epistemology are inexorably intertwined, and that writing instruction is not remedial but a premiere place for creating sophisticated student thinkers. The institutional cache of critical thinking offers such composition researchers an important opportunity to more specifically detail writing's role in developing critical thinkers.

Works Cited

Barad, Karen. *Meeting the Universe Halfway: Quantum Physics and the Entanglement of Matter and Meaning.* Duke UP, 2007.

Basgier, Christopher. "Engaging the Skeptics: Threshold Concepts, Metadisciplinary Writing, and the Aspirations of General Education." *The WAC Journal*, vol. 27, 2016, pp. 17–35.

Bean, John C. *Engaging ideas: The Professor's Guide to Integrating Writing, Critical Thinking, and Active Learning in the Classroom.* John Wiley & Sons, 2011.

Beaufort, Anne. *College Writing and Beyond: A New Framework for University Writing Instruction*. UP of Colorado, 2008.

Bryant, Sarah, Noreen Lape, and Jennifer B. Schaefer. "Transfer and the Transformation of Writing Pedagogies in a Mathematics Course." *The WAC Journal*, vol. 25, 2014, pp. 92–105.

Callon, Michel. "The Sociology of an Actor-Network: The Case of the Electric Vehicle." *Mapping the Dynamics of Science and Technology*, edited by Michel Callon, Rip Arie, and John Law, Palgrave Macmillan UK, 1986, pp. 19–34.

CCCC Executive Committee. "Principles for the Postsecondary Teaching of Writing." *Conference on College Composition & Communication*, 2015, www.ncte.org/cccc/resources/positions/postsecondarywriting. Accessed 5 May, 2017.

Cooper, Marilyn M. "The Ecology of Writing." *College English*, vol. 48, no. 4, 1986, pp. 364–75.

Council of Writing Program Administrators. "WPA Outcomes Statement for First-year Composition." 3rd ed., *WPA*, 2014, www.wpacouncil.org/positions/outcomes.html. Accessed 12 May, 2017.

Davies, Martin. "Critical Thinking and the Disciplines Reconsidered." *Higher Education Research & Development*, vol. 32, no. 4, 2013, pp. 529–44.

Ennis, Robert H. "A Taxonomy of Critical Thinking Dispositions and Abilities." *Teaching Thinking Skills: Theory and Practice*, edited by J. B. Baron & R. J. Sternberg, W H Freeman/Times Books/ Henry Holt & Co, 1987, pp. 9–26.

Facione, Peter. "Critical Thinking: A Statement of Expert Consensus for Purposes of Educational Assessment and Instruction." American Philosophical Association, 1990.

Fleckenstein, Kristie S., Clay Spinuzzi, Rebecca J. Rickly, and Carole Clark Papper. "The Importance of Harmony: An Ecological Metaphor for Writing Research." *College Composition and Communication*, vol. 60, no. 2, 2008, pp. 388–419.

Fulwiler, Toby. "Showing, Not Telling, at a Writing Workshop." *College English*, vol. 43, no. 1, 1981, pp. 55–63.

Latour, Bruno. *Science in Action: How to Follow Scientists and Engineers through Society*. Harvard UP, 1987.

Lotier, Kristopher M. "Around 1986: The Externalization of Cognition and the Emergence of Postprocess Invention." *College Composition and Communication*, vol. 67, no. 3, 2016, p. 360.

McPeck, John E. "Critical Thinking and Subject Specificity: A Reply to Ennis." *Educational Researcher*, vol. 19, no. 4, 1990, pp. 10–12.

Moore, Tim John. *Critical Thinking and Language: The Challenge of Generic Skills and Disciplinary Discourses*. Bloomsbury Publishing, 2011.

Naess, Arne. "The Shallow and the Deep, Long-Range Ecology Movement. A Summary." *Inquiry*, vol. 16, nos. 1–4, 1973, pp. 95–100.

Newcomb, Matthew. "Sustainability as a Design Principle for Composition: Situational Creativity as a Habit of Mind." *College Composition and Communication*, vol. 63, no. 4, 2012, pp. 593–615.

Rhodes, Terrel. *Assessing Outcomes and Improving Achievement: Tips and Tools for Using the Rubrics.* Association of American Colleges and Universities, 2009, www.aacu.org/publications-research/publications/assessing-outcomes-and-improving-achievement-tips-and-tools-using. Accessed 11 May, 2017

Russell, David R. "Rethinking Genre in School and Society: An Activity Theory Analysis." *Written Communication*, vol. 14, no. 4, 1997, pp. 504–54.

A Tale of Two Prompts: New Perspectives on Writing-to-Learn Assignments

ANNE RUGGLES GERE, ANNA V. KNUTSON, NAITNAPHIT LIMLAMAI, RYAN MCCARTY, AND EMILY WILSON

Many claims have been made in the past four decades about the efficacy of writing as a means of fostering student learning in a variety of disciplines. Yet, reviews and meta-analyses of publications about the implementation of writing-to-learn (WTL) pedagogies show mixed results. Ackerson's review of thirty-five studies, for example, found little empirical evidence for conceptual learning as a result of WTL. Similarly, Rivard concluded that "A number of issues must be addressed before the research base that supports writing to learn becomes widely accepted by science educators" (975). Investigating the relationship of writing assignments to effects on learning, Durst and Newell found that taking notes and answering comprehension questions may enhance retention, but that more analytical writing engendered "complex understandings" or conceptual understandings (386). Similarly, Bangert-Drowns et al. (2004) observe that "the simple incorporation of writing in regular classroom instruction does not automatically yield large dividends in learning" (51). Finally, Ochsner and Fowler call for more precision in defining key terms and for empirical evidence of WTL's "actual (rather than presumed) effects on students' education" (134).

To address the limited evidence that WTL pedagogies actually engender students' conceptual learning, Rivard recommended analysis of writing tasks or assignments to determine which ones promote knowledge transformation. Bangert-Drowns et al. (2004) responded by coding writing tasks according to five variables: informational, personal, imaginative, metacognitive reflection, and feedback, and they found that metacognitive reflection showed a statistically significant relationship to more positive effects of writing to learn. Feedback proved too complicated to code accurately, and the other three variables showed no effect. Arnold et al. (2017) analyzed genres of writing assignments and found that essays engendered elaboration and organization that supported conceptual learning while note-taking and highlighting did not. With these exceptions, there has been little response to Rivard's call for more analysis of WTL *assignments*.

Since the publication of Bangert-Drowns et al., however, assignments have received increased attention within writing studies. Melzer's 2014 analysis of 2,101 assignments from one hundred universities revealed how many assignments are underconceptualized, providing students with no indication of audience or purpose and relying on terms like *essay* and *research paper* with little attention to the ways genres are enacted in different disciplines. Anderson et al. showed statistical correlations between enhanced student learning and writing prompts that included three features: interactive writing processes, clear expectations, and meaning-making activities. A systematic review of published studies about WTL by Gere et al. (2019) provided empirical evidence that assignments that include the three features identified by Anderson et al., combined with the metacognitive elements recommended by Bangert-Drowns et al., yield verifiable conceptual learning.

While this body of work provides valuable tools for measuring the quality of WTL assignments, it does not address how students understand and take up such assignments. In response to this research gap, our association with M-Write, a university-wide program focused on integrating WTL pedagogies into large enrollment gateway courses, provided us with both the exigency and opportunity to explore how students take up WTL assignments. The goal of the M-Write project is to foster deeper conceptual learning in large-enrollment foundational or gateway courses with writing-to-learn pedagogies. The several thousand M-Write students who have participated in this program each semester write responses to carefully crafted prompts that create a rhetorical context, specify a genre, and require the application of knowledge to real-world situations. Through these assignments, they engage with Anderson et al.'s categories of clear expectations and meaning-making activities. Additionally, using an automated system, they participate in peer review and are guided by upper-division students called Writing Fellows; through these activities, they engage with the Anderson et al. category of interactive writing processes. Finally, drawing on their experiences in peer review, they write a revision, thus addressing Bangert-Drowns et al.'s category of reflective metacognition.

Building on Herrington's (1985) finding that assignments need to be integrated into the context of a given course, we created assignments that called upon key concepts of the given discipline. Given that the writing assignments asked students to call upon memory of concepts they had learned recently and translate both genre and conceptual knowledge into a new context, the concept of *uptake* proved useful in our analysis. As articulated by Freadman (2002), uptake builds on Austin's (1962) speech act theory by specifying the processes that intervene as a statement is taken up as action. In particular, she emphasizes the process of selection as students choose from among multiple memories that they then translate into a new context. Rounsaville (2012), expanding upon Freadman, explains that the concept of uptake gives language to the ways students call upon and translate the recent memories of subject matter learned and the more distant memories of previous learning and experiences to draw upon. This process of translation reformulates learning for new contexts. For our students this meant translating both subject matter and genre knowledge into written responses called for by a given assignment. Building on large-scale analysis of assignments across the disciplines (e.g., Melzer) and student learning across writing experiences (e.g., Anderson et al.), we determined that looking at writing students produced in response to M-Write assignments through the lens of uptake could provide valuable information about the learning effects of WTL pedagogies.

Working with a faculty member in statistics, we developed and implemented two prompts that adhered to the principles outlined by Bangert-Drowns et al. and Anderson et al. and called upon key concepts in the field of statistics: the Caffeine Studies prompt, where students were prompted to relate statistical information from two studies about caffeine to their grandparents, and the Chocolate and Cycling Prompt, where students were asked to take on the role of consultants drawing on statistical research as a means of advising the Tour de France team on cyclists' diets. Both prompts are showcased below as figures 1 and 2.

> *Objective*: Popular media sometimes inaccurately present the results of research studies and, as a result, make inappropriate claims and draw unreliable conclusions. When popular media writers combine multiple studies and do not have a sound understanding of the statistics, this can be accentuated. These issues, paired with a lack of understanding regarding study development and statistical analysis of the results, can lead to false perceptions of the scientific findings. Your grandparents are sometimes confused by all the contradictory scientific claims they see in the news. Recently, they read an article in *The Washington Post* that claimed to offer some scientifically substantiated advice about caffeine consumption. After having read the article, your grandmother is convinced both she and your grandfather are consuming too much caffeine. Your grandfather disagrees with her. They've asked you to help them interpret the article. Using both *The Washington Post* article and the *Food and Chemical Toxicology* study it references, write your grandparents an email that explains to them what kinds of questions they need to ask before they can determine whether they are consuming "too much" caffeine, and how to figure out what kind of consumptions habits the sample study is talking about. To do this, summarize the study's research question(s), including a basic description of the study design, what the study was measuring, and the statistical method(s) they used. Include references to the explanatory variable, response variable and any confounding variables; you may need to explain what these mean. Include in your email an argument about whether or not your grandparents should trust the claims made by *The Washington Post* and how they should interpret the results.

> *Items to keep in mind:*
>
> - When we read your drafted email, we will play the role of your grandparents with minimal statistical literacy who are trying to understand the complexity of the statistics underlying scientific claims.
> - Cite your external references (both the news article and study as well as any additional references) using MLA format.
> - Since you are explaining this to your grandparents, you should take care to carefully edit and proofread your email.
> - This should be an email of between 350–500 words.
>
> **References:**
>
> Mitchell, D. C.; Knight, C. A.; Hockenberry, J.;Teplansky, R.; Hartman T. J. Beverage caffeine intakes in the U.S. *Food and Chemical Toxicology*. 2014.63. Berman, J. "What's real and what's myth when it comes to caffeine?" *The Washington Post* 11 July 2016.

Figure 1. Caffeine Studies Prompt

In crafting this assignment, we called upon the three features that Anderson et al. identified as correlating with enhanced student learning. In their definition, *interactive writing processes* involve student writers communicating orally or in writing with one or more persons at some point between receiving an assignment and submitting the final draft. This interaction might include getting feedback from a peer, a friend, or an instructor, and it might be carried out in required peer review sessions, conferences with instructors, or a session at a campus writing center. For M-Write, interactive writing processes took the form of automated peer review, interaction with upper-class Writing Fellows, and occasional consultation with professors.

Anderson et al. describe *meaning-making writing tasks* as those that require students to engage in some form of integrative, critical, or original thinking. This dimension includes asking students to apply a course concept to a real-life situation, provide concept-based evidence to support an argument, or to evaluate a claim using a course concept. Each M-Write assignment, like the one above, asked students to apply course learning to a new context. Specifically, this assignment required the meaning-making activity of explaining the study, design, and use of discourses of statistics with terms like *confounding variable*. Anderson et al.'s description of *interactive writing processes* is evinced by the procedural elements embedded in the curriculum: after students drafted responses to this assignment they used the automated peer review tool to respond to one another's drafts. Finally, for Anderson et al., *clear writing expectations* focus on making sure that students understand what they are supposed to do and providing them with the criteria by which their writing will be evaluated, as the level of detail offered by the above-quoted prompt suggests. In addition, the assignment calls for the genre of an email addressed to the grandparents' question. This, along with "items to keep in mind" as well as the specification of which aspects of statistics should be included, was designed to make the expectations of the assignment clear. To assure that students could provide one another effective peer review, as well as to reinforce clarity of expectations, we gave students the following rubric:

1. This email should be written using language that your grandparents can understand. What parts were clearly written? What parts were hard to understand?
2. Evaluate the summary of the research question(s). The email should include a description of the study design, including if the study is experimental or observational, the sample size, and population of the study. What is explained well? How can the description be improved?
3. There should be a description of the method of statistical analysis the study used and
4. an analysis of the statistical significance of the results. What was missing or hard to understand?
5. The roles of the explanatory variable, response variable, and any confounding variables should be described. Which variables are described well? Which variables are missing or unclear?
6. Comment on whether the writing makes a coherent argument about caffeine consumption. What is missing from the discussion of if the claims made by the media are supported by the statistical results of the study?

Here, we provided further detail on what students needed to include regarding features of the study, statistical significance, and variables of the study, thus adhering to the *clear writing expectations* principle outlined by Anderson et al. After they completed peer review, students were required to write a revision of their original drafts, a process that added an element of metacognition to their writing experience (Johns; Ferris & Hedgcock); this curricular feature reinforces the metacognitive element recommended by Bangert-Drowns et al.

Another prompt used in the statistics class followed a similar pattern; for more detail, see figure 2.

Objective: You have been hired by the U.S. bicycle team to help them train for the Tour de France. The head trainer recently read an article, which claims that consumption of dark chocolate results in increased oxygen consumption during cycling. The experimental setup consisted of a randomized crossover design where the oxygen consumption of $n = 9$ male participants was measured in two trials after participants consumed either dark chocolate or white chocolate. A crossover design is a repeated measurements design such that each subject receives the two different treatments (dark chocolate versus white chocolate) during the different time periods, i.e., the patients **cross over** from one treatment to another during the course of the experiment. The order of which treatment was received in the first time period was randomized. Prior to receiving the first treatment, each participant underwent baseline measurements. Data was gathered and analyzed as depicted in the table below.

Maximal Oxygen Consumption* (Note: $n = 9$ for each condition)

	Baseline	White Chocolate	Dark Chocolate
Mean (ml/kg min)	41.89	41.84	44.52‡
Std dev 5.4	5.6	6.43	
p-value† -	0.071	0.037	

†p-value is for statistical comparison with respect to baseline
‡Dark Chocolate: 95% Confidence Interval for the population average change in maximum oxygen consumption (over baseline) is 0.21 ml/kg min to 5.05 ml/kg min.

The trainer knows you have some statistics background and wants your opinion about whether or not dark chocolate should be added to the athletes' diets. Based on the results from the article, write a memo to the trainer explaining what the statistics show and make an argument for or against inclusion of dark chocolate in the athletes' diet. Your memo should include a little discussion about of how a crossover design affects the data analysis. Describe what the p-values indicate about the results, and the meaning of statistical significance. Finally, comment about the provided confidence interval, including both an interpretation of the confidence interval itself and the meaning of the confidence level.

Items to keep in mind:

- When we read your memo, we will play the role of the trainer with minimal statistical literacy who is trying to understand the significance of these results.
- If you have any references, be sure to cite them using MLA format.
- Since you are explaining this to the head trainer, you should take care to carefully edit and proofread your memo.
- This should be a memo of between 350-500 words of core content (i.e. not including header or references). See the Purdue OWL website for information about how to draft a memo: https://owl.english.purdue.edu/owl/resource/590/1/
- You should not include your name on this initial draft (to keep the peer review anonymous).
- Data from: Patel, R. K.; Brouner, J.; Spendiff, O. Dark chocolate supplementation reduces the oxygen cost of moderate intensity cycling. *Journal of the International Society of Sports Nutrition.* 2015 12:47.

Figure 2. Chocolate and Cycling Prompt

Here, as in the previous assignment, we grounded the assignment in real-world data, specified the features students needed to include, and added details designed to help them produce the best possible memo. Students followed the same process of peer review, using this rubric:

1. This memo should be written to be understandable to someone with minimal statistical literacy. Comment on whether this was achieved. What parts were hard to understand?
2. The relationship between crossover design and data analysis should be discussed. What did the discussion do well? What additional information should be included?
3. Comment on the discussion of statistical significance. What is explained clearly? Which elements are missing?
4. There should be a description of p-values and what they indicate about the results. What is described well? How can the description be made clearer?
5. Comment on the explanation of the difference between a confidence interval and confidence level. Are there any aspects that are missing? What is made clear?

We launched these two prompts with the hope that our pedagogical goals of enhancing students' comprehension of statistical concepts like experiment design, variables, p-value, crossover design, standard deviation, and so on would be achieved as they composed their written responses. To evaluate whether students were demonstrating their understanding of statistical concepts, we analyzed their writing to determine the amount and type of learning evident there. We assessed students' uptake of these two prompts in an attempt to understand the extent to which prompts that followed the guidelines proposed by Bangert-Drowns et al. and Anderson et al. fostered the desired level of conceptual learning. Each assignment required students to call upon their memory of statistical terms and concepts and to translate them into the new contexts of writing an explanation to grandparents and a trainer. Despite their similarities, these prompts differed in terms of genre—email versus memo—and in the quality of translation required. The first asked students to both summarize and evaluate key features of a study, while the second focused on the more limited space of crossover design and p-values. These differences led us to expect that student uptake of these two assignments might differ.

Methods

Students enrolled in the Introductory Statistics course had the option of selecting an "honors" credit for the course for completing writing assignments in addition to the regular coursework. Students who opted to participate in these additional writing assignments consented to the analysis of their writing for the purposes of this research. Of just over 200 students, 150 chose to participate, though not all finished the course or completed every prompt. Students were given three writing prompts, including the two described above. They wrote drafts and submitted them for electronic peer review, with drafts circulated anonymously to other participants, who used the provided rubric as a basis for feedback. Participants also had the option of meeting one-on-one or in small groups with undergraduate writing fellows who were hired to attend lectures and hold office hours to give feedback on writing and help with the drafting process. These fellows were students who had previously taken the courses and were identified by the instructor as highly-successful students. To prepare for supporting WTL assignments, they enrolled in a course focused on processes of writing. After drafting, peer review, meeting with fellows, and revising, students submitted final drafts of their writing. They were graded on a credit/no-credit basis, based on their general display of statistical information and engagement in all stages of the writing process.

Once we collected participants' responses to these two prompts, we began the scoring process to determine how well students were incorporating statistical knowledge into their writing. This scoring was kept separate from the scoring associated with students' grades. Using the rubric provided to students, we met in norming sessions with the entire group of evaluators, which consisted of all researchers and doctoral student members of our research team, alongside undergraduate writing fellows. We established a five-point scale with ones indicating no significant statistical knowledge and fives indicating a high level, sometimes incorporating statistical concepts that were not part of the current unit of study. Next, we divided into pairs to read and score each of the 201 pieces of writing, 97 that addressed the prompt focused on caffeine and 104 that responded to the prompt focused on chocolate. In cases where both members of the pair did not agree on a score, we called for a third reader to ensure reliable scoring across readers.

To understand the ways students take up the genres invoked by these prompts, we identified cases for closer analysis of student writing. Since the average scores for the email to grandparents and memo as a consultant were, respectively, 2.49 and 3.56, we began our analysis by looking at work from students who fell near that range. However, because 43% of the students scored a 4 on the memo from a consultant assignment, we were interested in expanding our range to include those students. If students had generally earned scores in the 2 range for one assignment, then moved to a range at or near a 4, what were they doing differently across the assignments? Therefore, we identified students with differentiated scores, meaning that they scored within the 2 range on the email to grandparents and then subsequently scored a 3 or 4 on the memo to consultants. In doing so, we started with the sampling strategy identified by Patton as "typical case sampling," which involves "select[ing] cases that represent an average trend in a data set" (268). Pragmatically, this sampling range provided us with a greater number of students to contact for consent to analyze and write about their responses, but this choice was also important in that it identified cases that were typical of the larger data set and eliminated students who were either getting significant amounts of statistical information wrong (which generally moved them to the 1s category) or who were going beyond the expectations of the prompt by including discussion of additional statistical concepts (which generally moved them into the 5s category).

Of the student writing identified in this way, we further narrowed our sample by employing purposeful random sampling (Patton); six student writers were selected randomly from the list of names for closer analysis. We read each piece to identify how students had succeeded or failed to incorporate statistical information and what their writing illustrated about student uptake and the exigencies of the assigned genre. Of these six students, five wrote emails to grandparents and memos as consultants that were consistent with the trends described below. One student, we discovered, had scored low on the email to grandparents because of what seemed to be a misunderstanding of the prompt, which led the student to write an email advising his grandparents how to set up a test to see if they fell in the safe range of caffeine consumption but neglected to include other statistical concepts targeted by the prompt. The remaining five students were contacted via email for consent to use their writing in case studies; three responded affirmatively, and we present a discussion of two below as typical of our findings.

To further understand student uptake in terms of both subject matter and genre knowledge, we contacted participants for follow-up interviews. Two students responded and we conducted face-to-face interviews, grounded in discussion of both prompts and responses the participants had written. We asked students to reread each prompt, then asked them to describe what the prompt seemed to be asking them to do, what difficulties (if any) they had faced when writing, and what effects the audience and genre had on choices the student made. These interviews were transcribed and coded thematically. Taken together, the larger collection of scores, analysis of student writing samples, and student interviews provided us with a more rounded perspective of student uptake.

Results

When the initial scoring of student writing was completed, we immediately noticed a marked difference between the scores of the email to grandparents and the memo from the consultant, as figure 3 demonstrates. In the former, students were less successful in incorporating their statistical knowledge effectively. In contrast, in the latter, they were able to display statistical knowledge in clear and useful ways that were relevant to the task at hand. Certainly this is at least partially related to the sequencing of the assignments and the general progression expected in any course, as students develop better understandings of content and assignment structure over time. However, the extreme difference in scores suggests that there might be other factors underlying such difference.

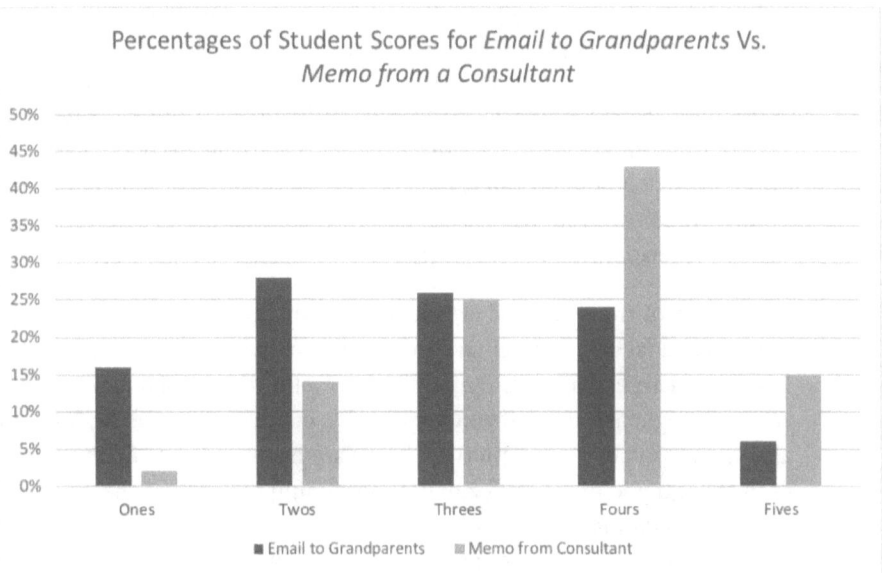

Figure 3: Students' scores for the two respective assignments

One way to understand this trend was to investigate how students' writing illustrated levels of uptake relevant to the discourses of statistics and to the genres demanded by each prompt. In this investigation we found Kimberly Emmons' distinction between generic and discursive uptake helpful. Emmons defines generic uptake as "the selection and translation of typified forms and social roles" and discursive uptake as the translation of "key phrases rather than patterns of social organization" (192). Genre's social organization, in Emmons' terms, includes identities, ways of knowing, goals, and emotion, all of which shape students' uptake of every genre. During the scoring of writing produced in response to the two prompts considered here, the importance of genre and its accompanying social organization was immediately apparent. Most consultant memos were immediately recognizable as approximations of the genre, with headers, mock consultant firm names, and visual layouts drawing on templates for memos that the students found (several students used the same template, in fact). Similarly, all students formatted the email to grandparents with features common to an email or letter, opening with a salutation and closing by using "love" or "your favorite grandson" or similar genre-appropriate choices. But beyond these visible genre conventions, students' choices of language and framing reflect deeper differences in the ways these two assignments prompted students to deploy their statistical knowledge.

In the more personal genre of the email to grandparents, students framed their research questions to provide personal advice instead of directly displaying statistical knowledge. A good example of this tendency can be seen in Miranda's email where she focused on more general statements from the article (in bold), not the actual statistical discussion. Even when variables discussed in the article are referenced, she does so without discussing them explicitly as variables, as the underlined portions show. Instead, Miranda chose to write about alternate explanations in a personalized way that makes the relationship to the statistical concepts hard to determine.

> **According to the scientific article, too much caffeine intake results in anxiety, headaches, and nausea.** So it would be a good idea to start looking to see if you are experiencing any of these symptoms, or all of them, in which case you might assume that you may need to cut down on caffeine. You can also monitor your sleep patterns—if you are having trouble falling asleep even though you drank coffee hours ago, timing may not be the problem. *The problem may be how much coffee you drank as opposed to when you drank it.* So if you are experiencing any sleep problems then maybe you can say that you've had too much caffeine and cut down on it and monitor your sleep patterns again. *Although, of course you can't conclude that caffeine is the only problem—there may be other underlying health problems.*

Miranda has made fairly rhetorically savvy choices for this genre and its intended audience. The underlined portions of the email draw her grandparents' attention to the importance of considering a range of variables, without getting bogged down in the technicalities of talking about variables as such. Unfortunately, this choice makes it difficult to assess the depth of her knowledge of these statistical concepts. Genre-based exigencies that determine what an email to grandparents might address to best suit the needs of its audience created a conflict with the assignment-based exigency to display discourses of statistics. Miranda's translation process emphasized the generic uptake at the expense of the discursive uptake of key terms from statistics.

However, in the same student's memo as a consultant to a Tour de France team, she frames her questions in ways that foreground the study methodology much more directly, maintaining a register that is more technical and specialized. Miranda identifies an important consideration—that this was a crossover study—and notes that this could have an effect on the results. She used *treatment condition* rather than a more commonplace phrasing like *the first chocolate they ate might affect how they respond to the second chocolate*. This choice is important in that it allows the student to use the terminology of a statistician, but it also creates a more distant and generalizable scientific register. When writing that crossover studies create the possibility for effects from one treatment condition to influence the second treatment condition, Miranda is able to explain not only the factors underlying this particular case, but to display an understanding of how research methods can be interpreted in general.

> After examining the results of the crossover study, I suggest that dark chocolate should be included in athletes' diets. **However, there are some things to keep in mind. Because this was a crossover study, there could be some effects from the first treatment condition on the second condition.** This means that if an athlete took dark chocolate first and it did in fact have an effect, some of this effect could still remain as the athlete takes the second treatment condition (white chocolate).

This student, whose earlier writing did not succeed in displaying the required statistical knowledge effectively, is able to introduce audience-specific questions and then explain how to answer them, discussing both the study results and the statistical implications of these results that might be of interest to her audience. Most notably, Miranda is able to explain in ways that highlight, rather than downplay, statistical concepts:

> In addition, our 95% confidence interval for the difference in baseline oxygen consumption and the dark chocolate oxygen consumption is (0.21ml/kg min, 5.05 ml/kg min). *What this means is* that we are 95% confident that the true population mean increase in oxygen consumption lies somewhere between 0.21-5.05 ml/kg min when athletes consume dark chocolate. *This interval also means that* if we were to repeat this study multiple times, we would expect 95% of our confidence intervals to contain the true population mean difference in oxygen consumption when athletes consume dark chocolate.

The use of *this means* does not signal a translation to simpler non-statistical concepts, but highlights the ways that statistical analysis can predict future results with, in this case, high levels of confidence.

However, it is not only the case that certain genres might suggest to students that certain information be included or omitted. Instead, it seems as if particular genres actively constrain or encourage students' abilities to incorporate statistical knowledge. As we discuss further below, this constraining tendency aligns with Rebecca Nowacek's suggestion that prior genre knowledge can lead students down paths that produce writing that does not fulfill the requirements of the assignment at hand (41). Indeed, our analysis suggests that prompts that ask students to imagine themselves in ostensibly authentic writing situations but also display knowledge for an instructor might simply be asking students to do two things that seem incompatible or creating a mixed message like the course described in Herrington's (1985) study.

In those cases it is perhaps unsurprising to find students breaking with genre conventions to fit the requirements of the classroom assignment. For example, Jada breaks with the expectations of an email to grandparents a bit, including significant information like the recommended daily dose and the average amount of caffeine in a coffee (in bold), but then goes directly back to the more audience-friendly and genre-appropriate personal tone (underlined), a shift that is signaled immediately by a direct address, an explicit marker of personal opinion, and an exclamation.

> Furthermore, **it would take a lot of coffee to exceed the FDA's daily-recommended dose of 400 mg/day**, which is stated in one of this article's references, which is a statistical overview of caffeine consumption by age group in the *Food and Chemical Toxicity Journal*. **According to this publication, the average cup of coffee has 95.2 mg of coffee in 8 fl. oz.** *You would have to drink four cups of coffee to reach the recommended dose. Personally, my morning cup is enough to get me going! Just thinking about drinking four cups of coffee is enough to make my hands shake.*

Jada seems conscious of the need to incorporate references to the assigned text, including academic-style source introduction and integration, as well as specific numbers, all of which leads to a straining of the email to grandparents genre. The need to name an academic journal, for instance, seems superfluous, unless the real reader is an academic who requires sources to be cited. This mixed generic uptake renders the text somewhat ineffective as either an email or as a display of statistical knowledge.

Like Miranda's though, Jada's memo from a consultant provides explanation that successfully displays high levels of course-appropriate statistical knowledge while maintaining genre and audience expectations. Responding to a request to analyze the reliability of the findings in a piece of published research, Jada is able to provide two levels of explanation. In the bolded examples, she provides her reader access to language, defining *null hypothesis* and a *p-value* of less than 5%. It is notable that even these translations of statistical terms into more everyday phrasings maintain a more technical register, compared to her language in the email to grandparents. Even more notable though is Jada's ability to go beyond explanation of meaning, moving toward explanation of implication, as the underlined section shows.

> Thus by the p-test, with 95% confidence, the null hypothesis (**that there is no difference between the baseline metabolic measurements and the post-dark chocolate diet metabolic measurements**) can be rejected, because the p-value was less than 5%. **In other words**, there was less than a five percent chance of this event occurring. *This means that it is reasonable to assume that*

> the population-mean oxygen consumption is greater for the test subjects after consuming the dark chocolate.

While the email to grandparents genre required this student to force statistical information somewhat awkwardly into the text, the genre of the memo from a consultant left space for Jada to use terms and concepts from class, explain them in complex ways that displayed her authority, and move toward the discussions of more complex implications that can be drawn from those more basic explanations. Her writing demonstrates a translation process appropriately balanced between generic and discursive uptake.

This detailed analysis of student writing showed the importance of genre and audience in students' uptake of these two prompts. For more direct information about students' uptake we conducted interviews with two statistics students: Amy, who achieved high scores on both prompts, and Eric, whose two responses were less successful. Amy scored a 4 on the memo to a consultant and was one of only a handful of students to score a 5 on the email to grandparents. In talking through her approach to the caffeine prompt, Amy said: "I think I probably had to read the study that was cited a few times, maybe read it once through to get a sense of it and then again to pick apart the different statistics that were mentioned. Then I guess I put myself in the shoes of someone who hadn't been learning stats at all just to make sure 'cause I know one of the main things was really to use language that would be understandable for anyone." She began the process by thoroughly reading and re-reading the study in order to get a sense of the statistical knowledge underlying the article. It was only once she had a firm grasp of the required conceptual knowledge that she then put herself "in the shoes of someone who hadn't been learning stats at all," that she began crafting language that would adequately bridge the gap between her audience's understanding and the understanding that the article required.

In contrast, Eric, who received a score of 2 on the email to grandparents assignments, described an approach that seemed to start with the audience and work backward to the assignment: "I think I took an informal enough approach to it so it could seem like I was writing it to my grandparents. I think I did a decent job of explaining the statistical part of the *Washington Post* article so that somebody who didn't understand statistics could understand it." And yet, Eric realized that there were issues with his writing in terms of communicating conceptual knowledge. He reflected that he "might have been able to do a better job explaining the process of how to draw the conclusions instead of just saying what the numbers are, explaining what they mean and explaining what the conclusions are." Concerns with the social organization of the genre seemed to be a key hang-up for Eric in determining how to respond to this prompt. He noted that, "I think I was definitely conscious of it, trying to—trying to make it as informal as possible . . . I honestly don't know how I could improve on that.

That's probably the toughest part of this prompt." Focusing on generic uptake may have prevented Eric from diving into the statistically-informed discursive uptake the prompt demanded; he said that in retrospect he "might have been able to do a better job explaining the process of how to draw the conclusions."

Discussion

Our analysis of student responses to the two prompts shows that even when assignments include some version of all of the features identified by researchers like Anderson et al. they do not always enable students to engage effectively with course concepts. This led us to look again at the Anderson et al. features communicated through the prompts to determine what led to the differences in students' ability to articulate statistical concepts.

The feature of interactive writing processes was a constant across both of our WTL assignments: the *memo from a consultant* and the *email to grandparents*, both involved having students write drafts, engage in peer review, and receive feedback from an undergraduate writing fellow before revising and submitting their final drafts. Because both assignments used such similar processes, the difference in student performance could not be attributed to this feature. However, the other two features that Anderson et al. identify—clear writing expectations and meaning-making in writing tasks—deserve more attention.

As mentioned previously, Anderson et al. argue that instructors need to provide students with an accurate understanding of what they are being asked to do and the criteria by which instructors will evaluate their work to increase the likelihood that they can take advantage of the affordance of WTL activities. The two prompts discussed here did include detailed instructions along with rubrics for evaluation, but "clear writing expectations" did not anticipate the various forms student genre and discourse uptake could take. When students wrote to the Tour de France team, the register in which they wrote and their inclusion of course concepts addressed the social organization that accompanies a professional memo directed to a national organization. Based on students' successful writing for this prompt, their uptake of this genre included statistical discourses with features like complex syntax, high-level register, and genre-appropriate tone, as befitting a consultant's report to their client.

In the *email to grandparents*, however, student writing illustrates the extent to which high-level register features and explicit discussion of statistical concepts did not fit the expectations of this genre. The conflict experienced by students in our study is reminiscent of the incident that Nowacek describes, in which a student's incoming knowledge of the genre of a personal diary interfered with the stated goals of an assignment where students were expected to write diary entries detailing the material conditions of medieval life. Although the student transferred her genre knowledge of the diary genre by writing a personal, introspective account of her character's life, she missed the point of the assignment, which was to demonstrate an understanding of medieval life using the discourses of the field. Nowacek's study offers another example of how a prompt can lead students to demonstrate generic uptake and neglect the discursive uptake that can demonstrate their understanding of course concepts.

Communicating via a memo provided students with a more likely way, in Gogan's sense of approximating likeliness, to relay their statistical knowledge; students' and instructors' expectations were in alignment with how a professional communicates their specialized knowledge to an organization requesting their consultation services. Students as a whole did not fare as well in the genre of an email to their grandparents. Because the genre and audience for this assignment were not adequately aligned to the conceptual purpose of the writing assignment, students were presented with two contradictory sets of expectations. One sentence in the prompt tells students, "write your grandparents an email that explains to them what kinds of questions they need to ask before they can determine whether they are consuming too much caffeine" and a few sentences later, students are told to "include reference to the explanatory variable, response variable and any other confounding variables." As a result, students had to navigate between either a genre-appropriate informality or a display of proficiency in statistical discourses for the instructor-as-evaluator, often leading to a blurring of the two. The relatively small number of students who, like Amy, concentrated on the three variables required by the prompt succeeded with this prompt.

Finally, as discussed earlier, Anderson et al. found that students need opportunities to make meaning with their writing and to engage in integrative, critical, or original thinking (207). How easily students can make meaning within the constraints of a WTL assignment depends on several factors, among them distance and aspiration: What is the distance between the real situation of writing in response to a professor's assignment and the imagined rhetorical situation offered by the assignment? To what extent does the imagined rhetorical situation of the writing prompt tap into students' aspirations? What we found was that the closer the real classroom situation and imagined situations embedded in the assignment and the more aspirational qualities that were present in a prompt, the easier it was for students' uptake to demonstrate effective meaning making. As Eodice et al. found, student aspirations play a key role making writing meaningful.

In both WTL assignments, the genre required students to hold in their minds an imaginary audience and exigence that would direct the ways in which they made meaning in their responses. But the reality was that they were writing to a professor and some writing fellows for a statistics class at a large public midwestern university. The two rhetorical situations existed in dynamic tension for the student-writers who sought to write meaningfully for both audiences. We hypothesize that the tension was somewhat easier to resolve when the real situation of writing for a professor and the imagined rhetorical situation of writing for, say, an employer were closer to each other rather than far apart. We conducted subsequent interviews with two other M-Write students, Amy and Eric, in order to shed further light on student uptake of these two prompts. These participants confirmed, too, that students' uptake focused on course concepts rather than rhetorical features demonstrated deeper conceptual learning.

Another dimension of students' uptake of these two assignments centers on the perceived stakes in each rhetorical situation presented. While each offered a clear context and audience for student writers, the grandparent audience led Eric's uptake, and probably that of many other students, away from providing detailed information about "what [the numbers] mean" because he was trying to make [his explanation] as informal as possible." In writing an email to their grandparents about something as pedestrian as caffeine intake, the stakes were fairly low. The grandparents may choose to follow the grandchild's recommendation or not—either way, little was lost or gained. On the other hand, part of what was at stake in the memo to a consultant is job performance, accolades, and possible future job opportunities. Those stakes are not unlike the stakes tied to course grades, at least from a first- or second-year student's perspective—doing well in a class will lead to good grades and possibly other opportunities (such as desirable internships) in the future. The students' writing task in the "memo as a consultant" was similar to a task they were used to doing: creating a product and having their performance evaluated.

Another factor that contributed to the students' uptake may have been the difference in how well students were able to make meaning in the *memo from a consultant* assignment as opposed to the *email to grandparents* assignment since the memo prompted students to imagine themselves as professionals while the email did not offer this aspirational connection. It gave many of them a way to make meaning beyond the classroom. By putting them in a role that many of them would aspire to, this writing-to-learn assignment let students borrow authority from that imaginary role, and perhaps write with more motivation and confidence as a result. The prompt's opening sentence, "You have been hired by the U.S. bicycle team to help them train for the Tour de France," makes the prompt a scaffold to a real-world activity, with a clear line from present work to future work. In Eodice et al's terms, this prompt invites students to be more agentive. In contrast, the *email to grandparents* did not contain the same aspirational or anticipatory socialization (Feldman; Lortie) in terms of career mobility. While some students might have been motivated by real-world applications outside the classrooms that allowed them to assist family members, the assignment didn't suggest any professional applications. There was not much borrowed authority to be had, and rather than creating a clear through-line from present work to future work, the grandparent assignment was a kind of cul-de-sac; a worthy end, perhaps, but an end in itself and not a means of writing their way into a professional world. As Brandt suggests, "'writing as worldly work' functions aspirationally in the lives of young writers . . ., exciting dreams of their future selves and inviting them into precocious engagement with some of the most powerful genres of the culture" (97); it should come as no surprise, then, that when asked to take on a professional stance, students seemed more engaged and agentive as writers and as learners.

Implications

We believe that the uptake we've witnessed in students' interviews and written responses to these prompts have important implications for improving how instructors craft WTL assignments. First, our findings shed additional light on the importance of genre and disciplinary discourses. Instructors need to attend to how different genres with their attendant social organization, the roles and expectations they carry, create space for the display of certain kinds of knowledge. Genre, as Bawarshi notes, acts upon writers, leading to communication in different registers with different audiences. The chosen genre should create a broad platform for presenting conceptual understanding in the respective discipline. If the genre called for by the WTL assignment demands that the student make a choice between using disciplinary discourses showing what they know or writing well for the genre, it may impede rather than promote student success.

Instructors may also want to consider the distance between real and imagined rhetorical situations. If students are asked to write for a situation that is vastly different in terms of stakes and demands of ethos from writing to an instructor or professor in a college classroom, the tension may be counterproductive rather than generative.

Finally, a useful question to ask about an assignment is what kind of aspirational quality it has and in what way it might be perceived as a scaffold to a desirable future role. The way an assignment is constructed can go a long way toward supporting students in making meaning of their learning and clearly conveying their knowledge of course concepts.

This research may be particularly critical given Anderson et al.'s finding that well-designed writing curricula may have a positive influence on students' "Personal and Social Development," which they define as "learning independently, understanding oneself, understanding other people, developing a personal code of values and ethics, and contributing to the community" (211). In other words, well-designed WTL assignments (which, ideally would be integrated throughout the curriculum) may not only have positive effects on academic learning, but they may also influence students' overall development, both as people and as global citizens.

Works Cited

Ackerman, John M. "The Promise of Writing to Learn." *Written Communication*, vol. 10, no., 3, 1993, pp. 334–70.

Anderson, Paul, Chris M. Anson, Robert M. Gonyea, and Charles Paine. "The Contributions of Writing to Learning and Development: Results from a Large-Scale Multi-Institutional Study." *Research in the Teaching of English*, vol. 50, no. 2, 2015, pp. 199–235.

Arnold, Kathleen M., Sharda Umanath, Kara Reilly Walter B. McDaniel, Mark A. March, and Elizabeth J. Marsh. "Understanding the Cognitive Processes Involved in Writing to Learn." *Journal of Experimental Psychology Applied*, vol. 23, no. 2, 2017, pp. 115–27.

Austin, John L. *How to Do Things with Words*. Harvard UP, 1962.

Bangert-Drowns, Robert L., Marlene M. Hurley, and Barbara Wilkinson. "The Effects of School-Based Writing-to-Learn Interventions on Academic Achievement: A Meta-Analysis." *Review of Educational Research*, vol. 74, no. 1, 2004, pp. 29–58.

Bawarshi, Anis S. *Genre and the Invention of the Writer: Reconsidering the Place of Invention in Composition*. Utah State UP, 2003.

Brandt, Deborah. *The Rise of Writing: Redefining Mass Literacy*. Cambridge UP, 2015.

Durst, Russell K. and George E. Newell. "The Uses of Function: James Britton's Category System and Research on Writing. *Review of Educational Research*, vol 59, no. 4, 1989, pp. 375–94.

Emmons, Kimberly. "Uptake and the Biomedical Subject." *Genre in the Changing World*, edited by Charles Bazerman, Adair Bonini, and Débora Figueiredo, The WAC Clearinghouse and Parlor Press, 2009, pp. 134–57.

Eodice, Michele, Anne Ellen Geller, and Neal Lerner. *The Meaningful Writing Project*. Utah State UP, 2017

Feldman, Daniel Charles. "A Contingency Theory of Socialization." *Administrative Science Quarterly*, vol. 21, 1976, pp 433–52.

Ferris, Dana R. and John Hedgcock. *Teaching L2 Composition. Purpose, Process, and Practice*. Routledge, 2014.

Freadman, Anne. "Uptake." *The Rhetoric and Ideology of Genre: Strategies for Stability and Change*, edited by Richard M. Coe, Lorelei Lingard, and Tatiana Teslenko, Hampton Press, 2002, pp 39–53.

Gere, Anne Ruggles, Emily Wilson, Naitnaphit Limlamai, Kate MacDougall Saylor, andRaymond Pugh. "Writing and Conceptual Learning in Science: An Analysis of Assignments," *Written Communication*, forthcoming.

Gere, Anne Ruggles, ed. *Developing Writers in Higher Education: A Longitudinal Study*. U of Michigan P, 2019.

Gogan, Brian. "Expanding the Aims of Public Rhetoric and Writing Pedagogy: Writing Letters to Editors." *College Composition and Communication*, vol. 65, no. 4, 2014, pp. 534–59.

Gunel, Murat, et al. "Writing for Different Audiences: Effects on High-School Students' Conceptual Understanding of Biology." *Learning and Instruction*, vol. 19, no. 4, Aug. 2009, pp. 354–67.

Herrington, A. J. "Writing in Academic Settings: A Study of the Contexts for Writing in Two College Chemical Engineering Courses." *Research in the Teaching of England*, vol. 19, no. 4, 1985, pp. 331–61.

Johns, Ann. "Students and Research: Reflective Feedback for I-Search Papers." *Feedback in Second Language Writing: Contexts and Issues*, edited by Ken Hyland and Fiona Hyland, Cambridge UP, 2012, pp. 162–81.

Lortie, Dan C. *Schoolteacher*. U of Chicago P, 1975.

Melzer, Dan. *Assignments Across the Curriculum: A National Study of College Writing*. Utah State UP, 2014.

Nowacek, Rebecca S. *Agents of Integration: Understanding Transfer as a Rhetorical Act*. Southern Illinois UP, 2011.

Ochsner, Robert and Judy Fowler. "Playing Devil's Advocate: Evaluating the Literature of the WAC/WID Movement." *Review of Educational Research*, vol. 74, no. 2, 2004, pp. 117–39.

Patton, Michael Quinn. *Qualitative Research & Evaluation Methods: Integrating Theory and Practice*. SAGE, 2015.

Reynolds, Julie A., Chris Thaiss, William Katkin and Robert J. Thompson. "Writing-to-learn in Undergraduate Science Education: A Community-Based, Conceptually Driven approach." *CBE Life Science Education*, vol. 11, no. 1, 2012, pp 17–25.

Rivard, Leonard P. "A Review of Writing to Learn in Science: Implications for Practice and Research." *Journal of Research in Science Teaching*, vol. 31, no. 9, 1994, pp. 959–83.

Rounsaville, Angela. "Selecting Genres for Transfer: The Role of Uptake in Students' Antecedent Genre Knowledge" *Composition Forum*, vol. 26, 2012, compositionforum.com/issue26/selecting-genres-uptake.php.

Schiavone, Aubrey and Anna V. Knutson. "Pedagogy at the Crossroads: Instructor Identity, Social Class Consciousness, and Reflective Teaching Practice." *Class in the Composition Classroom: Pedagogy and the Working Class*, edited by Genesea M. Carter and William H. Thelin, Utah State UP, 2017, pp. 19–39.

Swofford, Sarah. "Reaching Back to Move Beyond the 'Typical' Student Profile: The Influence of High School in Undergraduate Writing Development." *Developing Writers in Higher Education: A Longitudinal Study*, edited by Anne Ruggles Gere, U of Michigan P, 2019.

More Than a Useful Myth: A Case Study of Design Thinking for Writing Across the Curriculum Program Innovation

JENNA PACK SHEFFIELD

In May 2017, my university sent me to the Association of American Colleges and Universities (AAC&U) Institute on General Education and Assessment in Chicago, Illinois. In addition to enjoying the deep-dish pizza and rediscovering student life through sleeping in dorm rooms, I had the pleasure of hearing Stanford's Helen Chen, their director of e-Portfolio Initiatives, discuss the institute's theme: *design thinking*. At the time, I had been the director of my university's fledgling writing across the curriculum (WAC) program for two years, and while I was not at the institute in that capacity, I quickly went from being slightly skeptical about the concept of design thinking to, instead, not being able to ignore all of the ways in which design thinking could be employed in the context of WAC program design and sustainability. As Chen spoke, I kept seeing ways in which this concept could potentially invigorate our program.

As such, in this article, I argue that design thinking can be used as a strategy for addressing structural or curricular problems in WAC programs. I begin by describing how design thinking has been defined in other fields such as engineering and architecture. I then define the Stanford d.school's five modes of design thinking and discuss how I applied these modes to a design-thinking process in my own university's WAC program to address problems related to faculty resistance and meeting students' needs. I end by explaining how other administrators may use this interdisciplinary heuristic to analyze and wrangle with administrative WAC problems.

Decoding Design Thinking

Put simply, design thinking is a creative problem-solving approach. It is typically employed in the context of architecture and art/design disciplines but has more recently been applied in engineering, business management, and education contexts as well (Matthews and Wrigley; Purdy; Rowe). Many companies, such as global design company IDEO and General Electric, now use design thinking as a tactic for inciting new innovations regarding anything from re-structuring departments to creating new products (Brown; Moggridge). At least in business settings, design thinking has proven to have favorable outcomes, including better economic performance in the marketplace (Matthew and Wrigley; Moultrie and Livesey).

Essentially, engaging in design thinking means applying a designer's mindset or sensibility to complex or "wicked" problems. Drawing upon the theories of Horst W. J. Rittel and Melvin M. Webber, Richard Marback writes in a 2009 *CCC* article that *wicked problems* are "not solvable through greater command of information. Wicked problems are wicked because they are never finally solvable" (W399). These ill-defined problems, according to *Design Thinking* author Peter Rowe, have no definitive formulation (41). In fact, Rowe suggests, different formulations of the problem at hand imply different solutions, and proposed solutions to wicked problems are not necessarily correct or incorrect because plausible alternative solutions could be proposed (41).

To contend with so-called wicked problems, designers are said to employ a design-thinking approach. Richard Buchanan, inspired by Rittel and Webber's wicked problems concept, defines design thinking as problem-solving activity but also as reflective practice, emphasizing the connection between theory and practice. In "Wicked Problems in Design Thinking," Buchanan takes a process perspective, breaking down four areas of the world in which design is explored—symbolic and visual communications (such as graphic design), material objects, activities and organized services, and complex systems or environments for working, playing and learning (Buchanan 9–10). In other words, design thinking is a reflective practice that can be applied to a wide variety of subject matters, processes, and products. While Buchanan's work is relatively theoretical, some scholars and practitioners have also made moves to formalize methods for engaging with design thinking. As James Purdy notes in "What Can Design Thinking Offer Writing Studies," John Chris Jones, who was the "founder of the design methods movement," established a three-step process: "diverge, transform, converge" (Purdy 627). For Jones, design begins with divergence, in which the designer brainstorms and researches, escaping old assumptions and discovering what the problem actually is that the designer is attempting to resolve (64). Transformation is a creative phase involving setting objectives, identifying critical variables, and finding patterns, which ultimately allows designers to define the problem (Jones 66). Then, convergence involves selecting an appropriate solution to the problem.

Tim Brown, CEO and president of global design company IDEO, also writes about specific design-thinking methods in his book, *Change by Design: How Design Thinking Transforms Organizations and Inspires Innovation*. Having successfully employed design thinking for countless projects in his firm, Brown suggests there are three "overlapping spaces" of design thinking: inspiration, ideation, and implementation (16). Perhaps inspired by Jones, Brown describes the inspiration space as the space in which ideas are gathered; ideation involves turning insights into ideas; and implementation means turning ideas into a concrete action plan (Brown 16). Brown also suggests that design thinking is a dance between four mental states: convergent thinking (eliminating options and making choices), divergent thinking (multiplying options to create choices), synthesis (putting pieces together to form a whole), and analysis (breaking apart complex problems) (66–71).

Many of these ideas from Brown and Jones are present in the "design thinking" modes articulated by the Stanford d.school, which is the model that I use throughout the rest of this article. The Stanford model articulates five modes: empathize, define, ideate, prototype, and test. In the sections that follow, I describe these modes in more detail. No matter what method is being used, all design thinking practitioners emphasize that it is primarily about human-centered innovation (rather than technology or organization-centered innovation), and it is an iterative, collaborative process.

It is important to note that design thinking has been critiqued as well, with some suggesting it is little more than an empty buzzword. Don Norman, the founder and director of the Design Lab at the University of California, San Diego and former VP of advanced technology at Apple, writes in a 2010 online article that design thinking is a "useful myth." Norman's point is that design thinking is nothing more than a name for something innovators have been doing "throughout recorded history, long before designers entered the scene" ("Design Thinking: A Useful Myth"). In other words, breakthroughs in a variety of fields stem from people and processes that do not need to apply the term design thinking to what they do. Norman implies that design consultancies even use the concept as a public relations tool to mystify the work they do. Yet, Norman revisits his position a few years later in "Rethinking Design Thinking." He suggests that while, yes, design thinking is practiced "in some form or another by all great thinkers," in design, "there is an attempt to teach it as a systematic, practice-defining method of creative innovation" (Norman, "Rethinking Design Thinking"). For Norman, design thinking is critical as a way to encourage individuals and teams to "question the obvious, reformulate our beliefs, and to redefine existing solutions, approaches, and beliefs" ("Rethinking Design Thinking"). In short, design thinking is the application of a tried and true process for tackling complex issues and opportunities that is used by those with and without design backgrounds.

While the concept of design thinking is typically used in engineering, architecture, design, and even business management contexts, the concept has indeed been invoked in rhetoric and composition scholarship. Most notably, Carrie Leverenz argues in "Design Thinking and the Wicked Problem of Teaching Writing" that writing instructors should teach writing as a design process, create wicked writing assignments, and foster experimentation through prototyping. In "What Can Design Thinking Offer Writing Studies?," James Purdy draws comparisons between the multimodal composing process and design thinking. However, design thinking, to my knowledge, has not yet been applied to WAC. While Purdy does acknowledge that design thinking offers a model for how we might think about situating writing in the academy, his focus is more on the parallels between the composing process and design thinking as he codes composition journals for the different ways in which they invoke the concept of design (620). In this article, I want to suggest that design thinking can be applied productively to WAC administration, specifically.

While most of the WAC literature focuses on practical tips for program administration based on narratives of experienced administrators or on theorizing writing pedagogy rather than program administration, Michelle Cox, Jeffrey Galin, and Dan Melzer's recent book, *Sustainable WAC: A Whole Systems Approach to Launching and Developing Writing Across the Curriculum Programs*, does theorize program administration, drawing from theories outside of the field. Cox, Galin, and Melzer offer a theoretical framework for WAC program development grounded in complexity theory and systems theory. While systems thinking and design thinking developed independently in different fields (engineering/biology versus architecture/design, respectively), these approaches have some similarities and even overlaps. Systems theory involves thinking at the institutional level about the ways in which systems shape behavior (Cox, Galin, and Melzer 17). It is a recursive process that requires involving "actors in the system" in an attempt to "paint a rich picture of the system" (Cox, Galin, and Melzer 32). To employ this approach, for example, the authors describe a WAC director gathering a group of stakeholders to consider their goals for writing on campus, create alternative models for the system, and look for points of leverage for making change. In many ways, a design-thinking process would look similar. One of the major differences is that in systems theory, the stakeholders are the designers (in this case, the WAC director and, say, a campus writing committee), whereas in design thinking, the stakeholders are those observed and studied by the design team, such as students and faculty (Pourdehnad, Wexler, and Wilson). In other words, design thinking seems to more strongly emphasize a human-centered approach involving empathy with "users"—or the individuals/group for which one is designing. Another difference is that while systems thinking is more about seeing wholes (interrelationships rather than things (Shaked and Schechter), design thinking involves a "dance among four mental states"—convergent thinking, divergent thinking, analysis, and synthesis (Brown 66–71). Yet, the holistic approach to analyzing a system that is embodied in systems thinking can augment the creative idea development process of design thinking with greater consideration of the complexities of a system and power dynamics. Systems thinking may be more valuable for initial program development, but design thinking can be rather quickly (depending on the context and goals) and cheaply applied for innovation at any stage of a WAC program's lifespan. Brown reminds readers about the value of design thinking when he says, "Design thinking taps into capacities we all have but that are overlooked by more conventional problem-solving practices" (4).

The "Wicked Problem" of WAC

If design thinking is supposed to be applied to wicked problems, then the first question we as administrators might ask ourselves is, "Is WAC a wicked problem?" I would argue that both the acts of implementing and sustaining a WAC program can pose a variety of wicked problems worth exploring, and using wicked problems as a construct for understanding problems in WAC may allow us to address these problems differently.

There are a variety of common problems that WAC program administrators find themselves faced with. Many struggle with how to assess program effectiveness or monitor instructor compliance (Bazerman et al.; Carter; Cox, Galin, and Melzer; McLeod); how to deal with resistance from chairs to support faculty course releases or lower class caps or resistance from faculty who are frustrated by top-down, administratively launched curricular initiatives or who feel overburdened (Sandler); how to work with faculty who may be overly focused on grammar instruction to the detriment of higher-order concerns (Cole); or more generally how to deal with disciplinary differences in writing conventions and pedagogical approaches (Sandler). Some are faced with questions of who owns WAC and where WAC should be located in terms of place or administrative affiliation, and others worry about student perceptions of writing-intensive courses, noting that students (often at the advice of advisors) shy away from these courses due to concerns that the courses are more work (Cox, Galin, and Melzer 82–85). The sustainability of WAC programs is also an important issue arising in recent books and articles, and many of the above problems are why administrators worry about the sustainability of their programs.

These issues can be considered wicked problems because there is not necessarily one correct answer. Various solutions can be provided, and sometimes the actual problem itself is difficult to define. The problem also changes shape depending on the stakeholders under consideration, and the problem itself may change as one works to try and address it. Possible solutions to the problem also vary depending on the context. Traditional processes cannot solve wicked problems; these problems, in fact, cannot be indefinitely solved but they can be moderated or tamed. To illustrate, consider the question of where WAC should be located in terms of administrative affiliation. Does WAC belong to the English department? Should it reside in a center for teaching and learning (CTL)? Should it be run by a full-time administrator or a faculty member with a course release, and who does the director/coordinator report to? Different stakeholders would have different answers to these questions, and their answers are not necessarily right or wrong. Based on a concern that few faculty are participating in the WAC program, the Provost may pull WAC out of the English Department and into the CTL because he feels faculty across campus do not see WAC as interdisciplinary, but this may cause problems for the English department faculty who feel writing is their territory. Perhaps the move out of the English department does garner broader interdisciplinary participation, but the director, who has an English background, leaves out of frustration, and a director who lacks a writing background opens up new problems. Perhaps the problem was not really about faculty disliking that WAC was owned by the English department and the move to the CTL does not boost participation—hence the problem itself was not clearly defined. Perhaps engineering faculty do not want WAC under English but business faculty do, so the problem changes shape depending on which faculty are being considered.

Looking at WAC problems as wicked problems might, at first glance, cause an administrator to think that she should not even bother trying to work on these problems because they seem so impossible. However, this construct should actually empower us to feel that we can manage problems while reminding us that it is perfectly acceptable that we will be unable to find one perfect answer. In other words, the wicked problem concept has the potential to encourage administrators to tackle a problem that they might have otherwise deemed beyond their control or abilities. Identifying a wicked problem in WAC administration can remind us to focus on a specific user (the person or group for which we are trying to solve a problem) and to design a "solution" based on the specific stakeholder we want to address at any given time. Designating these problems as wicked also helps us to consider all the various complexities inherent in a problem and reminds us that new problems will emerge as we work on taming the initial issue; the wicked construct can help us troubleshoot and plan ahead. Ultimately, design thinking, and particularly the five modes I discuss in the next section, will help WAC administrators wrangle with these wicked problems. Yet, as Barbara Walvoord notes in the "Getting Started" chapter of Susan McLeod and Margot Soven's *Writing Across the Curriculum: A Guide to Developing Programs*, we should avoid the problem-solution model of WAC because if "WAC is seen only as a solution to a particular problem, then everyone expects that, if WAC is successful, the problem will be solved and WAC can end" (11). While the concepts of wicked problems and design thinking deal with the notions of problems and solutions, these concepts actually allow us to avoid this problem-solution model because they remind us that the kinds of problems we are faced with will continue to transform, and we will need to continually innovate, collaborate, and adjust.

At my university, there are a variety of wicked problems that I could attend to, but in this article, I focus on the most pervasive—which is the university's inability to offer enough writing-intensive courses to meet student demand. First, I will offer some context about our program and my role in its leadership. I started as the writing across the curriculum director at the same time that I first joined the faculty as an assistant professor of English. The university was in the process of implementing a new core curriculum, which would include one writing-intensive (W) course that all students would be required to take prior to graduation. As part of this change, the university removed one of our two required first-year writing courses. As a new faculty member, I was not privy to many of the conversations that led up to this change. I was not clear on the motivations behind the decision to implement WAC, nor did I know who made the decisions. Even after asking a variety of stakeholders to clue me in, I never really received the solid answers I was looking for. It *was* clear to me, however, that many faculty were resistant to this change. The "good luck with that" joke and chuckle that accompanied any conversation I had about WAC was a good indicator, and I was also warned by my chair and a Core Curriculum Task Force Committee that it would be difficult to get some chairs and faculty on board.

The major aspects of the "W" requirement and certification process were decided on before I arrived. We have a WI-based WAC program that follows an instructor-based approach, meaning that the W course designation is attached to sections of courses taught by instructors who have participated in our full-day orientation workshop and completed a course proposal. The proposal requires faculty to demonstrate how their courses meet the W requirements, such as that instructors should offer explicit instruction in writing, assign writing to learn (WTL) activities, give feedback on writing, and engage students in revision. During the semester they teach the W course, faculty are also asked to attend one 1-hour workshop to continue the professional development opportunity. W sections are currently a mix of general education courses and upper-level courses in the major, and section offerings have grown from ten to approximately twenty-five a semester, but by next year (AY 2019–2020) we need to be at around forty sections per semester to meet student need. When I arrived, I wrote a proposal to the provost to request a faculty stipend for those who would teach W courses, and the negotiated result was a $500 "start-up" stipend offered once—hence, the stipend is associated with participation in the workshop and proposal process and paid out during the semester the faculty member first teaches the W class, but faculty who teach courses again do not receive any compensation or release. Based on what was agreed to in relationship to the stipend, I was quite concerned about the sustainability of the program. Some faculty were motivated by the twenty-person class cap, such as history faculty who already taught writing-heavy sections with 30–35 students, but others' courses were already capped at 18–20 for a variety of reasons.

By the time I was introduced to design thinking, my initial sense of my program's wicked problem was that we did not have enough W-designated courses to meet the core curriculum requirement, which was ultimately a question of program sustainability. Given that sixty-two percent of the National Census of Writing WAC program respondents indicate that their institutions require all students to take writing-intensive courses taught by departments other than English or writing, this is likely a common problem. This problem also seems straightforward at first glance, so why did I consider this a wicked problem? Primarily because there was no easy answer and because different formulations of the problem would require different solutions. For example, the problem could have been that we did not have enough courses because my communications and recruitment were not effective, or, instead, we did not have enough courses because faculty wanted compensation for teaching the courses because they perceived them to be extra work. It could have been that faculty did not want to deal with students' resistance because many of our students did think W courses were "more work." The issue could also have been that department chairs could not afford to cap classes at twenty students. These different formulations of the problem would obviously lead to different approaches to a solution. Depending on the variety of problems and the different stakeholders facing these problems, I would need to tackle the issue in different ways—and I did so by drawing on concepts from design thinking.

A Case Study in Design Thinking for WAC

To apply design thinking to WAC, I used the Stanford d.school's design-thinking model—not only because it was the model that influenced me at the AAC&U Institute but also because it is arguably the most prevalent contemporary model invoked by businesses and academics, as Stanford is "at the forefront of applying and teaching Design Thinking" (Interaction Design Foundation). While these modes—empathize, define, ideate, prototype, and test[1]— are typically presented in order, they are intended to be iterative. In what follows, I define each mode, and after the mode's definition, I explain how I used that mode to tackle my program's wicked problem. While I wish I could share that I have engaged in a full-scale design-thinking process with a large team and measurable results, my own attempts at and successes with design thinking are certainly a work in progress; however, I would like to share a few elements of how design thinking informed some innovations on my campus.

1. Empathize

The first mode, empathize, is perhaps the most important of all modes because of its emphasis on a human-centered approach to creative problem solving.[2] Before a

---

1. Some scholars, such as Purdy, draw on a six-step process delineated by Jim Ratcliffe on the d.school K–12 wiki, but the most current instantiation by Stanford has five steps. Ratcliff's model includes understand, observe, define, ideate, prototype, and test. The current model takes "understand" and "observe," lumping these into the category of "empathize."

2. Many of the tools and methods mentioned in this section are drawn from the Stanford d.school's "Design Thinking Bootleg Deck," which is the latest iteration of strategies available on their website that were created by students, faculty, and designers from around the world.

designer can solve a problem, she needs to identify the user (the people for which she is trying to solve a problem) and truly understand their concerns. In this mode, the designer (1) *observes* users in the user's context, (2) *engages* users through interactions such as interviews, and (3) *immerses*, which essentially means that the designer wears the user's shoes, aiming to personally experience the reality of the user (d.school Hasso Plattner Institute of Design at Stanford i).

In this mode, the designer is supposed to assume a beginner's mindset by avoiding value judgments, questioning everything, finding patterns, and truly listening (d.school Hasso Plattner Institute). It is suggested that asking many "why" questions will help designers access empathy. This process ultimately is intended to help designers (in this case, WAC/WID directors) "grasp the needs of people you are trying to serve," according to Brown (9).

The elements of design thinking that inspired me the most, when I heard Chen discuss the concept, were the empathy mode and the iterative nature of the process. As such, I came back from learning about design thinking inspired to learn more about the faculty I work with and embracing the fact that I should go back and make changes to my program based on what I learned from these insights. This is not to say that prior to learning about design thinking, I did not care about or think about the faculty across my university. Quite the opposite. In fact, there were likely times when I worried too much about what they thought or felt; however, I had not specifically taken an opportunity to be *strategic* about determining their needs and feelings.

To engage with the empathy phase in my own design-thinking process, I first had to determine my users. Although the ultimate issue was related to students' needs, my users were faculty—faculty who I needed to continually teach W courses so that we could offer enough sections. Having the empathy mode in the back of my mind helped me to see that I needed more one-on-one time with the instructors where I gleaned their emotions about the program without allowing my own insecurities, biases, or assumptions to get in the way. To observe, engage, and immerse, I made a key change to my normal program structure. In lieu of our typical one-hour required mini workshop, I instead asked each faculty member to come to a 30–45 minute meeting in my office. By this time, I felt that I had a strong enough relationship with most of the faculty (I was in the third year of my program) that they would understand my intentions were not to police them but to learn from them. Luckily, I did have some program dissenters in this group because a few of the faculty had been strong-armed into the program by their chairs. This allowed me to garner the perspectives of a range of faculty. While I framed these meetings primarily around me being a resource for them, I also took the opportunity to engage them by asking many questions about

---

With a Creative Commons Attribution-Non Commercial Sharealike 4.0 license, the bootleg is available for any WAC director to download and use.

the workshop and course development process, how their course was going, what concerns they had about students' writing, if they would continue to teach W courses in the future, and why or why not. Especially for those who were resistant to being a part of the program or were not likely to teach a W course again, I was reminded by design-thinking principles to dig deep—moving beyond just the fact that faculty were resistant to trying to discover the exact *sources* of the resistance.

I also asked them to bring in course materials, such as a graded student paper or a rubric or a writing activity handout, so we could workshop their materials. This also enabled me to observe them in context. While this is not quite the same as sitting in on one of their classes or asking them to use a think-aloud protocol while grading (these strategies would perhaps better embody the "observe" category of the empathy mode), I selected an approach that felt natural and embedded in the local context. It did allow me to put myself in their shoes as I looked at the writing they received from their students or learned about their assessment struggles.

Another way I learned from stakeholders in the empathy phase was to begin surveying them. Much like I am sure other WAC directors do, I created a post-workshop survey, a student-experience survey, as well as a survey sent to department chairs for feedback about the process. I also held "WAC open office hours," or information sessions, that were open to anyone on campus. The main goal was to answer questions about the W process, but it also gave dissenters the opportunity to give me feedback on the program. While these information sessions were not terribly well attended, I did get the opportunity to speak to a few people who might have otherwise never taken the opportunity to present me with their perspective.

These informal interviews, surveys, and information sessions helped me gather a range of opinions and insights, looking for patterns that helped me formulate a more specific problem definition, which I discuss in the following section.

2. Define

After a designer engages with the empathy mode, she begins to *define* the problem. It is important to use the insights gleaned from the empathy mode in order to carefully craft a definition of the problem at hand. Rather than just calling it a problem statement, design thinkers call this a "point of view," which is an actionable problem defined by the user insights (d.school Hasso Plattner Institute ii). A strong point of view, according to the Stanford Bootleg Deck, allows for the generation of many possibilities and preserves emotion. In defining the problem, the Stanford team suggests describing the user and choosing your favorite insight that "represents the most powerful shift in your own perspective," then articulating what would be game-changing for the user, assuming the insight is correct (11). Perhaps the tip most poignant to WAC administrators is the d.school's assertion that a good point-of-view is one that "saves you from the impossible task of developing concepts that are all things to all people" ("An Introduction to Design Thinking" 3). How many administrators have tried to come up with a solution to a problem that makes everyone happy and ultimately failed? Design thinking emphasizes that a strong problem statement narrows the issue enough that the administrator does not have to please all people—only the specifically identified stakeholders on a specifically identified, actionable issue.

For my own design thinking activity, I used what I learned in the empathy phase—from the surveys and interviews and discussions of course materials—to more clearly formulate a problem. Based on what I learned in the empathy phase, the clearest two issues I could see were that (1) faculty felt insecure about how to manage the grading load and give enough in-class time to instruction about writing, which made them not want to teach a writing-heavy course, and (2) they felt teaching this type of course was extra work with little compensation. What came as a surprise to me was that a course release was considered much more valuable to most faculty compared to a stipend. The emotions behind this seemed to stem from faculty feeling overworked and undervalued, which is certainly not an uncommon phenomenon. I was also not surprised that the faculty members were concerned about the grading load, but I was not aware that so many were struggling with finding time to offer explicit writing instruction in class or that this issue was enough to make them not want to run a W class. Because writing is the content in most of my courses, it was difficult for me to get past my own biases and common practices to realize this was an issue. I was also surprised to learn that the faculty did not have a problem with our instructor-based approach because they saw how people teaching other sections of the same course may not use writing pedagogy strategically, and they did not have a problem with the proposal process, which was something I had worried was burdensome for the faculty and could cause them not to create a new W class.

As such, I had a more unique point of view to work with moving forward, one that allowed me to focus on specific issues and get rid of certain concerns of my own that I realized were not major problems. According to the Interaction Design Foundation, a good problem statement focuses on your users' need rather than your own. So, I had to keep faculty's needs in mind above my own need for more W courses. While my wicked problem was the overall issue needing resolution, my point of view as I moved into the ideate phase was slightly different. According to the foundation, designers need to combine three key ideas: user, need, and insight. Applying this to my scenario, my problem may have been defined as such: Faculty (*users*) need to feel adequately compensated and supported (*need*) because they are concerned about the grading load and having adequate time to offer writing instruction in class, and they ultimately feel undervalued (*insight*). This problem was defined broadly enough to allow for the generation of multiple ideas, but it was specific enough to be approachable.

3. Ideate

The next mode, *ideate*, is where ideas are born. The key to ideating, in design thinking terms, is to come up with ways to solve the actionable problem statement by generating as many ideas as possible, suspending judgment (Purdy 627). As such, the goal is quantity over quality, and most of the literature on design thinking argues that design thinkers at this phase should not initially consider constraints (a difference between design thinking and systems thinking) so that they can move beyond obvious solutions. One of the goals of ideation includes uncovering "unexpected areas of exploration," likely because constraints are not there to impede great ideas (iii). Yet, in some models, such as Tim Brown's, constraints are acknowledged, but in a different way than a more traditional approach to change. Brown suggests that designers discover which constraints are important and establish a framework for evaluating them. These constraints—feasibility, viability, and desirability—are overlapping, and a design thinker is to bring these in balance (18). With any model, the key seems to be to avoid letting a particular constraint get in the way of innovative ideas. In other words, designers should at least avoid passing judgment or evaluating ideas in the early phase of idea generation because the best innovations often stem from what some may view as bizarre ideas. As Brown notes, starting with the constraint of what will fit within current models makes change slow and incremental (Brown 18–22). Designers begin to build constraints back in more strategically as they begin to prototype and test.

Most of my program's ideation phase was conducted with the help of our first-year writing director and our writing programs coordinator, in addition to a session with my campus WAC committee. One particularly fruitful session during a reading day involved mapping out on a whiteboard our programs' (writing across the curriculum, first-year writing, and the writing center) successes, goals, gaps, and connections, and considering innovative possibilities. We also worked to ensure that what I had learned in the empathy phase was connected to the ideas we generated. We produced a wide variety of ideas focused on our defined problem. It was quite difficult to avoid passing judgment and throwing out ideas that did not seem feasible, but having design thinking in the back of my mind did help me focus on avoiding assessing quality in the early phases. This is the point in which, during any normal change process, I likely would have thrown out some of the ideas that we ended up succeeding with.

We selected three main ideas to move forward into prototyping. The d.school recommends creating voting criteria, such as "the most likely to delight," "the rational choice," and "the unexpected" ("An Introduction to Design Thinking"). While we did not use these specific terms to categorize our ideas, we did ensure the ideas ranged from practical to risky.

1. Our most "outlandish" or "unexpected" idea was to propose what we called a W banking system. Faculty would be able to "bank" credits each time they taught a writing-intensive course, and after four credits they would receive a course release, during which time they could catch up on research or work on designing new courses, and so forth. This idea was risky because it would be costly to backfill courses and was unlikely to get support from central administration; however, while I normally would not have let this idea even come out of my mouth, we aimed to take it seriously in the prototype phase. We felt that this idea could address the issue of faculty feeling better compensated and valued for their work.

2. Another idea, the "rational choice" in the d.school's terms, was to ask for more top-down support from the provost and deans, simply beginning to make it an expectation that faculty regularly participate in these processes. Part of the idea was to request that the expectation to teach a W course be built into the faculty handbook and into new faculty orientation. I had already been making suggestions along these lines, but the problem was how to make this happen in a meaningful way (or how to make administrators listen).

3. The third idea, perhaps the "most likely to please," was the implementation of a writing fellows program. While there are many different instantiations of writing fellows programs, our goal was to make fellows available only to writing-intensive faculty, and the fellows would be experienced writing center tutors who would work closely with W faculty to offer writing workshops to students focused on discipline-specific writing strategies articulated by the faculty member. We felt this option might best help support faculty who were concerned about the grading load and in-class instruction, as the tutor and faculty member could collaborate about how to improve student writing and move some instruction outside of normal class time. (Importantly, writing fellows do not grade for the faculty.) While many other universities already have a writing fellows program, our university writing center was only a few years old and without this process, we likely would not have made a step in this direction for a few more years because we were perhaps not as aware of faculty needs... or perhaps not as willing to take on risks.

4. *Prototype*

When a good idea is selected (or, ideally multiple ideas are selected), designers begin to *prototype*, which simply means to put the idea into any physical form. While this seems the most obvious for products, almost any idea can be prototyped. A new organizational structure for a business can be plastered up on Post-It Notes, or a role-playing activity can be designed to enact a new way for handling customer service scenarios. A design-thinking prototype should be created cheaply and relatively quickly. According to Brown, a prototype "should only command as much time, effort, and investment necessary to generate useful feedback and drive an idea forward" (90). This quick approach is due to the fact that the purpose of prototyping is to generate conversations and allow the team to learn, explore, and test. Brown even notes that a more refined prototype might not receive as much feedback because it feels complete. In fact, prototyping is often conducted on multiple ideas to help a team decide which to move forward with.

We began prototyping for our writing fellows program idea by using a mind-mapping approach on a whiteboard and then later composing an outline. This outline turned into a proposal written by our writing programs coordinator to myself and the first-year writing director about the ins and outs of the writing fellows program. Once we gave our coordinator feedback, we asked her to then turn it into a more formal proposal directed at the provost, which would include some changes in our overall budget request for the upcoming year.

For the banking system idea, I again used the genre of a proposal for prototyping because a proposal would eventually have to be directed through the provost. As the d.school recommends, I used this proposal prototype to "start a conversation," "test possibilities," and "problem-solve" ("An Introduction to Design Thinking"). As I worked on the protoype proposal, I decided that this idea would have a better chance of getting off the ground if it was framed around our university's emphasis on expanding high-impact practices (HIPs). As such, I started conversations with our service learning director, common course coordinator, and honors program director to test possibilities. We refined the idea to suggest that faculty who taught four high-impact courses (service-learning, honors, common course, writing intensive) could bank credits towards an eventual course release within a three-year timeframe. We created a variety of stipulations and requirements, and we added a portfolio requirement for students and faculty for program assessment. Portfolios were something the university had wanted but had been unable to get traction on, so we felt this was a good opportunity to garner further support by connecting our proposal to broader university goals. Another major university priority that had not been getting enough traction was our goal for a center for teaching and learning (CTL). As such, as we prepared our "high-impact practices incentive package," we described how we envisioned this opportunity leading to the creation of a CTL in which those instructors being honored for teaching high-impact courses would become CTL teaching fellows.

Related to feasibility, a major constraint we came up against as we prepared our prototype was that even if we created this incentive for faculty, we could get bottlenecked by chairs because getting buy-in for our courses is related to department needs. In this way, creating the prototype actually led to a redefinition of the problem because chair buy-in was not originally an issue that I discovered in the empathy phase. To offer an example, W and service-learning courses are capped at twenty, so chairs cannot always afford to cap classes at twenty because they have to find adjuncts to teach additional courses or sometimes have courses they cannot staff with adjuncts. As such, we also wrote into the proposal different ideas for department-level incentives; these ideas ranged from priority classroom selections for departments offering the most HIP courses to small budget increases for the most active departments, with the extra money going towards taking students to conferences. It was incredibly helpful to involve the other campus administrators in this process, as they each brought unique ideas and reminders of constraints to the prototype phase.

For our second idea related to top-down support, we used a white board and Post-It Notes to begin drafting what we called a "quota system." A major challenge with getting top-down support for WAC in the early stages at my university was that there was no accountability. For example, a dean could strongly encourage departments to start creating W courses, but the departments were not being required to do so and nothing negative happened if they did not participate. Of course, it would be terrible if the university could not meet student need, but somehow because this was everyone's problem, it was also no one's problem. Our attempt with a quota system was to arm the provost with specific numbers the university would need. When we ideated, we came up with different approaches, such as asking for an even number of W courses to be taught across all five of our colleges, making it a requirement that each faculty member teach one HIP class each year as part of their yearly contract, and so forth. Yet, we finally settled on the following: We first determined how many W courses were needed across the university, and we then broke that down by the *percentage of instruction* offered by each of the university's colleges. That then gave us a recommendation for the approximate number of W sections each college should offer. While this was only a rough estimate, it would give us something to work with that held each college accountable based on the amount of courses taught overall within the college.

As we prototyped, we began to see two ideas merging together. The quota system was helpful but still did not necessarily offer much motivation on its own. As such, we worked the quota system into our high-impact proposal, suggesting that a college's ability to meet these numbers would also serve as a way of measuring the proposed department-level or college-level incentives. Remembering to always go back to what we learned in the empathy mode helped us stay on the right track as we continued making changes to the proposals. We saw that we needed more than one solution, as the Writing Fellows program would give more pedagogical support while the HIP proposal would help faculty feel valued and better compensated.

5. Testing

The final mode, testing, means taking the opportunity to receive feedback on the prototype and refine the solutions. The Stanford team suggests, "Prototype as if you know you're right, but test as if you know you're wrong" (v). In other words, the testing mode is the time to be critical and consider the feasibility of the prototype. This mode may indeed reveal that the designer has framed the entire problem incorrectly. It can be useful to let the user experience the prototype without the designer offering a lot of context that could influence the user's experience.

For my context, testing was difficult because we could not exactly enable users to experience our prototypes. However, we did share our ideas with as many constituents as possible throughout various phases in the process (W instructors, department chairs, associate provosts, the faculty senate chair, and more), and we did so even when our ideas were early, sketchy drafts. One important decision we made was to call both the writing fellows program and the HIP incentive packages "pilots," and as such, we will be testing them, learning from users, and likely going back to the drawing board as we learn, engaging with the recursive nature of design thinking. Figure 1 shows a visual representation of the design-thinking process for our program's particular wicked problem.

Again, perhaps one of the most important points about the design-thinking process is that it is iterative. As figure 1 shows, testing and prototyping were particularly iterative for us because we continually made changes as we received feedback. At every step, the WAC team should consider how what they learn in one mode informs the other and may require changes to ideas, solutions, or prototypes.

I am pleased to share that the writing fellows program was easily approved. W faculty already eagerly signed up for our pilot, filling the program within an hour of the invitation email. We feel that this additional layer of support will motivate faculty and help them feel supported. A much larger win for us will be the HIP proposal. It was indeed tentatively approved by the provost and shared with campus deans and associate provosts. The potential budget impact is now being explored by campus stakeholders, and while we have not yet been guaranteed that this program can begin in fall 2018, it looks promising. Perhaps even more significant, talks of a campus CTL have ramped up largely in the context of these conversations about the incentive proposal. We feel these programs will connect well to the concerns that were prioritized during the empathy phase.

"Wicked" Problem: Program Sustainability Through Adequate Course Offerings

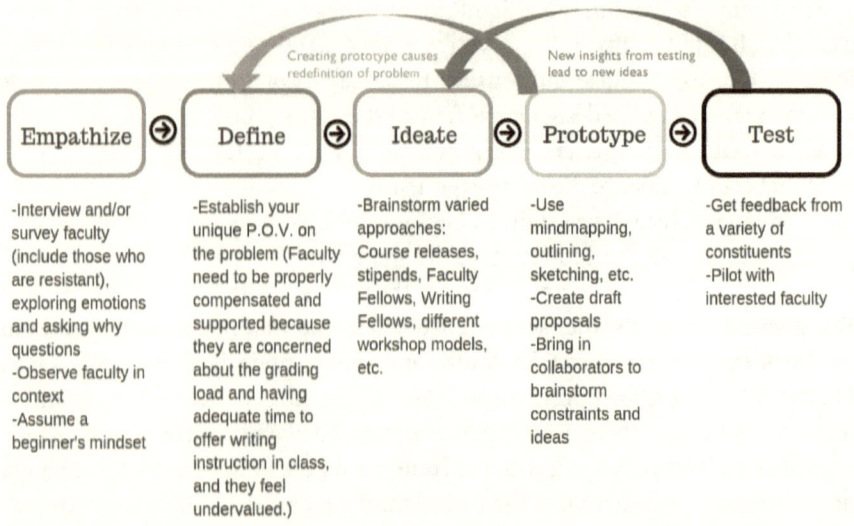

Figure 1. Design Thinking Map for Program Sustainability Issue

Given that wicked problems are shifty and never fully resolvable, we know we will need to continue to innovate. It remains to be seen if these initiatives will meet the goal of satisfying students' need for W courses, but we are confident that our approach is directly connected to faculty's concerns. We also have back-up plans in place in case our HIP proposal does not get final approval, and many of those ideas were also part of our ideation phase. However, the design thinking process certainly got us further than we would have gotten without it.

As I have noted, my own foray into innovation was certainly inspired by design thinking, but I also did not come close to exhausting the different ways in which design thinking can be applied to a variety of scenarios. There are many other innovative ways of working through wicked problems with design thinking. In the empathy mode, WAC directors could observe a faculty member while he or she grades papers using a think-aloud protocol. The director could run a W class herself or try to write a paper in another discipline in an attempt to "step into the students' shoes". She could partner instructors for classroom observations and collect and analyze the results to garner empathy insights. In the prototype mode, administrators can use mindmapping, sketching, outlining, storyboarding, and even role playing, such as acting out a committee's reactions to a new process change. Testing can occur in a variety of ways—from users actually using a mock product to users reviewing the org chart for a new reporting structure and offering feedback. The WAC director may sit in on a class if a new classroom pedagogy is being tested. There are innumerable ways to enact the five modes.

Applications for WAC Administrators

Design thinking allows WAC administrators to learn more about their programs and their problems with an eye toward focused solutions. The empathy mode encourages WAC administrators to (1) avoid bringing in their own biases or assumptions and (2) experience what their local users experience by actually witnessing their feelings, emotions, and challenges, rather than making educated guesses about these aspects of the users' experiences. The define mode allows administrators to hone in on a specific problem, making it more manageable and focused. This mode also encourages administrators to ensure that the problem definition is strongly connected to the empathy insights. The ideate mode allows for the generation of radical ideas. (Let's allow students to run WAC workshops. Let's get rid of workshops and move to departmental consulting.) The uniqueness of design thinking here is that the administrator is encouraged not to let typical concerns (about budgets, resources, staffing, etc.) get in the way of innovative ideas. Administrators can learn from the prototyping mode that their ideas are doable, and they can begin to problem-solve and diagnose the roadblocks they may encounter along the way, addressing feasibility and viability. From a heuristic point of view, administrators also learn from testing not only through the opportunity to receive feedback on their ideas but by getting the reminder to determine if the ideas actually meet the needs and desires revealed in the empathy phase, as well as if the ideas match the original problem. Prototyping and testing also allow administrators the opportunity to make progress with an idea but to avoid the pitfall of devoting exorbitant amounts of time to a solution that will never come to fruition or that will not bring about change.

As Don Norman notes, people who know a lot about their field tend not to question the fundamentals of their knowledge ("Rethinking Design Thinking"). The goal with design thinking is to allow designers to question their basic assumptions and do so in an informed way led by insights from stakeholders. As writing program administrators, we may not always question the basic fundamentals of composition pedagogy, and in some cases, a particular instructor's context or a particular discipline's conventions may require different ways of thinking about composition pedagogy best practices; design thinking can remind us to question some of our assumptions and redesign programs (or start up programs) with others' values at the forefront.

Of course, there are limitations to the design-thinking process. Perhaps the chief among them is time. It is not easy to find the time to engage in these activities and to find others willing to do so. One important thing to remember is that design thinking is, by nature, collaborative. Maybe directors/coordinators can enlist their on-campus writing committees or devoted instructors in their programs or even students (through an experiential/service-learning type of classroom opportunity) to conduct observations or interviews. Another important thing to remember about design thinking is that it focuses on the users and the unique problem/point of view. As such, as administrators, we should pick and choose which tactics we can employ that are manageable and tailored to the user and problem we are focusing on at the moment, thus narrowing the scope of the work. Another frustration with design thinking is that some of the ideas that generate the most excitement may end up not working once constraints are built back in. However, even implementing small elements of this overall framework into one's approach to WAC program development and sustainability may help foster innovation.

Design Thinking as Empowering Mindset

Readers may wonder if I really needed design thinking to make the changes I have described. For me personally? Yes. For others? Perhaps yes, perhaps no. The question itself hearkens back to Don Norman's early critique of design thinking as a "useful myth," when he argues that it is simply what innovators have been doing throughout recorded history. Yet, when Norman doubles back on this critique a few years later, he suggests that design thinking is unique in that is offers a "systematic, practice-defining method of creative innovation" ("Rethinking Design Thinking"). For me, the value of design thinking came from adopting it as a strategic mindset. It empowered me to explore opportunities that I normally would not have given more than a moment's thought. I cannot emphasize enough how getting the provost to make steps forward with the HIP proposal was a huge win in my campus context, and I simply cannot imagine myself having moved forward enough to come up with a viable proposal if I had not been influenced by the creative practices of design thinking. Specifically, taking the extra step to collect strategic data in the empathy phase, and then using those narratives to inform not only my prototype but the actual presentation to the provost, were both extremely helpful. Actually sitting down and "prototyping" my ideas also made a big impact on the process, and frankly, just having a name and strategy for this approach forced me to take the time to engage with some of these activities. As I continue to work with design thinking in the future, one thing I can improve upon is immersing myself, learning how to put myself in the shoes of the faculty with whom I work. I also can see opportunities for more creative prototypes as I take more time to engage with the process, and I need to work on bringing in collaborators early in the process.

Of course, design thinking is not the only way to approach innovation in WAC, and others may find different approaches more suited to their personalities or goals. However, the systematic, iterative, human-centered, empathy-driven modes of design thinking, I argue, can be usefully applied to a wide range of problems that we may encounter in our programs. Design thinking offers a different way of thinking about and tackling our sometimes "wicked" problems.

Works Cited

"An Introduction to Design Thinking: Process Guide." *d.school*, dschool-old.stanford.edu/sandbox/groups/designresources/wiki/36873/attachments. Accessed 15 April 2018.

Bazerman, Charles, et al. *Reference Guide to Writing Across the Curriculum*. Parlor Press, 2005.

Brown, Tim. *Change by Design: How Design Thinking Transforms Organizations and Inspires Innovation*. HarperCollins, 2009.

Buchanan, Richard. "Wicked Problems in Design Thinking." *Design Issues*, vol. 8, no. 2, 1992, pp. 5–21.

Carter, Michael. "A Process for Establishing Outcomes-Based Assessment Plans for Writing and Speaking in the Disciplines." *Language & Learning Across the Disciplines*, vol. 6, no. 1, 2003, pp. 4–29.

Cole, Daniel. "What if the Earth is Flat? Working with, Not Against, Faculty Concerns about Grammar in Student Writing." *The WAC Journal*, vol. 25, fall 2014, pp. 7–35.

Cox, Michelle, et al. *Sustainable WAC: A Whole Systems Approach to Launching and Sustaining Writing Across the Curriculum Programs*. National Council of Teachers of English, 2018.

Dam, Rikke, and Teo Siang. "Stage 2 in the Design Thinking Process: Define the Problem and Interpret the Results." *Interaction Design Foundation*, interaction-design.org/literature/article/stage-2-in-the-design-thinking-process-define-the-problem-and-interpret-the-results. Accessed 1 July 2018.

d.school Hasso Plattner Institute of Design at Stanford. "Design Thinking Bootleg." *d.school*, dschool.stanford.edu/resources/design-thinking-bootleg. Accessed May 25, 2018.

Jones, John Chris. *Design Methods, 2nd Edition*. Wiley, 1992.

Leverenz, Carrie. "Design Thinking and the Wicked Problem of Teaching Writing." *Computers and Composition*, vol. 33, 2014, pp. 1–12.

Marback, Richard. "Embracing Wicked Problems: The Turn to Design in Composition Studies." *College Composition and Communication*, vol. 61, no. 2, 2009, pp. W397–W419.

Matthews, Judy, and Wrigley, Cara. "Design and Design Thinking in Business and Management Higher Education." *Journal of Learning Design*, vol. 10, no. 1, 2010, pp. 41–54.

McLeod, Susan and Miraglia, Eric. "Writing Across the Curriculum in a Time of Change." *WAC for the New Millennium: Strategies for Continuing Writing Across the Curriculum Programs*, edited by Susan McLeod et al., National Council of Teachers of English, 2001, pp. 1–27.

Moggridge, Bill. "Design Thinking: Dear Don . . ." *Core77*, 2 Aug. 2010, core77.com/posts/17042/design-thinking-dear-don-17042. Accessed 12 March 2018.

Moultrie, James, and Livesey, Finbarr. "International Design Scorecard: Initial Indicators of International Design Capabilities." Institute for Manufacturing, University of Cambridge, www.naylornetwork.com/IDC-nwl/assets/090406int_design_scoreboard.pdf. Accessed 5 April 2018.

National Census of Writing. Swarthmore U, writingcensus.swarthmore.edu/. Accessed 6 June 2018.

Norman, Don. "Rethinking Design Thinking." *Core77*, 19 Mar. 2009, core77.com/posts/24579/rethinking-design-thinking-24579. Accessed 10 March 2018.

—. "Design Thinking: A Useful Myth." *Core77*, 19 Mar. 2009, core77.com/posts/16790/design-thinking-a-useful-myth-16790. Accessed 10 March 2018.

Pourdehnad, John et al. "Systems & Design Thinking: A Conceptual Framework for Their Integration." *Organizational Dynamics Working Papers*, vol. 10, 2011, pp. 1–16.

Purdy, James. "What Can Design Thinking Offer Writing Studies?" *College Composition and Communication*, vol. 65, no. 4, 2014, pp. 612–41.

Rowe, Peter. *Design Thinking*. MIT Press, 1986.

Sandler, Karen Wiley. "Starting a WAC Program." *Writing Across the Curriculum: A Guide to Developing Programs*, edited by Susan McLeod and Margot Soven, Sage, 1992/2000, pp. 35–42.

Shaked, Haim and Chen Schechter. "Seeing Wholes: The Concept of Systems Thinking and its Implementation in School Leadership." *International Review of Education*, vol. 59, no. 6, 2013, pp. 771–91.

Walvoord, Barbara. "Getting Started." *Writing Across the Curriculum: A Guide to Developing Programs*, edited by Susan McLeod and Margot Soven, Sage, 1992/2000, pp. 9–22.

How Exposure to and Evaluation of Writing-to-Learn Activities Impact STEM Students' Use of Those Activities

JUSTIN NICHOLES

That writing, "a knowledge-making activity," aids learning represents accepted knowledge in writing studies (Estrem, 2015, p. 19). Research has established that writing is linked to important educational outcomes in higher education (Arum & Roksa, 2011; Astin, 1992; Light, 2001) and that specific features of writing assignments most effectively facilitate deep learning (Anderson, Anson, Gonyea, & Paine, 2015, 2016). Traditionally occupying one end of McLeod's (1992/2000) writing-across-the-curriculum (WAC) approach continuum, writing-to-learn (WTL) approaches generally reflect a view of writing as a mode of thought (Arnold et al., 2017; Emig, 1977; Estrem, 2015) and may include assignments such as journaling, class-note summaries, and imaginary dialogues (Fulwiler, 1982; Young, 1984/2011) and other ungraded writing assignments aimed at promoting "learning" defined not simply as memorization but as "*discovery*, as a way of objectifying thought, of helping separate the knower from the known" (McLeod, 1992/2000, p. 3). Much of the literature on WTL outcomes, though, has used a more specific measurement of learning, specifically *learning achievement*, defined as and measured by recall of course content.

What is known about WTL experiences in relation to learning achievement is that WTL has produced modest but positive effects (Bangert-Drowns, Hurley, & Wilkinson, 2004). Short in-class WTL experiences have had greater effects than longer experiences, feedback on WTL assignments has generated no visible impact, and metacognitive WTL tasks have been more effective than personal writing (Bangert-Drowns et al., 2004). In exploring cognitive processes involved in WTL activities, Arnold et al. (2017) found that essay-like responses measuring recall of content led to better achievement, suggesting, as did Newell (1984), that WTL may be most effective when it leads to elaboration upon and reorganization of material. Nevid, Ambrose, and Pyun (2017) found that brief higher-order WTL assignments, defined as assignments "in which students needed to apply [a] particular concept to an example or to use the concept to analyze a process or mechanism" versus assignments that asked only for definitions or descriptions, were most impactful (p. 2). In their study of calculus students in a challenging R1 setting, Doe, Pilgrim, and Gehrtz (2016) found that students in a traditional lecture class were outperformed by students in a class where lecture time was reduced to make room for mainly writing and discussion, with the writing-class group doing better both on conceptual understanding and mathematical procedural knowledge. Finally, Gingerich et al. (2014) found that the effects of writing about course content was significantly greater than the effects of copying lecture slides in class, and recall of course content was still greater eight weeks after the WTL intervention.

Generally, then, writing as an activity and WTL in particular have been established as beneficial for learning achievement, yet a topic that remains less investigated in WTL literature is how students evaluate these experiences and how those evaluative judgments may relate to exposure to and adoption of WTL activities. Steffens (1991) argued for using WTL journaling in large history lecture classes and provided student reflections on the WTL experience, which showed students reporting that writing forced engagement with content and was useful for learning. In a paper that looked at learning achievement and student perceptions, Schurle (1991) found that, although writing substituting for homework did not help students outperform another group of students on college math tests, students perceived that writing enhanced their conceptual understanding of the material. Elder and Champine (2016) recently enhanced our understanding further of how college students understand WTL experiences: They reported that mathematics students judged problem-solving writing, or "writing to clarify student's thinking," as more useful for learning new content than narrative-mode writing (Conclusion section, para. 1). In the present study, I have aimed to add to WTL literature on students' evaluative judgments of WTL experiences in STEM (science, technology, engineering, mathematics) majors by measuring the degree to which STEM students' exposure to and evaluative judgments of WTL activity use in their STEM major were associated with voluntary use of those activities. While WAC/WID researchers have long emphasized the need to focus on observable learning outcomes rather than student or faculty perceptions of learning (Ochsner & Fowler, 2004), this study follows in the footsteps of researchers who have looked at how student writers' dispositions and writing-experience evaluations may be made manifest in self-directed learning behavior, such as strategy adoption and use, that may signal development and writing skill and knowledge transfer (Baird & Dilger, 2017; Driscoll, 2011; Driscoll & Powell, 2016; Driscoll & Wells, 2012).

This study also aims to contribute to STEM-specific writing-complemented learning. As a recent special issue linking WAC and writing in the disciplines (WID) to high-impact educational practices (HIPs) in the journal *Across the Disciplines* reaffirms (Boquet & Lerner, 2016), since its start in the 1970s, **WAC/WID has always been about helping students navigate and become members of disciplinary communities that have their own specialized literacy practices** (Russell, 2002). In STEM fields, specialized literacy practices have been described as involving informative-genre writing, for instance through lab reports on science experiments. **Described elsewhere** as a HIP (Kuh, 2008), a uniquely effective way to engage STEM students in STEM-community academic practices has been course-based research experiences (Hanauer & Bauerle, 2012; Hanauer, Graham, & Hatfull, 2016; Hanauer, Hatfull, & Jacobs-Sera, 2009; Hanauer et al., 2006). Undergraduate research experiences generally have been linked to STEM-student persistence (Gardner & Willey, 2016; Goonewardene, Offutt, Whitling, & Woodhouse, 2016; Jones, Barlow, & Villarejo, 2010; Schultz et al., 2011) and intent to become research scientists (Hanauer et al., 2016). Mainly, the educational experiences described above may be said to fall on the learning-to-write (LTW) or WID end of McLeod's (1992/2000) WAC-approach continuum. This WID focus may reflect what Reynolds, Thaiss, Katkin, and Thompson (2012) referred to as a relative neglect of WTL in STEM programs. Yet, linking a signature pedagogical feature of WAC/WID, namely WTL activities, to how students evaluate and use activities in their own, self-directed learning (Zimmerman, 1989, 2002) could provide a powerful additional argument for the value of WAC/WID in higher education. After all, students' perceptions of what they are doing in their courses and programs matter. In his evidence-based theory of college student persistence, for instance, Tinto (2015) has noted that students' perceptions that their curriculum provides relevant and meaningful learning experiences impact students' motivations to stay in college.

In my emphasis on WTL, I should note here that I do not wish to advance a theoretical distinction between WTL and LTW. WAC/WID practitioners and researchers have long advocated integrated perspectives that consider the implications of composition research broadly speaking without focusing through the lens of exclusively WTL or LTW (Melzer, 2014; Thaiss, 2001). In my reference to McLeod's (1992/2000) traditional WAC-approach continuum, I wish to highlight the interconnected nature of writing in college in general, and my focus in this study on WTL is meant to narrow the scope of my analysis to specific in-class writing activities meant to assist STEM students in engaging with course content. While LTW places emphasis on learning as well as on socialization into disciplinary communities (Carter, Ferzli, & Wiebe, 2007), my aim here is to shed light on activities that may take place in class, reserving, then, genres such as lab reports and persuasive/informative genres for future research.

To guide inquiry, I posed the following research questions:

1. To what writing-to-learn activities do STEM majors report being exposed?
2. What writing-to-learn activities do STEM majors report using?
3. How do STEM majors' exposure to and evaluations of writing-to-learn activities in their STEM majors relate to use of those activities?

Method

Study Design and Hypotheses

The purpose of this study was to measure the relationships among STEM students' exposure to, evaluations of, and use of WTL activities. A quantitative design using inferential difference and association tests was used. To explore whether evaluation of WTL activities differed depending on degree of exposure and use, participants were categorized into two groups for Mann-Whitney U testing of difference: those who reported being exposed to and using three or more WTL activities, and those who reported being exposed to and using fewer than three. To further explore whether greater exposure and evaluation were associated with greater use of WTL activities in STEM classes, Spearman's rho tests were used.

Hypotheses for this study can be stated as follows:

- *Hypothesis*: Students with greater exposure to and higher evaluations of WTL activities will use more WTL activities than students with less exposure and lower evaluations.
- *Null Hypothesis*: There will be no difference in evaluative judgments of WTL activities among students based on degree of exposure and use of WTL activities.

Participants

Participants were invited to participate in two ways: a web-based survey (via Qualtrics) that was emailed to STEM majors with the help of professors in students' departments and hard-copy versions of the survey distributed and collected in the opening minutes of first-year mathematics sections for STEM majors. Students were invited to pass the survey on to a STEM-major peer. Participation in this study was voluntary and anonymous, and it was carried out under supervision of the research site's institutional review board.

Table 1 details characteristics of participants who took the survey ($N = 134$).

Table 1

Participants' Characteristics

Category	Characteristic	Number
STEM Major	Anthropology	1
	Biochemistry	8
	Biology (Molecular)	27
	Chemistry	7
	Chemical Engineering	1
	Computer Science	28
	Engineering	1
	Geography	2
	Geoscience	11
	Health Science	1
	Mathematics	29
	Natural Science	9
	Physics	6
	Psychology	1
	Wildlife Science	1
Location	Midwestern/Great Plains	6
	Southern	12
	Western	9
	Eastern	107
Level of Education	Graduate	24
	Undergraduate	110
Self-Identified Gender	Female	59
	Male	72
	Preferred Not to Answer	3
Age	18-25	115
	26-35	18
	36-45	1

Instruments

The survey (Appendix A) followed items from Schmidt's (2004) writing-to-learn attitude survey (WTLAS). WTL activities included in items in the WTLAS are (a) in-class impromptu focused writing; (b) brainstorming, freewriting, or listing ideas before writing; (c) brief summaries or microthemes about points in reading assignments; (d) peer-critiquing of a classmate's writing; (e) personal-experience writing to see connections between content and a student's life; and (f) journaling (Schmidt, 2004, p. 462).

Data Analysis

After checking of core assumptions of the survey data, a Shapiro-Wilk test ($p < .05$) indicated data was not normally distributed. Nonparametric Spearman's rho association and nonparametric Mann-Whitney U difference tests were then chosen as most appropriate. In addition, the result of Cronbach's Alpha to test internal reliability of the *evaluation of writing to learn activities in STEM majors scale* ($\alpha = .80$) was within an acceptable range (Nunnally, 1967) to create a composite variable also used in the analysis.

Results

To What Writing-to-Learn Activities Do STEM Majors Report Being Exposed?

The median for WTL exposure was 3, with a minimum of 0 and maximum of 7. While more than half of all participants reported being exposed to three or more of these WTL activities (69/134, [51.5%]), fewer than half reported being exposed to fewer than three (65/134, [48.5%]). Only two participants reported never being exposed to a WTL activity. Of those who did report exposure, a majority reported being exposed to pre-writing (88/134, [66%]) and summarizing (85/134, [63%]). Fewer than half reported being exposed to peer-critiquing (60/134, [45%]) and in-class impromptu writing (53/134, [40%]). Some reported being exposed to reflective writing (39/134, [29%]), personal writing (36/134, [27%]), and journaling (34/134, [25%]).

What Writing-to-Learn Activities Do STEM Majors Report Using?

The median for WTL use was 3, with a minimum of 0 and maximum of 7. While more than half of all participants reported using three or more WTL activities (68/134, [50.7%]), fewer than half reported using fewer than three (66/134, [49.3%]). Only one participant reported not using at least one WTL activity. A majority reported using pre-writing (102/134, [76%]). More than half reported using summarizing (77/134, [58%]). Some reported using reflective writing (43/134, [32%]); peer-critiquing (40/134, [30%]); personal writing (37/134, [28%]); in-class impromptu writing (36/134, [27%]); and journaling (30/134, [22%]). Aside from these, one student indicated using creative writing, one indicated using poetry, and one indicated using proof writing as alternative WTL activities.

How Do STEM Majors' Exposure to and Evaluations of Writing-to-Learn Activities in Their STEM Majors Relate to Use of Those Activities?

In evaluating the usefulness of WTL activities in STEM courses, participants reported a composite mean of 3.85 on a 5-point Likert scale, indicating they mainly understood WTL activities as supporting their learning in STEM classes. See Table 2.

Table 2

Means and Standard Deviations for Exposure, Evaluation, and Use of WTL Activities

Item	M	Mdn	SD
WTL Exposure	2.99	3.00	1.90
WTL Evaluation	3.85	3.86	0.67
WTL Use	2.80	3.00	1.55

In measuring the relationship among these variables, Spearman's rank correlation coefficient (Spearman's rho) test of association indicated that there was a statistically significant positive relationship between exposure to WTL activities and use of WTL activities, $r_s = .26, p = .003$, as well as between evaluation of WTL activities and use of WTL activities, $r_s = .40, p < .001$. These relationships can be described respectively as weak and moderate (Cohen, 1988). Finally, there was no statistically significant relationship between exposure and evaluation. Ultimately, the greater students' reported exposure to and evaluation of WTL activities, the greater their likelihood was of using them.

After the checking of core assumptions, nonparametric Mann-Whitney U tests were run to check for differences between participants who reported being exposed to three or more WTL activities ($n = 69$) and those who reported being exposed to fewer than three ($n = 65$).

Table 3

Means and Standard Deviations for Evaluations of Usefulness of WTL Activities by Exposure

Item	M ≥3/<3		SD ≥3/<3	
Summarizing	4.23	3.94	.75	.93
Pre-writing*	4.16	3.85	.90	.91
Peer-reviewing*	4.16	3.72	.92	1.13
Personal-experience writing*	3.84	3.42	.99	1.13
Impromptu in-class writing	3.81	3.68	.91	.90
Journaling	3.52	3.29	1.13	1.14
Composite (α = .80)*	3.99	3.70	.59	.71

Note. *$p < .05$. **$p < .01$. ***$p < .001$. Differences significant at the $p < .05$ level. A five-point Likert scale was used: 1 = strongly disagree, 2 = disagree, 3 = neither agree nor disagree, 4 = agree, 5 = strongly agree.

As reflected in Table 3, results showed that positive evaluation of WTL activities overall was significantly greater for students exposed to three or more WTL activities ($Mdn = 4$) than for students exposed to fewer than three ($Mdn = 3.86$), $U = 1674.50$, $p = .011$. In addition, when students were exposed to three or more WTL activities, they also reported significantly more positive evaluations of the following: pre-writing ($Mdn = 4$, $Mdn = 4$, $U = 2009.50$, $p = .021$); peer-reviewing ($Mdn = 4$, $Mdn = 4$, $U = 1723.50$, $p = .014$); and personal-experience writing ($Mdn = 4$, $Mdn = 4$, $U = 1764$, $p = .024$).

Table 4 below presents evaluations of WTL activities based on reported use. After the checking of core assumptions, nonparametric Mann-Whitney U tests were run to check for differences in how participants evaluated WTL activities in STEM classes between participants who reported using three or more WTL activities ($n = 68$) and those who reported using fewer than three ($n = 66$).

Table 4

Means and Standard Deviations for Evaluations of Usefulness of WTL Activities by Use

Item	M ≥3/<3		SD ≥3/<3	
Summarizing**	4.31	3.86	.74	.91
Pre-writing**	4.28	3.73	.69	1.03
Peer-reviewing*	4.16	3.73	.94	1.10
Impromptu in-class writing*	3.93	3.56	.76	1.01
Personal-experience**	3.93	3.33	.97	1.11
Journaling***	3.75	3.06	1.08	1.09
Composite (α = .80)***	4.09	3.59	.49	.73

Note. *$p < .05$. **$p < .01$. ***$p < .001$. Differences significant at the $p < .05$ level. A five-point Likert scale was used: 1 = strongly disagree, 2 = disagree, 3 = neither agree nor disagree, 4 = agree, 5 = strongly agree.

Results showed that positive evaluation of WTL activities overall was greater for students using three or more WTL activities ($Mdn = 4.14$) than for students using fewer than three ($Mdn = 3.86$), $U = 1312.50$, $p < .001$. In addition, when students used three or more WTL activities, they also reported significantly more positive evaluations of the following: impromptu in-class writing ($Mdn = 4$, $Mdn = 4$, $U = 1805$, $p = .035$);

pre-writing ($Mdn = 4$, $Mdn = 4$, $U = 1561.50$, $p = .001$); summarizing ($Mdn = 4$, $Mdn = 4$, $U = 1627$, $p = .003$); peer-reviewing ($Mdn = 4$, $Mdn = 4$, $U = 1715$, $p = .012$); personal writing ($Mdn = 4$, $Mdn = 4$, $U = 1562.50$, $p = .001$); and, journaling ($Mdn = 4$, $Mdn = 3$, $U = 1485.50$, $p < .001$).

Results, then, establish that greater exposure to and evaluation of WTL activities were systematically associated with greater use of WTL activities in this sample of STEM students. It was also the case that no meaningful differences were found as a result of subgroup analysis that compared participants by major, location, level of education, gender, or age.

Discussion

This study explored the degree to which STEM students' exposure to and evaluations of WTL activity use in their STEM majors were associated with reported use of those activities. Because WTL theory and prior research have established that WTL generally if modestly supports learning, I hypothesized that students with greater exposure to and more positive evaluations of WTL activities would report using more of those activities. Data analysis led to rejection of the null hypothesis, which stated that no statistically significant difference or association would be found, and to three main findings: (a) STEM majors in this sample reported being exposed to and using a range of WTL activities, with more than half reporting using three or more activities to learn STEM-course content, and, as reported exposure went up, so too did reported use, suggesting that greater exposure is associated with greater use; (b) STEM majors here positively evaluated WTL activities; and (c) STEM majors who were exposed to a greater number of WTL activities and who more positively evaluated those activities also reported using more of them.

In her recent book on the literacy narratives of scientists, Emerson (2016) noted that scientists she interviewed reported having undergraduate experiences mainly "devoid of authentic opportunities to engage as writers of science" (p. 202). Emerson suggests that we question whether WAC programs are adequately reaching undergraduate programs "and whether they are designed to meet the needs of our science students" (p. 202). The findings here, however, hint that WAC's reach may have the capacity to extend into the way students manage their own learning through WTL activities, even if further work may be required to explore whether undergraduate programs provide authentic WID experiences.

The findings reported here also potentially reflect a problematic issue regarding trends in higher education to assign informative genres or modes of writing while neglecting personal, expressive, or poetic writing experiences (Melzer, 2014). Participants in this study reported being exposed to and using mainly pre-writing and summarizing while only about 30% reported being exposed to and using reflective writing, personal-experience writing, and journaling. The story may be more complicated when looking at STEM majors, of course, because signature genres such as the chemistry lab report, while essentially informative genres, may be designed to communicate with specific scholarly communities and mimic genre moves reinforced in published reports, suggesting something different from more teacher-student, transactional writing to inform. Still, the results here showing STEM students' relative lack of reported exposure to and use of more reflective, expressive WTL activities should motivate WAC practitioners to continue our work of emphasizing the value of such writing for writers.

Additionally, that STEM majors in this sample positively evaluated WTL activities further supports research on students' perceptions that writing has face validity when presented or used as a way of learning (Elder & Champine, 2016; Schurle, 1991; Steffens, 1991). Summarizing and pre-writing were reportedly especially valued WTL activities. Though the survey instrument used here was not sensitive enough to shed light on how summarizing or pre-writing were specifically used, it may be that these activities encouraged the kinds of elaboration and reorganization of course material that WTL researchers have long identified as especially impactful for content recall and learning achievement (Arnold et al., 2017; Bangert-Drowns et al., 2004; Newell, 1984). Not only does WTL enhance coverage of class content, an important issue for STEM professors who may have varying definitions of what coverage means for them (Scheurer, 2015), but also students believe in WTL. And perceptions matter. In his evidence-based theory of college student persistence, Tinto (2015) has noted that students' perceptions that their curriculum provides relevant and meaningful learning experiences impact students' motivations to stay in college.

The systematic differences measured here between those participants who used many and those who used few WTL activities are also striking. If this result reflects that students use more WTL activities because they find that those activities help them succeed in their specific departmental and disciplinary communities, this finding may reflect and add to knowledge derived from Bangert-Drowns et al. (2004), who concluded that longer-lasting WTL interventions had more significant effects on learning achievement than shorter ones. Along with longer sequences of WTL experiences, wider exposure to a variety of activities seems to be useful as well.

Limitations and Directions for Future Research

The findings above must be considered in light of the study's limitations. This study sampled from STEM students from different majors. STEM majors' writing experiences would be expected to differ by department and discipline; as Melzer (2014) has argued, each class that students encounter, even within a department or discipline, may be said to constitute a unique discourse community (Swales, 1990, 2017) students are charged with understanding and navigating. More work is needed to determine the experiences of students in particular departments and similar STEM majors. Another limitation concerns the sensitivity of a survey instrument, which necessarily limits participants' chances to elaborate or add nuance. It is important to note, too, that participants in this study self-reported strategy exposure and use, making it possible that students who remembered their strategy exposure and use most explicitly were the ones who were able to recall the potential efficacy or appearance of efficacy of those strategies. Of importance here, then, is an understanding of the value of explicit instruction and discussion of WTL usage in STEM settings. The goal may be to nurture the kind of students Driscoll (2011) referred to as those "explicitly connected students" who can explain how previous writing instruction transfers to future disciplinary writing situations (Student Attitudes About Future Writing section, para. 10). Finally, an argument can be made for other ways of defining WTL activities and experiences, and therefore of measuring variables in relation to WTL exposure and use. My use of items from a previously validated survey captured general activities and experiences but not specific genres written in class, such as those that have long been discussed in WTL and WAC literature in general (Fulwiler & Young, 1982; Young, 1984/2011).

Future research might explore individual voices of students through qualitative designs, such as case-study or phenomenology research, to nuance big-picture patterns established here. A fuller understanding of WTL activities would be helpful. Preliminary results of my academic life narrative research into STEM majors indicate that reflective, autobiographical writing has potential to nurture STEM students' performances of disciplinary identities and work in service of institutional priorities, specifically student engagement and retention (Nicholes, 2018). Additional research might explore how WTL activities support deep engagement with course material as well as in-class identity work that may support students' reflections of themselves as members of disciplinary communities. Further research seems to be called for to illuminate the practices of departments and programs of different STEM majors to see what may be prized, supported, and reinforced regarding in-class and disciplinary literacy experiences. Exciting work on understanding how departments understand threshold concepts that define their disciplinary, more WID-related writing has been reported by Wardle, Updike, and Glotfelter (2018). Regarding directions for WTL-related writing research, I have found it fitting (Nicholes, in press) to draw on the work of science educators and theorists such as Hadzigeorgiou (2016), who has emphasized the central role of imagination in science education. The wonder especially younger students feel for science, for instance, has been described as a mediating variable or even prerequisite for conceptual understanding (Hadzigeorgiou & Fotinos, 2007).

WTL activities that prompt this kind of imaginative writing related to science, such as science fiction prototyping (Atherton, 2016; De Lepe, Olmstead, Russell, Cazarez, & Austin, 2015; Draudt et al., 2015), could complement more LTW, disciplinary writing that has been credited with prompting socialization into disciplinary communities (Carter et al., 2007).

Overall, though more sensitive qualitative designs are needed to understand participants' reasons for using WTL, such as case-study or phenomenological designs that look to understand how students define and understand the experience of WTL, the present study establishes patterns between WTL exposure, evaluation, and use in one sample of STEM students, offering direction for future research and WAC practice.

References

Anderson, P., Anson, C. M., Gonyea, R. M., & Paine, C. (2015). The contributions of writing to learning and development: Results from a large-scale multi-dimensionality study. *Research in the Teaching of English, 50*(2), 199–235.

Anderson, P., Anson, C. M., Gonyea, R. M., & Paine, C. (2016). How to create high-impact writing assignments that enhance learning and development and reinvigorate WAC/WID programs: What almost 72,000 undergraduates taught us. *Across the Disciplines: A Journal of Language, Learning, and Academic Writing, 13*. Retrieved from http://wac.colostate.edu/atd/hip/andersonetal2016.cfm

Arnold, K. M., Umanath, S., Thio, K., Reilly, W. B., McDaniel, M. A., & Marsh, E. J. (2017). Understanding the cognitive processes involved in writing to learn. *Journal of Experimental Psychology: Applied, 23*(2), 115–27. doi:10.1037/xap0000119

Arum, R., & Roksa, J. (2011). *Academically adrift: Limited learning on college campuses.* Chicago, IL: University of Chicago Press.

Astin, A. W. (1992). What really matters in general education: Provocative findings from a national survey of student outcomes. *Perspectives, 22*, 23–46.

Atherton, E. (2016). Science fiction prototyping at work. *Computer, 49*(8), 109–111. doi:10.1109/MC.2016.229

Baird, N., & Dilger, B. (2017). How students perceive transitions: Dispositions and transfer in internships. *College Composition and Communication, 68*(4), 684–712.

Bangert-Drowns, R. L., Hurley, M. M., & Wilkinson, B. (2004). The effects of school-based writing-to-learn interventions on academic achievement: A meta-analysis. *Review of Educational Research, 74*(1), 29–58.

Boquet, B., & Lerner, N. (2016). Introduction to the ATD special issue on WAC and high-impact practices. *Across the Disciplines: A Journal of Language, Learning, and Academic Writing, 13*. Retrieved from http://wac.colostate.edu/atd/hip/intro.cfm

Carter, M., Ferzli, M., & Wiebe, E. N. (2007). Writing to learn by learning to write in the disciplines. *Journal of Business and Technical Communication, 21*(3), 278–302.

Cohen, J. (1988). *Statistical power analysis for the behavioral sciences* (2nd ed.). Hillsdale, NJ: Lawrence Erlbaum.

De Lepe, M., Olmstead, W., Russell, C., Cazarez, L., & Austin, L. (2015). Using science fiction prototyping to decrease the decline of interest in STEM topics at the high school level. In D. Preuveneers (Ed.), *Workshop proceedings of the 11th International Conference on Intelligent Environments*, 1–11. Amsterdam, Netherlands: IOS Press.

Doe, S., Pilgrim, M. E., & Gehrtz, J. (2016). Stories and explanations in the introductory calculus classroom: A study of WTL as a teaching and learning intervention. *The WAC Journal, 27,* 94–118.

Draudt, A., Hadley, J., Hogan, R., Murray, L., Stock, G., & West, J. R. (2015). Six insights about science fiction prototyping. *Computer, 48*(5), 69–71.

Driscoll, D. L. (2011). Connected, disconnected, or uncertain: Student attitudes about future writing contexts and perceptions of transfer from first year writing to the disciplines. *Across the Disciplines: A Journal of Language, Learning, and Academic Writing, 8*(2). Retrieved from http://wac.colostate.edu/atd/articles/driscoll2011/index.cfm

Driscoll, D. L., & Powell, R. (2016). States, traits, and dispositions: The impact of emotion on writing development and writing transfer across college courses and beyond. *Composition Forum, 34.* Retrieved from http://compositionforum.com/issue/34/.

Driscoll, D. L., & Wells, J. (2012). Beyond knowledge and skills: Writing transfer and the role of student dispositions. *Composition Forum, 26.* Retrieved from http://compositionforum.com/issue/26/beyond-knowledge-skills.php

Elder, C. L., & Champine, K. (2016). Designing high-impact "writing-to-learn" math assignments for killer courses. *Across the Disciplines: A Journal of Language, Learning, and Academic Writing, 13.* Retrieved from http://wac.colostate.edu/atd/hip/elder_champine2016.cfm

Emerson, L. (2016). *The forgotten tribe: Scientists as writers.* Fort Collins, CO: The WAC Clearinghouse.

Emig, J. (1977). Writing as a mode of learning. *College Composition and Communication, 28*(2), 122–28.

Estrem, H. (2015). Writing is a knowledge-making activity. In L. Adler-Kassner & E. Wardle (Eds.), *Naming what we know: Threshold concepts in writing studies* (pp. 19). Logan: Utah State University Press.

Fulwiler, T. (1982). The personal connection: Journal writing across the curriculum. In T. Fulwiler & A. Young (Eds.), *Language connections: Writing and reading across the curriculum* (pp. 15–32). Urbana, IL: National Council of Teachers of English.

Fulwiler, T., & Young, A. (Eds.). (1982). *Language connections: Writing and reading across the curriculum.* Urbana, IL: National Council of Teachers of English.

Gardner, A., & Willey, K. (2016). Academic identity reconstruction: The transition of engineering academics to engineering education researchers. *Studies in Higher Education, 43*(2), 234–50. doi:10.1080/03075079.2016.1162779

Gingerich, K. J., Bugg, J. M., Doe, S. R., Rowland, C. A., Richards, T. L., Tompkins, S. A., & McDaniel, M. A. (2014). Active processing via write-to-learn assignment: Learning and retention benefits in introductory psychology. *Teaching of Psychology, 41*(4), 303–08. doi:10.1177/0098628314549701

Goonewardene, A. U., Offutt, C. A., Whitling, J., & Woodhouse, D. (2016). An interdisciplinary approach to success for underrepresented students in STEM. *Journal of College Science Teaching, 45*(4), 59–67.

Hadzigeorgiou, Y. (2016). *Imaginative science education: The central role of imagination in science education.* Cham, Switzerland: Springer.

Hadzigeorgiou, Y., & Fotinos, N. (2007). Imaginative thinking and the learning of science. *The Science Education Review, 6*(1), 15–23.

Hanauer, D. I., & Bauerle, C. (2012). Facilitating innovation in science education through assessment reform. *Liberal Education, 98*(3), 34–41.

Hanauer, D. I., Graham, M. J., & Hatfull, G. F. (2016). A measure of college student persistence in the sciences (PITS). *CBE-Life Sciences Education, 15*(4), 1–10.

Hanauer, D. I., Hatfull, G. F., & Jacobs-Sera, D. (2009). *Active assessment: Assessing scientific inquiry.* New York, NY: Springer.

Hanauer, D. I., Jacobs-Sera, D., Pedulla, M. L., Cresawn, S. G., Hendrix, R. W., & Hatfull, G. F. (2006). Teaching scientific inquiry. *Science, 314*, 1880–1881.

Jones, M. T., Barlow, A. L., & Villarejo, M. (2010). Importance of undergraduate research for minority persistence and achievement in Biology. *Journal of Higher Education, 81*(1), 82–115.

Kuh, G. D. (2008). *High-impact educational practices: What they are, who has access to them, and why they matter.* Washington, DC: Association of American Colleges and Universities.

Light, R. J. (2001). *Making the most of college: Students speak their minds.* Cambridge, MA: Harvard University Press.

McLeod, S. H. (1992/2000). Writing across the curriculum: An introduction. In S. H. McLeod & M. Soven (Eds.), *Writing across the curriculum: A guide to developing programs* (pp. 1–8). Fort Collins, CO: The WAC Clearinghouse.

Melzer, D. (2014). *Assignments across the curriculum: A national study of college writing.* Logan: Utah State University.

Nevid, J. S., Ambrose, M. A., & Pyun, Y. S. (2017). Effects of higher and lower level writing-to-learn assignments on higher and lower level examination questions. *Teaching of Psychology*, 1–6. doi:10.1177/0098628317727645

Newell, G. E. (1984). Learning from writing in two content areas: A case study/protocol analysis. *Research in the Teaching of English, 18*(3), 265.

Nicholes, J. (in press). Developing STEM interest and genre knowledge through science fiction prototyping. *The STEAM Journal*.

Nicholes, J. (2018). *Exploring how chemistry and English majors understand and construct disciplinary identities in relation to life, departmental, and writing experiences: Implications for WAC and retention*. (Doctoral dissertation). Retrieved from ProQuest.

Nunnally, J. C. (1967). *Psychometric theory*. New York, NY: McGraw-Hill.

Ochsner, R., & Fowler, J. (2004). Playing devil's advocate: Evaluating the literature of the WAC/WID movement. *Review of Educational Research, 74*(2), 117–40. doi:10.3102/00346543074002117

Reynolds, J. A., Thaiss, C., Katkin, W., & Thompson, J., Robert J. (2012). Writing-to-learn in undergraduate science education: A community-based, conceptually driven approach. *CBE-Life Sciences Education, 11*(1), 17–25. doi:10.1187/cbe.11-08-0064

Russell, D. R. (2002). *Writing in the academic disciplines: A curricular history* (2nd ed.). Carbondale: Southern Illinois University Press.

Scheurer, E. (2015). What do WAC directors need to know about "coverage"? *The WAC Journal, 26*, 7–21.

Schmidt, L. A. (2004). Psychometric evaluation of the Writing-To-Learn Attitude Survey. *Journal of Nursing Education, 43*(10), 458–65.

Schultz, P. W., Hernandez, P. R., Woodcock, A., Estrada, M., Chance, R. C., Aguilar, M., & Serpe, R. T. (2011). Patching the pipeline: Reducing educational disparities in the sciences through minority training programs. *Educational Evaluation and Policy Analysis, 33*(1), 95–114. doi:10.3102/0162373710392371

Schurle, A. W. (1991). Does writing help students learn about differential equations? *PRIMUS: Problems, Resources, and Issues in Mathematics Undergraduate Studies, 1*(2), 129–36.

Steffens, H. (1991). Using informal writing in large history classes: Helping students to find interest and meaning in history. *Social Studies, 82*(3), 55–58.

Swales, J. M. (1990). *Genre analysis: English in academic and research settings*. Cambridge, MA: Cambridge University Press.

Swales, J. M. (2017). The concept of discourse community: Some recent personal history. *Composition Forum, 37*. Retrieved from http://www.compositionforum.com/issue/37/swales-retrospective.php

Thaiss, C. (2001). Theory in WAC: Where have we been, and where are we going? In S. H. McLeod, E. Miraglia, M. Soven, & C. Thaiss (Eds.), *WAC for the new millenium: Strategies for continuing writing-across-the-curriculum programs* (pp. 299–325). National Council of Teachers of English: Urbana, IL.

Tinto, V. (2015). Through the eyes of students. *Journal of College Student Retention: Research, Theory, and Practice, 19*(3), 254–69. doi:10.1177/1521025115621917

Wardle, E., Updike, A., & Glotfelter, A. (2018). Using Threshold Concepts and Disciplinary Teams as the Backbone of WAC Seminars, IWAC 2018, Auburn University, Auburn, AL.

Young, R. E. (1984/2011). *Toward a taxonomy of "small" genres and writing techniques for use in writing across the curriculum.* Fort Collins, CO: The WAC Clearinghouse.

Zimmerman, B. J. (1989). A social cognitive view of self-regulated academic learning. *Journal of Educational Psychology, 81*(3), 329–39. doi:10.1037/0022-0663.81.3.329

Zimmerman, B. J. (2002). Becoming a self-regulated learner: An overview. *Theory Into Practice, 41*(2), 64–70. doi:10.1207/s15430421tip4102_2

Appendix A: Writing-to-Learn Evaluation Survey

1. In what department or program are you studying?

    ☐ Biochemistry
    ☐ Biology
    ☐ Chemistry
    ☐ Computer Science
    ☐ Geoscience
    ☐ Mathematics
    ☐ Physics
    Another _____

2. At what level are you studying?

    ☐ PhD
    ☐ Master's
    ☐ Bachelor's
    ☐ Associate's
    Another _____

3. With what gender do you most identify?

    ☐ Male
    ☐ Female
    ☐ Another _____
    ☐ Prefer not to answer

4. How old are you?

    ☐ 18-25
    ☐ 26-35
    ☐ 36-45
    ☐ 46-55
    ☐ 56-above
    ☐ Prefer not to answer

5. Please rate the degree to which you agree with the following statements.

	Strongly Disagree	Disagree	Neither agree nor disagree	Agree	Strongly Agree
Impromptu focused writing during class in my major can help me solve problems or clarify concepts.	☐	☐	☐	☐	☐

	Strongly Disagree	Disagree	Neither agree nor disagree	Agree	Strongly Agree
Brainstorming, freewriting, or listing ideas before writing about topics related to my major can help me find out what I know and think about topics related to my major.	☐	☐	☐	☐	☐
Writing brief summaries can make me aware of the most important points in classes related to my major.	☐	☐	☐	☐	☐
Critiquing a classmate's writing for conceptual clarity can result in increased understanding of topics related to my major for both of us.	☐	☐	☐	☐	☐
Writing personal experience pieces can make me see connections between what I am learning in classes related to my major and my own life.	☐	☐	☐	☐	☐
Journal writing [journaling] can enhance my understanding of concepts and course materials related to my major.	☐	☐	v	☐	☐

6. Please mark which ways you use writing to help yourself learn.
- ☐ impromptu focused writing in class
- ☐ brainstorming, freewriting, or listing ideas
- ☐ writing brief summaries about readings
- ☐ critiquing a classmate's writing for conceptual clarity
- ☐ writing about personal experiences
- ☐ journal writing [journaling]
- ☐ reflective writing
- ☐ Another _____

7. Which, if any, of these activities have you been exposed to in classes in or related to your major?
- ☐ impromptu focused writing in class
- ☐ brainstorming, freewriting, or listing ideas
- ☐ writing brief summaries about readings
- ☐ critiquing a classmate's writing for conceptual clarity
- ☐ writing about personal experiences
- ☐ journal writing [journaling]
- ☐ reflective writing
- ☐ Another _____

Preparing Writing Studies Graduate Students within Authentic WAC-Contexts: A Research Methods Course and WAC Program Review Crossover Project as a Critical Site of Situated Learning

MICHELLE LAFRANCE AND ALISA RUSSELL

> What is important in the professional worlds we inhabit, and what new directions might curriculum development facilitate to better prepare students?
>
> —Joan Mullen

As we were composing this essay, the conveners of the Writing Across the Curriculum Graduate Organization (WAC-GO) released the results of their spring 2017 survey, which sought to capture the primary experiences, needs, and concerns of their fledgling membership. "What challenges do you face as a graduate student interested in and/or involved in WAC/WID work?" this survey asked. Just over half of the respondents (11 of 20) noted that their graduate program does not offer coursework on WAC/WID scholarship or administration. Additionally, 9 of 20 responded that they did not know "how to find or cultivate mentoring relationships in WAC/WID work" (WAC-GO, 2017). Despite this survey's limited sample size (a reflection of WAC-GO's early-stage membership), we believe these findings highlight a crucial, but little held, conversation in WAC/WID scholarship and research. In what ways are we preparing future writing studies leaders within authentic WAC-related contexts? And how might these authentic WAC-related contexts prepare future writing studies leaders to carry out their varied work?

As WAC professionals, we know the benefits of exposing students across educational levels to the highly situated contexts of writing outside of English. In fact, the field of WAC/WID has itself rested on the foundational assumption that it is difficult to understand the divergent ideals held about writing *writ large* without experiencing those differing (and occasionally competing) values, vocabularies, and practices first hand. Despite several decades of recognition in writing studies research that writing is a highly situated and rhetorical practice that is shaped relationally within communities of practice, graduate-level training in pedagogy, research methods, and the rhetorical theories of writing still largely take place within the comfortable confines of programs that are firmly embedded within English departments. And, many of these locations still largely traffic in generalist notions of writing. To introduce PhD students to the actualities of cross-curricular writing contexts—emphasizing an understanding of writers, writing, and writing instruction that characterizes scholarly and programmatic approaches to WAC but is often missing from studies of rhetoric, composition, and writing program administration—Michelle designed a crossover project that coupled a required PhD-level research methods course and an ongoing program review in a long-standing WAC program at George Mason University.[1]

This collaboration between the PhD research methods course and a WAC program found its footing by what television personality Bob Ross would call "a happy accident": under new directorship, the Mason WAC program[2] had undertaken a multi-year process of writing-intensive (WI) course review to examine the ways these courses were carrying out the criteria established by the Faculty Senate's WAC Committee. We named this effort the RE/View Project (RE/V). Here, Michelle faced a dilemma not uncommon to the directors of large, decentralized programs: with 86 WI courses in majors across colleges and no fewer than 125 faculty across ranks, the size and variety of the program posed a challenge for conducting comprehensive research of the WI courses. The PhD research methods course, English 702: Research Methods in Writing and Rhetoric, offered a pragmatic and dynamic opportunity. Inviting the nine PhD students enrolled in the course as full collaborators into the RE/V project meant we could extend the reach of the WAC program staff. The program would have the benefit of fresh energies and insights, as well. To assist with the coordination of the project's multiple pieces, Michelle invited graduate student, co-author Alisa, to support and assist with the design and implementation of this project.[3]

Ultimately, this collaboration revealed the importance of first-hand exposure to WAC research that we believe cannot be replicated by reading WAC scholarship or studying the structures of WAC programs and intitaitves from afar. As we observed, questioned, and interviewed the graduate students in the research methods course, we found that, for most of these students, involvement in the integrated processes of the class resulted in rich, and indeed "real world," learning and professional development experiences. It is one thing to learn from a research article or conversation in a writing studies seminar that writing is a highly situated and flexible response within communities of practice; it is quite another to see first-hand the messiness—and the many slippages between—definitions of writing that occur across faculty interviews, to witness the differences in pedagogical knowledge and application across different institutional and material contexts, to encounter the constraints upon non-English faculty who teach writing, or to observe those faculty surface their otherwise tacit and nuanced expertise as teachers of writing.

In this article, then, we wish to open a conversation about how and why we should support exposure to WAC contexts as a central component of graduate preparation in writing studies. We do so by describing the recursive and overlapping components of our crossover project, analyzing the course projects and reflective writing of students in our PhD seminar, and presenting the results of surveys and interviews with these graduate students. To be sure, our sample size (limited to the 9 students enrolled in the research methods course) and our data-collection activities (geared toward the reflexive learning moments about students' experiences) are too limited for us to be able to claim this crossover course as a definitive model for graduate student learning in WAC. However, the data we uncovered compel us to argue for the benefits of exposure to authentic cross-curricular writing contexts for graduate students in writing studies. We hope our exploration of this crossover project between a research methods course and a WAC program review (as one possible example) will encourage further work by others in the field around WAC-focused research and exposure to authentic contexts for graduate students across writing studies.

Toward the Research Methods Course as a Critical Site of Situated Learning

To open up this conversation, we ground our broad concern for the preparation of graduate students in the work of the research methods course—a location that allows us to situate the possibilities of PhD student training at the interstices of established, if distinct, conversations in the field. Many who teach graduate students in writing studies contexts anecdotally understand the good that comes of integrated (or "real world," if you will) learning. E. Shelley Reid (2004) has argued that our teaching and mentoring strategies for new graduate teaching assistants need to introduce students to the "messiness" of the actual contexts they will encounter; she argues we do this when our TA preparation courses provide a model of "undercoverage," a pedagogy that "emphasizes discoveries that lead to long-term learning over immediate competencies" (p. 16). Reid further argues that exposure to "the various institutional pressures . . . we face [that are] built into the systems in which we teach" (p. 18) provides crucial learning opportunities for those just beginning their professional work. Similarly, Rebecca Rickly (2007) observes that encountering the authentic "messiness" of the research process is particularly important for building resilient research practice. Moreover, for Rickly, producing more savvy researchers in the field requires a bit of a pedagogical sea-change in the required research methods curriculum; we must move away from a rote discussion of methods as "static" or "contained" content, instead turning our pedagogical attentions "to the actual practice of conducting empirical research" in the increasingly complex environment of the twenty-first-century institution (p. 2). Both authors make the case that exposure to authentic—and inherently disorderly—contexts are central to developing the critical capacities new teachers and researchers in the field rely upon. As we thought through how we might use WAC program review activities as the site of a research methods course, we agreed.

Less developed, though, are the professional and scholarly conversations about preparing graduate students for the multifaceted richness of WAC-program work. Some scholarly attention has focused on preparing graduate students to teach first-year composition courses (see, for instance, Estrem and Reid, 2013; Reid, Estrem, and Belcheir, 2012; Pytlik and Ligget, 2002; and Wilhoit, 2002, among others), while a handful of writing program administrators have also argued that explicit attention be paid to preparing graduate students for administrative roles and projects (see Charlton et al., 2011; Elder, Schoen, & Skinnell, 2015; Thomas, 1991; Stolley, 2015; and White, 2002, as some examples). Others, such as Rose and Weiser (1999), have argued that the research know-how of writing program administrators is a central component of effective administrative and intellectual work within a program.

Meanwhile, WAC scholars have tended to turn their research eye toward support for graduate students as writers within disciplinary and/or professional contexts (Casanave and Li, 2008; and Micciche and Carr, 2011; Mullen, 1999; Swales and Feak, 2004, among others) and/or preparing graduate students in the disciplines to teach writing (see, for instance, Rodrigue, 2012; Rodrigue, 2013; Strenski, 1992; and Winzenried, 2016). These arguments, models, and studies complement the numerous resources available in support of general WAC program development and design. Finally, a very small handful of scholars have discussed the design of the graduate research methods class and preparing graduate students to be effective researchers (Blakeslee and Fleischer, 2007; Nickoson and Sheridan, 2012; Rickly, 2007).

As we have little published research about graduate students encountering WAC-contexts, we turn to one study that does emphasize the impact of this exposure. Cripps, Hall, and Robinson's (2016) findings demonstrate that experience working in a WAC context positions graduate students to "operate in the interstices of the university, where they have an opportunity to observe and to learn what goes on behind the scenes"; the "liminality" of this position offers "a much broader picture, through practical experience, of how academia functions" (para. 6). Significantly, the authors argue, the experience affords these graduate students a stronger understanding of writing as a mode of learning. They write:

> We see from our survey and interviews that one of the primary things that [WAC Fellows] take away from the experience is a commitment to incorporating WAC and writing pedagogies into their teaching. [...] Traditional TAships usually remain within the field: a sociology TA teaches sociology, and professional development activities focus directly on teaching sociology. But a [WAC Fellow] whose own field is sociology may work closely with a

faculty member teaching a writing intensive course in biology and develop materials to help tutors work with students from that course. Our respondents tell us that this experience helps them in their own teaching, but the benefit comes in a broader pedagogical understanding of the relationship between writing and learning, rather than specific approaches to a particular subject matter. (para. 15)

Work as a WAC Fellow, in short, leads to an expanded understanding of the institution, its structures, values, and processes—but also to a more sophisticated understanding of writing and writing instruction.

Cripps, Hall, and Robinson's results, then, provide an initial blueprint for the possibilities of work within WAC contexts, especially as these results emphasize personal experiences in cross-curricular-contexts. Turning toward our own crossover project, we believed the review of WI courses would offer the PhD research methods students plenty of grounded and collaborative practice as a site of learning and reflection, but we also believed it was an opportunity for these graduate students to experience what those who do WAC work already know: that our values, sensibilities, vocabularies, teaching practices, and perceptions of student writers are often far more varied, more unpredictable, than we might suppose. It is often difficult to understand just how varied, how unpredictable, those contexts are until we experience them ourselves via work that carries us across the curricula on our campuses.

The question of how we might approach the pedagogical aspects of the PhD-level methods course was a bit thornier. We turned again to Rickly (2007), one of the few scholars in writing studies who has written about preparing graduate students as researchers, to direct our own efforts at course design. For Rickly, the methods course must offer a sense of (drawing from Law) the complex "entagle[ments]" of the research process and the sites we study, "allowing us to see research not as an ordered, neat, linear procedure, but one that is integrated, messy, and non-hierarchical" (p. 9). She offers six suggestions to guide the development of research methods courses, noting that graduate student researchers benefit from (a) opportunities to use methods already central to the work of the field, (b) coaching/mentoring to critically appraise and read current research, (c) the ability to conduct an actual research project, (d) support for carrying out that research, (e) being asked to critically appraise research sites, and (f) practice rhetorically tailoring chosen research methods to the particular exigencies of a project (p. 21–22). Guided by these suggestions, we approached our Research Methods Course/WAC Program Review crossover project as an opportunity to immerse writing-studies graduate students within an authentic WAC context as a critical site of situated learning.

Integrating a Research Methods Course with a WAC Program Review

Designing this crossover project required, as one might suspect, a great deal of foresight and early planning. Michelle sought to balance the learning opportunities described by Reid and Rickly, particularly the hands-on needs of graduate students as researchers in unfamiliar contexts, with the PhD programs' desire that the course also offer basic familiarity with the broader contexts of research in the field at large. The course design required us to think seriously about how all the moving parts of the collaboration offered a situated introduction to the realities of WAC work, as it subsequently met the needs of the WAC program, its faculty, and administrative audiences. We had to consider what we ourselves wanted to learn, and we also had to ask how the program's exigencies could also become a site of learning for students. The logistics of integrating readings about methodologies with actual *collaborative* research practice required some intentional tradeoffs (discussed below).

The time constraints of the typical semester timeline were rather daunting, as well: often it felt like there was too much to integrate into the class—readings that offered a sense of the larger processes of research project design; specific introductions to different types of methodologies (theoretical/abstract *and* foundational/practical); reading in particular areas of interest (e.g., writing-to-learn, genre across the curriculum, reading across the curriculum, transfer, WAC professional identities, etc.); and setting up a research project—from collecting the data to managing and coding the data to writing up the findings. In anticipation of these time crunches, we began our work on this crossover project a full year before the class rolled out, redeveloping previously established project protocols (including WI faculty surveys and interviews) and recruiting faculty participants. We hoped this early start date would allow us to develop a robust program review process and to anticipate issues that could derail the applied aspects of the PhD research methods course when it began in fall of 2015.[4] Additionally, we asked the PhD-level students to take and complete their CITI training before our first class session together so they could be added to our IRB application beforehand. As the semester began, then, newly certified and ready-to-go as learners and research assistants, each graduate student was invited into the ongoing RE/V Project as a full collaborator. All of these pre-course measures allowed us to recursively engineer the class environment and the RE/V project's protocol to reflect the integrations we sought and to manage the time commitments of effective research.[5]

In light of these points of integration, Michelle designed the syllabus to unfold around four recursive and overlapping frames: Methods and Frameworks (Mixed-Methods Research), Collaborative Data Collection (Qualitative/Quantitative), Comparative WAC/WID Contexts, and Data Analysis/Writing Up Research. Each frame offered introductions to key elements of writing studies research practice, the nuts and bolts of the project itself, and the messy contexts of WAC/WID work. We treat each of these frames below to demonstrate how we integrated these components toward our vision of offering authentic WAC contexts as a critical site of situated learning.

Methods and Frameworks (Mixed-Methods Research)

Anecdotally, we had gleaned that graduate students who had taken research methods courses often felt "bogged down" with the set-up, IRB approval processes, and recruitment of participants. These conversations revealed that students often did get their own "pilot" projects off the ground, but were frequently stymied with recruiting issues, unanticipated problems in data collection, and difficulties with data management. Pulling off a full project start to finish in a single semester was simply daunting and quite difficult. Because of these conversations, Michelle posited that it was important for graduate students to be simultaneously reading about research methodologies and engaged in hands-on practice. Moreover, it seemed important that graduate students be supported in understanding the practical realities of completing a research project. As such, methods (how to's) began to take precedence over methodologies (the frames for research practice) in the course design.

We knew we needed to ask students to begin data collection as early in the semester as possible. But before beginning work on data collection, students did need to be familiar with the overall process of designing a research project (from initial project proposal to data collection activities) and the writing up of data and findings. We also knew we would be remiss if we did not introduce students to the handful of historical debates characterizing conversations about research in writing studies, from how methodologies reflect key epistemologies and/or paradigms, to what counts as data, to the values that particular types of methodologies/methods accrue. We complemented these more theoretical readings with how-to readings that foregrounded the practicalities of conducting research; these readings touched on the foundational issues of project design, but also highlighted issues of ethics and consent, the practicalities of managing and coding data, and finally, strategies for writing up research findings.[6]

Collaborative Data Collection (Quantitative/Qualitative)

To provide the situated and personal context for their learning, graduate students were asked to conduct and transcribe two interviews with WI faculty. They then observed and took extensive notes on two different WI courses. Once the data-files were cleaned of any identifying information, they were collected and stored on a shared drive so that all graduate students would have equal access to the range of data that had been collected. Survey responses, syllabi, and other course documents that had been collected via the WAC program's efforts were also made anonymous and posted in the same drive. Quantitative data, such as "Drop, Fail, and Withdrawal Rates," enrollment figures, and other public forms of institutional and assessment data were identified and collated for use by students in the class should they choose. These multiple points of data provided the opportunity for triangulation and accumulative understandings of interview responses and observation notes—offering further context for the broader understandings of writing we hoped graduate students would develop.

Comparative WAC/WID Contexts

As full collaborators in this WAC-program review, graduate students also forayed into the literatures of WAC pedagogy and program administration to develop their own WAC-related research interests and questions by focusing on at least two of the collaboratively collected data sets described above. The diverse lines of inquiry the graduate students chose reveal how WAC-contexts allow for varied interests across writing studies, especially since most students were able to pursue research interests they already had coming into the course. Some of these interests included low stakes writing, the prevalence of teaching for audience, what genres students were being asked to write in, and how technology appeared to be integrated into courses. Once these lines of inquiry were chosen, graduate students were asked to revise one aspect of the program review protocol to better reflect that focus. Some students chose to create a new interview question for the scripts; others revised or reframed an existing question on the protocol; others yet developed new processes of data collection, such as observations and a rubric-like analysis of the WI syllabi. Some students also sought additional forms of institutional data that could be collected from other offices and resources on campus.

Data Analysis and Writing Up Research: The WAC Committee Memo

The research methods course culminated in three writing assignments centered around each graduate students' individual line of inquiry: a literature review, a final essay targeted to one of the field's major journals, and a "memo" to the faculty senate's WAC committee. These writing assignments brought together the full experience of the semester—reading in methods and methodologies, reading the literature of the field, collecting and analyzing data, and thinking like a program stakeholder. Each writing project asked students to share the insights they had gleaned from their analysis of the collaboratively-collected data by framing their findings via ongoing pedagogical and programmatic conversations central to the field of writing studies.

The memo to the faculty senate's WAC committee proved to be one of the more challenging and generative learning opportunities of the semester, suggesting that the processes of drafting these memos may reveal the critical learning that comes of encounters with authentic WAC contexts. Importantly, the memo assignment asked students to think like WAC-program leaders who drew from their research to advocate for WAC-program policy, making a case for this change in no more than three pages and addressing those changes to the body of faculty who oversee WI courses on Mason's campus. Seasoned program leaders will immediately recognize the daunting nature of these administrative balancing acts: contextualizing research findings in relation to a pedagogical conversation in the field *and* rhetorically framing a "policy request" within the conventions of a persuasive appeal is not an easy writing situation. We dare to assume that very few PhD students write extensively as program leaders, a standpoint that requires we pay close attention to the situated nature of a research context, align our arguments with our institutional knowledge, maintain a professional and non-threatening register, and present the complexities of writing, writing pedagogy, and the needs of student writers in succinct, direct, and compelling ways to an audience with (perhaps) a different relationship to those topics and their complexities.

Indeed, students did initially struggle with this balance and synthesis. The necessary brevity of the memo provided one element of difficulty; the memo needed to summarize the research exigencies of each project, including the research question, the project's data collection methods, and the stakes for writing instructors and students alike. The assignment also required that students include a brief pedagogical background culled from the published literature of the field (particularly best teaching practices), a short description of their project's findings, and a graphical representation of those findings (chart, table, or image). Writing persuasive and rhetorically-savvy policy recommendations proved an additional challenge for many in the class, especially those who were dismayed by their findings or who enthusiastically wanted to encourage attention to pedagogical principles they considered crucial to effective writing instruction.

These challenges in drafting the memos were perhaps one of the more significant learning moments to come of the Research Methods Course/WAC Program Review crossover project, as well as an important detail in our conversation about introducing graduate students to authentic WAC contexts. Many students in the class appeared a bit taken aback by *how little the conversations central to teaching writing in their familiar contexts (composition and/or English studies) had permeated the disciplinary and departmental contexts of the WI courses*. While these realizations were powerful and re-orienting for the graduate students in our class, the memo required that students take on a tone that did not reveal such investments. For example, one student's study that "explored how WI faculty built audience awareness into their classes and assignments," found that, despite the pedagogical gains offered by asking students to write to "wider, public, or disciplinary-specific audience," instructors of the majority of WI courses served as the primary audience for student writers (Jensen, 2016). Another report on "The Prevalence of Low Stakes Writing and Writing-to-Learn Activities in WI Courses" commented upon the ways in which "WI faculty who did not assign any low stakes writing in class were also the WI faculty who gave the most negative responses to the questions" (Lussos, 2016). Finally, a third author noted that, despite the strong statements of support for teaching and learning writing in digital environments from NCTE and our campus leadership more generally, faculty were often still uncertain about how they might integrate technology into their writing classes; moreover, the availability of up-to-date technologies in campus classrooms was a cause for concern, especially in light of the pervasive need to help students understand writing in digital contexts (McGregor, 2015).

As drafts moved through stages of revision, their authors were required to adapt their thinking, to modify their rhetorical stances, to shift the tone of their language, and to argue from more practically grounded positions. Ultimately, these graduate students had to viscerally confront what should be happening in writing courses: how to be most effective when dealing with other real people who have different ideas about writing and how it should be taught; how to speak as a knowing stakeholder who is invested in creating a sense of shared community; how to advocate for best practices; how to recognize the constraints upon faculty teaching writing in the disciplines. A "short" memo assignment at the end of the semester, then, presented the opportunity to develop crucial and more authentically-grounded rhetorical acumen—a synthesis of what they were learning about working effectively with others in "messy" WAC contexts.

In the end, of the total nine final memos to the WAC committee (and related projects) submitted, four were chosen to be presented to the WAC committee the following fall. Projects were selected based upon the potential of their research findings to be interesting and persuasive to audiences outside of writing studies and for how findings demonstrated elements of the WI course criteria and foundational WAC pedagogy in action. (Topics included: low-stakes writing, the prevalence of teaching for audience, what genres students were being asked to write in, and how technology appeared to be integrated into courses.) The graduate students who composed each memo gave a short presentation of their findings to the WAC committee and answered questions about their research. Following this meeting with the committee, Michelle worked with each author to revise the memos into program white papers and posted the revised drafts to the program's web page (which can be found at http://wac.gmu.edu/past-assessment-and-program-review-resources/). A fifth report on what and how students were asked to read in WI courses became the genesis for a additional study directed by program staff. In all—because of the emphasis on presenting persuasive arguments about core WAC pedagogies, with attention to what was already happening in WI courses and what was not—these memos and subsequent projects provided a rich and critical site of situated learning for these graduate students.

The Graduate Student Experience within Authentic WAC-Contexts

As with most experiments, we wanted to know what worked well, where our students found value in the collaborations and integrated moves we designed, and where, perhaps, we might have tried to do too much. To understand the graduate student experience in this Research Methods Course/WAC Program Review crossover project, we administered two anonymous surveys and conducted follow-up interviews via email to gain a better understanding of how graduate students saw the course functioning within their own scholarly development as researchers. We were also quite curious: Had the authentic contexts of the course influenced their thinking about work in WAC or other aspects of writing and writing instruction? We conducted the first survey (Survey 1; see Appendix A) as the semester's work in the Research Methods course came to a close, fall 2015. A follow-up survey (Survey 2; see Appendix B), to understand the longer-term impacts of student expereinces, was rolled out at the end of the following semester, spring 2016. A full year later, spring 2017, we conducted email interviews with three of our original nine graduate students.

As noted earlier, our data-gathering on student experiences is limited. After all, only nine students took the Research Methods course (this is typical enrollment for a course in our PhD program) and were thus available to survey and interview (making for a very low "sample" size in traditional qualitative research). Six of the nine graduate students responded to both surveys to share their experiences and thoughts on the course with us. Since our surveys were initially designed as a tool to inform the next iteration of the course, our protocol was not designed to account for those students who would simply choose to ignore our questions, and only three consented to be interviewed a year later. The low response rate was a real surprise for us. We must continue our conversation here with a question mark in place of the answers those students may have provided. Did they dislike working in WAC contexts? Did they dislike the course itself? Were they simply too busy to respond to our questions? Were they—like many of us involved in programs and communities—simply suffering from "survey fatigue?" We offer the absence of their voices as another piece of the puzzle that members of our field must begin to unpack should we want to understand how we may more effectively serve those who will pass through our graduate programs.

Overall, our six respondents did note, with some important caveats, that the authentic contexts of this crossover project enhanced their learning in ways that we feel are significant to share. We especially recognized three main benefits from their survey and interview answers: First, graduate students noted encountering (often for the first time) instructional values and sensibilities about writing outside of English, values that reflected quite different institutional contexts and cultures of writing than they may have supposed. Second, these encounters encouraged our students to think more broadly about writing studies pedagogies, especially how composition courses might better prepare undergraduate writers to move more freely across the curriculum; this often made a difference to how these graduate students conceived of and taught their own composition classes. Third, our students began to understand the quite specific rhetorical exigencies (local issues, situated audiences, and material concerns) that drive and give shape to effective research projects on sites of writing, especially those in WAC contexts. Overall, we believe these benefits contributed to graduate students' facility with writing research contexts and supported their development as writing studies leaders on many fronts; moreover, we are encouraged by the extent to which even students who were not intending to become WAC scholars identified the WAC contexts as a key element in their learning about research methods in writing studies.

Experiencing Campus Cultures of Writing Outside of English

Survey responses suggested that the graduate students' encounters with faculty and courses outside of English introduced them to previously unfamiliar campus cultures of writing, and these encounters highlighted the differences and complexities of these cultures. As one student wrote, "Loved the glimpses into writing that happens in other disciplines, and perceptions, attitudes." We find this short response significant, as it suggests a new awareness of the disciplinary differences that WAC professionals take for granted. Similarly, another student responded, "[I realized] the challenges a WAC program head faces when working with a variety of faculty (personalities, disciplines, experience, etc)."

Graduate students also commented on the challenges that faculty members outside of English face, a key understanding that we believe comes from the immersive WAC contexts the course offered. For example, in Survey 2, we asked, "Of the following 'learning moments' [concerning WAC] offered in our initial survey, which of the following remain significant examples of your learning in 702?" Table 1 shows the respondents mostly identified "the challenges instructors outside of English face when they include writing in their courses" and "the challenges and opportunities WAC programs face" respectively.

Table 1

Significant "learning moments" about WAC work one semester later

Significant "learning moments" about WAC work one semester later	Graduate Student Respondents (n=9)
The challenges instructors outside of English face when they include writing in their courses	6
The challenges and opportunities WAC programs face	5
What it means to have a WAC program on campus	4
Opportunities for and challenges in providing professional development to faculty who teach writing outside of English	4
The perceptions and attitudes of people outside of English	3
What it means to study WAC contexts	3
What it means to design courses to support student writers	3
What it means to direct a WAC program	2
What it means to be a student in writing courses outside of English	2

One respondent summed up their realizations about the situated nature of writing, the challenges of WAC-program contexts, and the institutional realities of campus cultures outside of English, by sharing:

> Writing really does mean different things to different disciplinary instructors. It's tough to characterize WAC other than to say that students engage in writing as a practice and create writing as a product. However, WI faculty almost universally believe that students should focus on writing and that the university should teach their students to write. That's a pretty powerful space for conversations about what writing is and might be in the disciplines and across the university. But, I'm not sure what can come from such conversations without some institutional support from administration. I can see why WAC is such a challenge, even though it seems to be an intuitively good idea to make sure that writing and writing instruction continues throughout undergraduate education.

Graduate student respondents also confided that their learning experiences changed how they interacted with colleagues outside of English; as one student explained, "I've begun to seek opportunities to talk to other disciplines about reading and writing." And, another student replied more specifically, "It's definitely made me want to interrogate [faculty in the disciplines] more about what they mean by 'bad writing,' how much they know about the WAC program, etc." Conducting authentic research in a WAC context made the concept of *pedagogical conversations across disciplines* real for and important to these students. Moreover, many respondents even noted the importance of research in conversations about WAC-program leadership: "Having a robust data set and research story to tell about the current landscape and needs is an important step in advocating for the importance of the program."

Thinking More Broadly About Writing Pedagogies

Survey responses also suggest that the Research Methods Course/WAC Program Review crossover project helped graduate students think more broadly about writing pedagogy and to reflexively shape their own teaching practices. For example, 5 student respondents in Survey 2 noted changing their own composition classes based on exposure to WAC contexts. One respondent shared: "I will be thinking more about how to tie in reading and writing and to ensure that students begin to see both as situated practices." Another noted, "I took the lessons that I learned about low-stakes writing in my own project and lessons about language acquisition and reading in my peers' projects and applied them to my teaching approach." Even more than reflecting on their own writing pedagogies, the 702 students also began to see the possibilities of writing pedagogies across the curriculum. One respondent confided:

> [My main takeaway from this project is] how important it is to examine the writing that is happening across the curriculum and what is being asked of students. Without that knowledge and view of the writing landscape, the way we teach writing and prepare students risks being disjointed, and even, at times, contradictory.

Another respondent similarly expressed that understanding the disciplinary writing and writing pedagogies on our campus "infomed[ed] the revision of some of our assignments and curricular goals in the classes [they] oversee." This respondent went on to explain, "In other words, knowing what writing happens at the upper-division levels across the curriculum can help me think through how to build in the necessary rhetorical and linguistic skills in our first-year writing courses." This student has in effect learned the ideals of the vertical curriculum in a way that will then authentically guide their teaching.

Students unanimously agreed that their conversations with faculty in the disciplines increased their knowledge of writing instruction in other disciplines. For example, one respondent noted, "I learned that teaching and learning writing in other disciplines is frequently limited to simply adding writing assignments to a typical course in a discipline. The course itself rarely ever includes lessons on writing." Additionally, these insights into how writing is taught or characterized in other disciplines were usually linked back to the field of WAC and of composition in general. For example, one respondent answered, "[One of the most important things I learned about WAC practices is] where the discussion has been and currently is in composition." This is a powerful realization for those interested in both composition and WAC programs—many of us come to this work from composition, but the contexts and the realities outside of these familiar contexts, as seasoned WAC program leaders know, are often quite different.

Encountering Situated Research Practices

Most importantly, our surveys demonstrate an increased awareness of how research projects unfold—authentically and messily (to recall Reid and Rickly)—in WAC contexts. In Survey 2, when asked, "Of the following 'learning moments' [concerning research processes] offered in our initial survey, which of the following remain significant examples of your learning in 702?" Our respondents indicated increased understandings of the processes and logistics that all program leaders must be ready to account for (Table 2).

Table 2

Significant "learning moments" about research one semester later

Significant "learning moments" about research one semester later	Graduate Student Responses (n=9)
How research can be messy and "iterative"	5
The process of coding	5
How long effective research takes	5
The ethics of research	5
Choosing methods carefully	4
The importance of triangulation of data	4
The nature and importance of protocols	3

Relatedly, graduate students also commented upon how the integrated research context prepared them for future projects, especially dissertation and more autonomous professional research. For example, one respondent noted, "I have begun to have more confidence in my ability to create meaningful and thoughtful projects." Another student observed that this crossover project had given them "a more cohesive picture of what a project should look like," which has increased their interest in "beginning to create [their] dissertation project." These responses reveal how these authentic WAC contexts influenced students' understandings of conducting research on a pragmatic level—organizing, posing and revising research questions, and grounding research questions within the work of a dyamic field *and* the slippery nature of all sites of writing. As they encountered the real world unpredictablities of research, graduate students' understanding of the resilience necessary to carry out effective research and work within the authentic contexts of the university deepened.

Follow-up interview responses lead us to conclude that exposure to authentic WAC contexts can have a meaningful impact upon the teaching and institutional savvy of graduate students. These experiences can also prepare them to use research as a listening tool to inform work with writing and writing instruction in multiple contexts. One respondent, for instance, noted:

> As a writing teacher, it was interesting to learn (through the WI faculty interviews) what aspects of teaching writing they influenced based on their perceived needs of students. These needs were sometimes at odds with my perceived needs of first year composition students. This is not to say that WI faculty were misidentifying these needs; on the contrary, they opened my eyes to things that I sometimes overlook or take for granted. This reminds me that the writing experiences of WI faculty are important for faculty who teach in more familiar contexts (composition, writing centers, etc.) need to hear as well. We can all learn from each other.

Another respondent spoke to one of the biggest hurdles we face within WAC progam work, particularly faculty development:

> I've also realized that most professors don't need to be convinced of writing's importance to the learning process and for entering disciplinary ways of knowing/doing: they don't have to have all the writing theory to understand how important it is that their students learn to write in the discipline. The problem is the PEDAGOGY . . . Valuing writing and knowing how to successfully teach/integrate writing into a "content" course are NOT the same thing.

In closing this section, we want to acknowledge that two respondents did share a frustration about the focused nature of the research entailed in the crossover project; these two students noted in their responses that they would have liked more latitude to change the RE/V protocol or to develop their own study. To be fair, not all students in the research methods course were necessarily interested in WAC-related work or its contexts; as employees of university offices and programs, or established professional and technical writers, they already had experiences outside of English, even if they had not studied the shape of writing instruction outside of English. These are valuable counterpoints for this ongoing conversation about preparing graduate students in writing studies through exposure to authentic WAC contexts, and, we believe, a further argument to establish an ongoing research-based conversation about mentorship and preparation of graduate students within writing studies.

Conclusion

> There's so much more to learn about research that I'm convinced one course cannot do it real justice.
>
> —Research Methods Course/WAC Program Review Graduate Student

Ultimately, we call for yet more explicit attention to and study of the ways in which authentic WAC contexts can act as a critical site of situated learning for graduate students in writing studies. We particularly believe that the authentic, and even chaotic, contexts of WAC programs have much to teach graduate students about the nature of writing, their students, their colleagues, and the university at large—as well as the situated and local nature of research practices. We are struck by how our crossover project compares to recent calls for the value of "teaching for transfer" in our undergraduate writing classes, a conversation that has refocused how many of us teach composition and support WAC-related conversations on our campuses. For example, Howard Tinburg's charge that the teaching for transfer approach "boldly charges students to develop a portable theory of writing applicable across broad and varied contexts, including the workplace" (para. 2) strongly resonates with our own reflections on this crossover project. We would offer a similar conjecture—the students who took part in our project were required to think in new ways about writing, often in the face of what they thought they already knew.

The significance of introducing graduate students in writing studies to the actualities of writing outside of English cannot be understated. The gains of awareness we saw are, we contend, unlikely to be replicated by reading publications by leaders in the field of WAC in a seminar. Just as we have shifted to better prepare our undergraduates for the varied and unique contexts they will encounter as they cross the curriculum as writers, so may we shift our work with graduate students to better prepare professionals in writing studies who will be colleagues, coaches, and teachers to those within *and* outside of English.

One of the graduate students from the crossover project puts the realizations at the heart of work in WAC-contexts into words for us:

> I think the biggest thing I've realized about writing is that every discipline (and then even different professors within the discipline) has a slightly different language for TALKING about writing. There are some common terms that float around—editing, formatting, argument, "good" sentences, literature—but everyone is using those terms slightly differently. No wonder students struggle with writing from course to course!

What might the core pedagogies of writing studies look like if more of our courses offered an integrated practicum that exposed them to WAC contexts? What would our research activities look like if more of our graduate students were exposed to the actualities of writing, writers, and writing instructors who lived quite comfortably outside of English?

Further, we want to suggest that these types of projects are themselves provocative sites of study; they have the potential to extend, enrich, and integrate our field's conversations about preparing graduate students to be effective leaders. They offer sites primed for the study of how ideas about writing and writers proliferate across institutional boundaries and the transfer of pedagogical ideas—a topic as important as the transfer of writing ability during the undergraduate degree process. Our project's findings suggest that there is work yet to be done around how required research methods courses might promote the wide variety of research and administrative skills our students will need to be successful once they enter their own professional spheres. We hope that others will join us in continuing this project, sharing their own course designs, local opportunities, and found knowledge uncovered by these experiments.

Echoing the epigraph from Joan Mullen that begins this essay, we saw throughout the ways in which this crossover project benefited the graduate students involved. From increasing the graduate students' knowledge of how to carry out a research project from start to finish, to a more situated knowledge of WI courses and authentic WAC contexts, to the ways writing functions within larger institutional structures within a university—the benefits were clear. The graduate students we worked with not only gained experience with the foundations of research, but came away with rich and grounded understandings of the contexts that make up the broader culture of writing on our campus, including (but hopefully not limited to) the highly situated nature of writing, the differing value systems that inform and shape ideals of writing, and the many constructions of writing at work in WI courses.

Acknowledgments

We would like to thank Amy Devitt, Shelley Reid, Justin Nicholes, and our two anonymous reviewers for their generous and thoughtful feedback.

Notes

1. George Mason University is the largest public university in Virginia, serving over 23,812 undergraduate and 11,092 graduate students (GMU, 2017). In February of 2016, the institution was recognized to be among the highest research institutes by the Carnegie Classification of Institutions of Higher Education (GMU, 2016). The Ph.D. in Writing and Rhetoric is in its fifth year, with 47 total students.

2. The WAC program was created in 1993 through a provost office initiative. The program's primary charge is to oversee the WI courses offered in each major and to support the professional development conversations of the faculty who teach those courses.

3. Alisa was not enrolled in the course, but acted as the program's research assistant and Co-PI on elements of the project's work.

4. We also hoped to establish a model that could be repeated (with variations) and built upon the next time Michelle would be scheduled to teach the Research Methods class in the PhD program.

5. Alisa visited the course to fully explain, complicate, and contextualize all of the processes that occurred before the course started, including the IRB application and the protocols.

6. Key readings included: Blakeslee and Fleischer's *Becoming a Writing Studies Researcher* (2007); Rubin and Rubin's *Qualitative Interviewing* (2012); Haswell's "NCTE/CCC's War on Scholarship" (2005); Smagorinsky's "The Methods Section as Conceptual Epicenter in Constructing Social Science Reports" (2008); Lillis' "Ethnography as Method, Methodology, and 'Deep Theorizing'" (2008); and Johanek's *Composing Research* (2000).

References

Belcher, D. (1994). The apprenticeship approach to advanced academic literacy: Graduate students and their mentors. *English for Specific Purposes, 13*(1), 23–34.

Belcher, W. L. (2009). Reflections on ten years of teaching writing for publication to graduate students and junior faculty. *Journal of Scholarly Publishing, 40*(2), 184–200. doi:10.3138/jsp.40.2.184

Blakeslee, A. M. & Fleischer, C. (2007). *Becoming a writing researcher*. New York: Routledge, 2007.

Cassanave, C. P. & Li, X. (2008). *Learning the literacy practices of graduate school*. AnnArbor: University of Michigan Press.

Charlton, C., Charlton, J., Graban, T. S., Ryan, K. J., & Stolley, A. F. (2011). *GenAdmin: Theorizing WPA identities in the twenty-first century*. Anderson, SC: Parlor Press, LLC.

Cripps, M. J., Hall, J., & Robinson, H. (2016). "A way to talk about the institution as opposed to just my field": WAC fellowships and graduate student professional development [Special issue on TAs and the teaching of writing across the curriculum]. *Across the Disciplines, 13*(3). Retrieved May 30, 2017, from http://wac.colostate.edu/atd/wacta/crippsetal2016.cfm

Curry, M. J. (2012). Transcending "traditional academic boundaries": Designing and implementing a science communication course for science and engineering PhD students. *Journal of the IATEFL ESP SIG, 40*, 4–7.

Elder, C. L., Schoen, M., & Skinnell, R. (2014). Strengthening graduate student preparation for WPA work. *WPA: Writing Program Administration-Journal of the Council of Writing Program Administrators, 37*(2), 13-35.

Estrem, E. & Reid, E. S. (2012). What new writing teachers talk about when they talk about teaching. *Pedagogy: Critical Approaches to Teaching Literature, Language, Composition, and Culture, 12*(3), 449–80.

George Mason University. (2016). *Mason achieves top research ranking from Carnegie*. Retrieved from https://www2.gmu.edu/news/182106

George Mason University. (2017). *About Mason*. Retrieved from https://www2.gmu.edu/about-mason

Jensen, A. (2016). *Will write . . . But for whom? An analysis of WI faculty's consideration of audience in assignment design and pedagogy*. Retrieved from http://wac.gmu.edu/past-assessment-and-program-review-resources/

Lussos, R. (2016). *The prevalence of low stakes writing and writing-to-learn activities in WI courses*. Retrieved from http://wac.gmu.edu/past-assessment-and-program-review-resources/

McGregor, B. (2015). *Technology access and use in writing intensive courses*. Retrieved from http://wac.gmu.edu/past-assessment-and-program-review-resources/

Micciche, L. R., & Carr, A. D. (2011). Toward graduate-level writing instruction. *College Composition and Communication, 62*(3), 447–501.

Mullen, C. A. (1999). "What I needed to know to get published": Teaching (frightened) graduate students to write for publication. *Journal on excellence in college teaching, 10*(2), 27–52.

Nickoson, L., and Sheridan, M. P. (2012). *Writing studies research in practice: Methods and methodologies*. Carbondale, IL: Southern Illinois University Press.

Pytlik, B. P. & Ligget, S. (2002). *Preparing college teachers of writing*. New York: Oxford University Press.

Reid, E. S. (2004). Undercoverage in composition pedagogy. *Composition Studies, 32*(1),15–34.

Reid, E. S., Estrem, H., & Belcheir, M. (2012). The effects of writing pedagogy education on graduate teaching assistants' approaches to teaching composition. *WPA, 36*(1), 30-73.

Rickly, R. (2007). Messy contexts: The required research methods course as a scene of rhetorical practice. In D. N. DeVoss and H. A. McKee (Eds.), Digital writing research: Technologies, methodologies, and ethical issues (pp. 337-97). New York: Hampton Press.

Rodrigue, T. K. (2012). The (in)visible world of teaching assistants in the disciplines: Preparing TAs to teach writing. *Across the Disciplines, 9*(1). Retrieved June 21, 2012, from http://wac.colostate.edu/atd/articles/rodrigue2012.cfm.

Rodrigue, T. K. (2013). Listening across the curriculum: What disciplinary TAs can teach us about TA professional development in the teaching of writing. *Teaching/Writing: The Journal of Writing Teacher Education, 2*(2): Article 5. Retrieved August 15, 2014, from http://scholarworks.wmich.edu/wte/vol2/iss2/5.

Rose, S. K., & Weiser, I. (1999). *The writing program administrator as researcher: Inquiry in action & reflection*. Portsmouth: Boynton/Cook.

Stolley, A. F. (2015). Narratives, administrative identity, and the early career WPA. *WPA: Writing Program Administration, 39*(1), 18-31.

Strenski, Ellen. (1992). Helping TAs across the curriculum teach writing: An additional use for the TA handbook. *Writing Program Administration, 15*(3), 68–73.

Sundstrom, C. J. (2014). The graduate writing program at the University of Kansas: A disciplinary, rhetorical genre-based approach to developing identities. *Composition Forum 29*. http://compositionforum.com/issue/29/kansas.php

Swales, J. M., and Feak, C.B. (2004). *Academic writing for graduate students: Essential tasks and skills*. Ann Arbor: University of Michigan Press.

Thomas, T. (1991). The graduate student as apprentice WPA: Experiencing the future. *WPA: Writing Program Administration, 14*(3), 41–51.

Timberg, H. (2017). Teaching for transfer: A passport for writing in new contexts. *Peer Review, 19*(1). Retrieved from https://www.aacu.org/peerreview/2017/Winter/Tinberg

Writing Across the Curriculum Graduate Organization. (2017). *Resource Survey Report, 2017*. Retrieved from https://www.facebook.com/WACGO/?hc_ref=ARSXrOFID9nJkZh-6rxg2iRCUoY6ZvVs_eMDsv61klPnKyLeQ689WzIh8Vh pstt1EJs&fref=nf

Wilhoit, S. (2002). *The Allyn Bacon teaching assistant handbook*. New York: Pearson Longman.

Winzenried, Misty Anne. (2016). Brokering disciplinary writing: TAs and the teaching of writing across the disciplines [Special issue on TAs and the teaching of writing across the curriculum]. *Across the Disciplines, 13*(3). Retrieved May 30, 2017, from http://wac.colostate.edu/atd/wacta/winzenreid2016.cfm

White, E. (2002). Use it or lose it: Power and the WPA. *The Allyn & Bacon Sourcebook for Writing Program Administrators,* 106–113.

Appendix A

Survey 1 (Initial End-of-Term Survey for 702 Students)

1. What is the most important thing you learned about research methods from this class/project?
2. What is the most important thing you learned about WAC practices or theories from this class/project?
3. What unique challenges did you face as a research assistant for the WAC RE/View Project?
4. If you could change one thing about your participation in this research project, what would it be and why?
5. How did participating as a research assistant for the WAC RE/View Project relate to and/or prepare you for your own research interests or goals?
6. What is your main take-away from this course and this project?

Appendix B

Survey 2 (Follow-Up Survey for 702 Students One Semester Later)

1. Of the following "learning moments" offered in response to our initial survey, which of the following remain significant examples of your learning in 702? (Please check all that apply). I learned more about . . .

    a. The nature and importance of protocols
    b. Choosing my methods carefully
    c. The ethics of research
    d. The importance of the triangulation of data
    e. The process of coding
    f. How long effective research takes
    g. How research can be messy and "iterative"
    h. The perceptions and attitudes of people outside of English
    i. What it means to have a WAC program on campus
    j. What it means to study WAC contexts
    k. The challenges and opportunities WAC programs face
    l. What it means to direct a WAC program
    m. What it means to be a student in writing courses outside of English

    n. The challenges instructors outside of English face when they include writing in their courses
    o. Opportunities for and challenges in providing professional development to faculty who teach writing outside of English
2. Did this collaboration increase your understanding about teaching writing in other disciplines or the people who teach writing in other disciplines?
3. What theories and practices from WAC have stayed with you since the 702 class/project?
4. Have any of your experiences in 702 changed how you teach composition classes?
5. Have any of your experiences in 702 changed how you interact with colleagues outside of English on your campus?
6. How did your experiences as a research assistant in the RE/View Project prepare you for your professional goals?
7. In what ways have you drawn on your participation as a research assistant in the RE/View Project to pursue your own research interests and goals?
8. What is your most lasting impression of the 702 course and RE/View Project now that another semester has passed?

"Stealth WAC": The Graduate Writing TA Program

CAMERON BUSHNELL AND AUSTIN GORMAN

The title of our essay comes courtesy of University of Toronto colleague, W. Brock MacDonald speaking at the 2018 International Writing Across the Curriculum Conference.[1] It seems to describe perfectly, and elegantly, the way that we think of the Graduate Writing Teaching Assistant (GWTA) Program discussed in this essay: the GWTA program permits a stealthy reintroduction of strategies and practices associated with a previous generation's programs for writing across the curriculum and writing in the discipline on our campus—importantly by recognizing a sometimes neglected university population already involved in teaching writing, graduate teaching assistants.

Let us say immediately that we are not at all opposed to the traditional method of building support for WAC and WID programs through faculty workshops. In fact, we look forward to a time when they might play a larger part in ongoing training and discussion about writing (and oral presentation) pedagogy. However, at our research-striving campus—where R1 status has just been achieved and "research very high" status is being sought in part through an expansion of doctoral programs—the timing is, shall we say, not ripe for a direct intervention with faculty on the subject of teaching, writing, and speaking pedagogies.

Additionally, to avoid any confusion that may arise from our title, which might seem to suggest that graduate students have been excluded from writing fellows and WAC programs, we note that "stealth WAC" refers to a particular kind of intervention that concerns both graduate students themselves and the program. On one hand, "stealth WAC" points to GTA's work in contexts such as training other TAs in the disciplines and in spearheading efforts to introduce WAC and WID concepts to faculty. Indeed, as a search of writing fellows programs on the *WAC Clearinghouse* shows, graduate students are already involved in cross-discipline writing instruction with their peers at many institutions of higher education. Thus, we acknowledge the important work that has already been done to include graduate students in WAC and WID programs, but also suggest that our program allows for efforts such as syllabi modification and informal writing that can alter writing outcomes even for disciplines with established curricula, thus representing a "stealthy" approach from our

---

1. MacDonald, W. Brock and Andrea Williams. "Connecting Writing and Disciplinary Knowledge: Teacher Formation in a WAC Program." Co-Presenters at IWAC Conference, June 3–6, 2018.

graduate student collaborators. On the other hand, but related, disciplinary TAs are often responsible for courses that require them to be involved with undergraduate student writing, but this contribution to their programs is often unacknowledged. TA supervisors may emphasize disciplinary content and gloss over TA writing responsibilities. Our program recognizes that there is writing instruction happening under the radar and capitalizes on an under-recognized resource, seeking to shape and support it, thus expanding WAC on campus.

Our particular program working with graduate teaching assistants offers a robust strategy for re-igniting conversations about WAC and WID. Austin Gorman, director of the campus writing center and myself, director of the Pearce Center for Professional Communication, piloted a program aimed at GTAs who assisted us in expanding efforts on campus to address writing as a necessary and urgent area of academic competence for undergraduate and graduate student populations. The Graduate Writing Teaching Assistant (GWTA) program, as we have called it, offered, in the pilot year, a cohort of nine GTAs, an opportunity to focus on writing as a process critical to: (1) student learning—in comprehending and in demonstrating understanding of content, (2) undergraduate workplace readiness—in explaining and using concepts and practices beyond the classroom, and (3) graduate student scholarship—in expressing clearly (in writing and in oral presentation) sophisticated concepts for a wide variety of audiences encountered in journals, conferences, and dissertation defenses. Although the program aimed primarily to increase and improve undergraduate writing in courses taught by graduate students, we always thought that graduate student writing would progress with increased attention on writing as process.

Our first group of GWTAs came recommended by their departmental faculty. To be accepted into the program, graduate students had to have teaching responsibilities in a lab or a classroom. Our interest was in identifying graduate teaching assistants (GTAs) who were committed to teaching and whose supervisors were supportive of their dedicating time to the improvement of writing instruction in their classrooms. We sought GTAs, as Austin notes in his section, because they, as a population, are pivotal—both literally and metaphorically. By definition, they have responsibilities to: (1) the undergraduates they teach, (2) the faculty for whom they are working as assistants, and (3) each other, as peers. Their multivalent perspective is shaped by their need to mediate among competing interests and demands. These three points comprise a GWTA's network, which is critical to the success of the GWTA program; Cameron elaborates them further below. In the section immediately following, Austin writes about the theoretical and practical considerations that have informed our venture into graduate teaching education. We conclude, as we have begun, with a joint reflection, ending with plans for the future iterations of this program.

Theoretical and Practical Considerations

Austin Gorman

Since its inception in the mid-1970s, WAC programs have struggled with the perennial question of faculty engagement; in particular, how to alter faculty misconceptions about writing (see: Fulwiler, Gorman, and Gorman, "Changing"); overcoming the "resistance" of recalcitrant colleagues in other disciplines (see: Swilky, "Reconsidering"; Swanson-Owens, "Identifying"); or, in the words of WAC pioneers Toby Fulwiler and Art Young in their polemical "Enemies of Writing Across the Curriculum," combatting the "entrenched attitudes that undermine the goals for writing across the curriculum" (292). In Fulwiler and Young's "Enemies," the antagonism between WAC directors and their putative cross-disciplinary collaborators rises to a fever pitch: "many faculty," they assert, "are apathetic, others insecure, even hostile, to any program that offers to assist them with their teaching" (293). While this sentiment may seem unnecessarily bellicose, the early innovators of WAC programs nonetheless identify the greatest obstacle standing in the way of the success of any WAC/WID/CCL initiative: namely, how to find university stakeholders with a desire to advance writing outcomes in their classrooms.

Approaches to WAC that focus mainly on administrative features of the program may fail to address the problem of how to secure a broad-based faculty "buy-in." Theorists of WAC collaboration, such as Barbara Walvoord, advise WAC to stay on the "faculty side" because "considerable faculty autonomy is likely to remain strong" (288). More recent approaches to the foundational question of faculty participation in WAC have emphasized disciplinary differences in writing as pedagogically productive and how we, as academically professionalized teachers of writing, should become more open to the "problems" of grammar that potential stakeholders from other disciplines want to see "fixed" in their undergraduate students' writing (see: Katherine Schaefer "Emphasizing"; Daniel Cole "Earth"). My own experience as the director of a writing center and writing fellows program at an R1 public college of more than twenty thousand students certainly confirms how important it is to listen to the concerns of faculty from other disciplines regarding their objectives in improving student writing. How rigidly one applies the canonical advice of Stephen North of attending to "process" over "product"—or, how one diplomatically explains to a professor in the STEM field that the primary duty of writing fellows is not to simply fix "bad" grammar, but rather to apply a holistic approach to teaching writing—involves matters of pedagogical theory, personal style, and, most importantly perhaps, the anatomy of one's educational institution. On this latter point, a large R1 university, which frequently caters to the sciences, will need to develop a WAC program that is more accommodating to those in other disciplines than would a smaller liberal arts college.

(We venture that many will find that this "goes without saying," but, like so many basic facts that determine the success or failure of any WAC program, it probably isn't said emphatically enough.)

While cross-disciplinary faculty involvement remains the eternal bugbear of the WAC mission, there has been a dearth of scholarly work on what faculty involvement is and how it might mesh with the best practices developed by WAC. As Heather Falconer rightly points out, in reference to "Statement of WAC Principles and Practices" (2014) by the International Network of WAC programs and CCCC Executive Committee, merely affirming that "writing in disciplines (WID) is most effectively guided by those with experience in that discipline" does not explain what "experience" and "expertise look like in practice" (123). Taking a slightly different tack, we might ask two questions: (1) what disciplinary experience and expertise is important for the collaborative project and goals of WAC? and (2) how can WAC administrators leverage this expertise in order to affect change across disciplinary thresholds?

Put a slightly different way, and taking a step back from macro-level concerns regarding WAC-program design, methodology, and assessment, we suggest the first question above might prompt the first decision: *where* and *who* are our stakeholders. Jeffrey Jablonski argues that "the limitation of most WAC studies is that they conceive of interdisciplinary collaboration as a research *method*, but not as an appropriate research *object*" (38; italics original). Taking collaboration seriously as an "object" of research, rather than as simply a part of one's "research methodology," draws us toward an inquiry into how to cultivate the appropriate institutional stakeholders as the first, and most important, determinant in the success (or failure) of any WAC program.

The faculty workshop of the original WAC programs codified our current notion of the relevant university stakeholders. Earmarking courses as "writing-intensive" and training faculty in writing pedagogy while capitalizing on their disciplinary expertise can appear outdated now because of the outsized role played by graduate teaching assistants in grading and assessing student writing. According to the US Bureau of Labor Statistics, from 1988 to 2016 graduate teaching assistants have risen much faster proportionally than the total number of graduate students. While it is difficult to offer definitive numbers with regard to how much writing assessment is done by graduate teaching assistants, much anecdotal evidence suggests that tenured and tenure-track faculty, particularly in the sciences, have offloaded the grading of written assignments to graduate students. This is certainly true of my own university where TAs in a number of high-profile disciplines are responsible for grading the majority of written assignments that undergraduates do within their respective majors.

In essence, the cross-curricular pollination that Chris Anson describes between tenured faculty in other disciplines and English graduate students has been replaced by an increasingly hermetic form of writing instruction in which (in the best-case scenario), the director of undergraduate studies trains TAs in undergraduate writing assessment in the genres appropriate to their particular discipline. While the quality of the training in writing assessment that TAs receive varies widely by institution and discipline, Falconer shows—in her case study of undergraduate biology courses—that "innovative approaches [to writing] *are* taking place" in the sciences (135). The question she leaves readers with is precisely what place the programs and literature of WAC/WID, with our unique pedagogies, might claim within these already robust fields of "innovative" disciplinary writing.

This brings us to our second question: How can WAC programs leverage disciplinary expertise to improve writing outcomes across a broad constituency of undergraduate and graduate writers at the university? Falconer indirectly points to the problem (i.e., faculty stakeholders will likely be reluctant to incorporate our pedagogies), but, like most WAC researchers, understands collaboration as a methodological problem (how can we "persuade" faculty stakeholders to want to incorporate our pedagogies), rather than a legitimate object of inquiry in its own right. To admit the simple truth that the majority of faculty in other disciplines view writing as someone else's problem to solve and will develop their own pedagogical approaches, which may be "innovative," but will also, oftentimes, exclude particular kinds of writing—low-stakes informal writing for example—that advance the acquisition of habits critical to the writing-to-learn model of pedagogy.

This points toward the innovation of Clemson's GWTA (Graduate Writing Teaching Assistants) initiative in leveraging the significant disciplinary expertise of nine graduate student TAs—four from mechanical engineering, three from PRTM (Parks, Recreation and Tourism Management), and two from English, to build sustaining relationships with the faculty in charge of training graduate TAs. In particular, we sought graduate students with both an interest in improving their own writing, which led us to include a significant number of international graduate students, and those with significant support from their discipline for advancing writing pedagogy.[2] In terms of WAC-program success, working primarily with graduate students, rather than faculty, has had numerous advantages. First and foremost, it capitalizes on the current reality of instruction at many large universities: increased numbers of graduate teaching assistants are responsible for undergraduate student work. This shift in

---

2. For the pilot year of our program we sought recommendations from program administrators in mechanical engineering, PRTM and English to identify graduate students for our program. We hope to move to an application process in future years. Additionally, we worked entirely with doctoral students—not out a particular strategic objective—but simply because the recommended students happened to be in doctoral programs in ME, PRTM and English. It might behoove us, in future iterations of this course, to work with more MA students, although at our institution, much of the teaching (save in some programs like English) is performed by doctoral candidates.

workplace structure has also indelibly changed how universities *assess* undergraduate work—namely, and for our purposes, the written work of undergrads—by giving graduate students a larger role in the evaluation and grading of this work. Simply put, if graduate students in mechanical engineering at our institution, which is an important and well-funded major in the School of Engineering, are charged with the grading of undergraduate lab reports, it makes little sense to hold WAC workshops for ME professors at this particular juncture.[3]

In addition to the prosaic point that WAC administrators should work with those *actually* responsible for the evaluation and teaching of writing within the disciplines, graduate students make for desirable collaborators because of their unique status in the university. As Irene Ward and Merry Perry contend, graduate students often "walk a tightrope between several subject positions: student, teacher, and scholar" (119). For Ward and Perry, faculty needs to be cognizant of how the multiple metaphorical hats graduate students are asked to wear can lead to a dizzying and alienating academic experience. As an instructor and administrator four years removed from a PhD program, I certainly have empathy for graduate students—particularly when it comes to the paltry stipends they receive—but the multiplicity of the roles graduate students endure is a benefit, rather than liability, when it comes to WAC. (We must insist, lest there be any confusion, that any graduate student expending time to take a WAC course and/or work as a WID ambassador should receive an additional stipend. Our graduate student collaborators received $1,500 in additional monies in the form of a professional development fund, which could be used for books, conference expenses, and other items related to their education.) The sundry professional identities that graduate programs require of their students make them particularly adept in transferring and translating their disciplinary expertise into different institutional contexts of the university.

It is the multiplicity of the professional roles that graduate students play—scholar, teacher, student, colleague—that enables them to so successfully understand other disciplinary codes. The reason, for instance, that the graduate colleagues in our program were able to apply the teaching of templates to their own pedagogical toolbox—unlike, as Faculty X explained to me, who'd be reluctant to introduce templates because they "didn't want to spoon feed their students"—was precisely because they were open to reframing their writing instruction. It was not the case that we required them to follow our pedagogical methods, but rather that graduate students are more open, given their position in the academy, to incorporating and employing cross-disciplinary techniques

---

3. Again, we do not want to dismiss the faculty workshop model entirely, but merely point to some of its limitations, particularly at our university at the present time. As it will be shown below, faculty participation was a critical element of our program outside the conventional faculty workshop model.

The Graduate Writing TA Program & Structure

Cameron Bushnell

Over the period of a one-year pilot program, we found that disciplinary graduate teaching assistants were excellent candidates for WAC instruction. As mentioned above, the GWTAs are at the center of a three-pronged network of undergraduates, faculty, and peers. The GWTA program was designed to maximize the GTAs medial positioning, structured around three main goals: (1) improving undergraduate writing through syllabi modifications that better prepared undergraduates for advanced coursework, capstones, and the workforce; (2) improving graduate writing and teaching in the disciplines through focus on writing as a process of learning, which had the added benefit of increasing consistency in teaching among fellow disciplinary TAs; and (3) assisting faculty by increasing departmental reputations in producing more accomplished writers among undergraduate and graduate populations.

The Overall GWTA Program Structure

The impetus for our program arose from an inheritance. Our university had been the site of a nationally recognized writing across the curriculum program, started by Art Young, an early proponent and initiator of the idea in the 1970s. Other scholars who have gone on to achieve great renown in the field complemented his work. After a period of low activity in the mid '00s, my predecessor began rebuilding a program through what had become two highly successful undergraduate intern programs in professional communication and in the writing center. Last year, Austin and I saw an opportunity to re-introduce WAC to our university through our large, teaching-active population of graduate teaching assistants.

The GWTA pilot program extended two semesters and revolved around a one-credit seminar each semester. The first semester involved instruction in theories and principles grounding writing, whether across the curriculum, in the disciplines, or in writing centers. It also required students to modify existing syllabi for the labs and courses the GWTAs taught to include more, and different kinds, of writing (specifically low-stakes writing and revision). The second semester involved practical application of those theories not only in their classrooms, but also in other venues; two major assignments focused on providing one-on-one "guest" writing instruction to peers seeking assistance at the university writing center and on preparing and delivering a "writing bootcamp" for the graduate school's professional development program. Evaluation of the pilot will be further discussed below.

Improving Undergraduate Writing

The GWTA program addressed the first, and main, goal of increasing and improving undergraduate experience with writing in the initial realization of graduate students as a great, untapped resource on campus. Disciplinary graduate students, in particular, are already deeply involved in writing, teaching, and, even, perhaps somewhat surprisingly, the process of teaching writing. Although we take for granted that English Department TAs teach writing, it is also true in other departments. The irony of GTAs ready involvement in teaching rests in a mistaken assumption by many faculty and administrators, who think that because TAs were accepted into competitive doctoral programs they also know how to write, teach, and even teach writing. Many GTAs find it embarrassing, if not impossible, to bring up the error given, in part, that much of the work that TAs do is critical, but nearly invisible, on campus.

Tanya K. Rodrigue argues in "The (In)Visible World of Teaching Assistants in the Disciplines" that TAs in doctoral programs, though assigned teaching responsibilities as part of their funding package, are often encouraged to prioritize research over teaching. Therefore, coupled with the fact that historically writing has often been considered less important than content in the disciplines, "the most challenging obstacles WAC administrators face are faculty resistance [...], and faculty disinterest" (2);[4] granting graduate students time to become better teachers is rarely a priority in graduate programs.[5] Rodrigue makes the case, however, that TAs are, despite the lack of recognition for it, already contributing to the teaching of writing by virtue of their multiple engagements with students. The work TAs do influences, directly and indirectly, undergraduate writing: from grading essays, discussing writing assignments, leading discussions, supervising laboratory and study sessions, and other interactions with students, graduate TAs already interact with students in ways that "relate to writing instruction."[6] This is the case, even though, as Rodrigue makes clear in her title (above), this contribution is not often noticed.

The GWTA program opened with a series of readings and discussions on WAC/WID principles and practices as encapsulated by the overarching goals of writing to learn and writing-to-demonstrate learning. The first half of the semester focused on tools that could be used directly with students—lessons in informal writing, grammar, organization, argument, revising, templates. At the crux of the first semester stood the Rubrics Assignment, which I will return to shortly. To conclude the first

---

4. Quote comes from the abstract.

5. Anecdotally, we often hear that various disciplines are aware of the importance of writing but are just not interested in taking on the task themselves. This potentially points to an opportunity for graduate TAs to fill a necessary but neglected, role.

6. Rodrigue, 2; cites: Strenski, Ellen. "Writing Across the Curriculum at Research Universities." *New Directions for Teaching and Learning*, vol. 36, 1988, pp. 31–41.

semester, we discussed strategies more applicable to their own writing—summaries, literature reviews, introductions, conclusions, and visual tools.

The Rubrics Assignment (a general description of all the assignments from the first semester is included in Appendix 1) was planned as the marker of before and after in the semester plans and tasked our students to modify and explain each element of the rubric to be used in grading their undergraduate essays or lab reports. All our GWTAs were teaching courses that had existing, department-designed rubrics that had to be followed. Modifications to the rubrics were to accommodate additional writing, including informal writing and revision, both of which were nearly unrepresented in existing syllabi.[7] The GWTAs were asked to collect two papers prior to the Rubrics Assignment—one informal and one formal essay. These student papers were to demonstrate the existing, ground-level writing capabilities of their undergraduates. After the Rubrics Assignment, (and after they had presented several lessons on writing as an adjunct to the disciplinary subject matter and had emphasized writing by including it in the rubric), the GWTAs were asked to collect two additional papers, again one informal, one formal. The difference between these groups of essays—the before and after sets—was assessed at the end of the year (more on assessment below).

Improving Graduate Writing

Interestingly, one of the main obstacles to writing instruction for TAs (i.e., institutional priority for publishing [over teaching and writing]) motivated the GWTA program and provided means to achieve our second objective: improving graduate writing through the study of writing as a process. In other words, most TAs are not only frequently more engaged with undergraduates than the supervising faculty—interacting more frequently in discussions and conferences and reading more papers—but also they are thoroughly involved in learning to write well themselves. The multivalence of graduate student existence, to return to a much earlier point, lends itself to employing many pedagogical strategies and methods, for a multitude of purposes, simultaneously.

In short, the GWTA program capitalized on this doubled effort toward good writing. Taking as a starting point the WAC principle that writing is integral to learning and demonstrating learning, we designed the GWTA program to be a site where GTAs could become better writers by learning more effective ways to teach writing. A recent study confirmed the value of writing to improve teaching, and we suggest also the teaching of writing. Judith Hiller, working with UK university science

---

7. The exception, unsurprisingly, was for the Accelerated Composition classes taught by English MA students. Because the working practices for these freshmen English courses was different from other disciplinary classes, we have decided in the second pilot to omit English department participants.

teachers-in-training, included in her education course a requirement for self-generated explanatory narratives of key concepts in conjunction with lesson planning. This relatively easy step greatly improved the teachers' ability to communicate crucial scientific concepts to their students. As Hiller states, "a process of writing narrative explanations of scientific phenomena [. . .] as part of a preservice teacher education course" revealed that "having coherent internal accounts to explain phenomena" was crucial to the new teachers' ability to transform subject knowledge into pedagogical content knowledge. In a mutually reinforcing strategy, writing for teaching purposes helped teachers grasp content through the effort to condense and synthesize concepts and resulted in more effective teaching practice. By logical extension, we suggest the act of writing narratives not only bolsters pedagogical content, but also improves facility with writing.

To this end, at various points throughout the first semester of our program, the GWTAs wrote one-page narratives that reflected both on the concepts in class and on how they had applied these concepts to their own writing (and writing instruction) in their particular subject areas. In the words of one student, and to their surprise, these narratives were immensely useful: actually "writing down what I was trying to explain in . . . like concept [sic] from engineering—helped me better understand my own thoughts . . . I think I could explain these ideas to students better too." Additionally, GWTAs commented at the end of the first semester, in final reflection essays, and in one-on-one exit interviews that their own writing improved as they thought about writing as a process and learned strategies for teaching writing. For example, several in the cohort noted that they benefited from learning about the writing genres and style conventions required in other disciplines. Others noted that in preparing for classroom low-stakes assignments, for introducing templates, and for one-on-one assistance to other graduate students, they learned strategies they could apply to their own work. And in a true vote of confidence in the GWTA program, one student suggested expansions to it, including offering a three-credit seminar and providing more opportunities to exchange their own writing for peer review.

Assisting Faculty

Finally, the GWTA program benefited from faculty support as the GWTA program proved valuable to faculty. We had the direct encouragement of faculty from all three departments that formed the first cohort—English, Mechanical Engineering, and PRTM—as evidenced by their recommendations of participants. Beyond this initial point, however, we were able to identify three distinct areas in which the GWTA program benefited faculty: (1) faculty participation in the seminar, (2) peer mentoring, and (3) dissertation preparation.

One of the faculty members sponsoring graduate students was so enthused about the GWTA program that she decided to attend the fall seminar in which we discussed writing pedagogy and practice. Our program helped her continue her own parallel, departmental initiative set on improving the quality of writing and communication skills of her graduate students. Although I wondered about the dynamics of having a faculty auditor in the pilot program, all concerns were banished in the first session. This faculty member was a great asset to the class, sometimes asking more penetrating questions during the seminar because of her long experience teaching and sometimes answering questions from a different disciplinary view, in this case social science, than either of us could provide (both Austin and I have disciplinary backgrounds in English).

A second faculty member, who manages all the teaching assistant schedules for his department, held regular TA meetings, during which he invited the GWTAs from his department to share with their TA colleagues points that would assist them in adding writing components to their lesson plans. Peer mentorship meant that the GWTA program benefited supervising faculty by having a trickle-down effect among TAs not in the program. Because the Pearce Center provided professional development funds for each of the participants, the cohort was relatively small; therefore, the peer sharing was especially valuable in reaching a larger population of GTAs than we could support directly.

Finally, a third faculty member who had no students in the first GWTA cohort was particularly gratified in having GWTA one-on-one support for a second-language doctoral candidate finishing his dissertation. As part of the second-semester practical applications, we assigned our GWTAs to work with their graduate students in one-to-one writing center format. The faculty member was so pleased with the interaction on behalf of her doctoral student that she offered remuneration to the GWTA and the program from her departmental budget.

Reflecting on the First Year; Looking to the Second

At the end of the first year, we realize that seizing the opportunity to increase the level of teaching preparedness among graduate students also recognizes the structural reality of higher education in which GTAs will be supplementing a growing contingent workforce.[8] Working with this neglected, but pivotal, group of graduate teaching assistants provides the university an attractive resource for teaching writing

---

8. Rodrigue cites numbers from a June 2009 report from the US Department of Education, published by the American Federation of Teachers: "contingent labor, including TAs, has increased over the past ten years, while tenured and tenure-track faculty positions have plummeted" (5; qtd. in Rodrigue 2). A 2014 AAUP Annual Report gives more details about this trend; from 1976–2011, part-time faculty increased 286%; full-time, non-tenure track faculty increased 259%, and full time tenured and tenure-track faculty increased 23% (qtd. in

for several, large and small, reasons. First, nationwide, graduate teaching assistants are key figures in university labs, teaching the majority of undergraduate courses.[9] Secondly, these teaching roles include not only work as graders or assistants, but also teachers of record, potentially influencing the quality of undergraduate education and the university reputation. Thirdly, even in a time of uncertainty for foreign students,[10] when according the Migration Policy Institute, "rising cost of U.S. higher education, student visa delays and denials, and an environment increasingly marked by rhetoric and policies that make life more difficult for immigrants,"[11] our university has continued to consistently attract well over two hundred new international graduate students per year for the past ten years. A program like GWTA can potentially benefit second-language teachers by helping them improve their competency in English and by focusing on teaching writing.

As shown in Figure 1, the first pilot year proved successful. Undergraduates improved in writing skills, as measured across five factors, including purpose, organization, analysis, research support, and design on both formal and informal assignments. The chart measures the improvement of undergraduate writing from papers collected after the Writing Design Assignment (see: Appendix) was implemented. While Graduate Student 1, 3, 6 and 7 showed consistent (even remarkable) improvement across our five factors, the dip in quality for Graduate Students 2 and 5 stands out as well. (It should be noted that our analysis was performed with the assistance of two PhD candidates from Rhetoric and Composition. We collated our assessment data and had a statistical margin of difference in evaluations of less than .05). The lack of improvement in G2 and G5 was mostly on the informal writing assignments, which leads us to conclude that cross-disciplinary biases about the usefulness of informal writing may have been a factor. We are examining ways to address this going forward. Overall, however, from our undergraduate papers (we had adequate data from six GWTAs) five of the seven showed improvements from 4–13% across all factors.

Champlin and Knoedler 2). Also see: pages 5–6 on the increased role of graduate students as instructors.

9. Gardner and Jones note: "Undergraduate teaching at research universities often rests solidly on the backs of graduate teaching assistants (GTAs) who teach large portions of the introductory curriculum" (31)..

10. The Migration Policy Institute reports: "the U.S. share of globally mobile students dropped from 28 percent in 2001 to 24 percent in 2017, while the overall number of international students more than doubled in the same period. In school year (SY) 2016–17, international enrollment in U.S. colleges and universities increased 3 percent from the prior year, the slowest growth rate since 2009–10. A total of 291,000 new international students enrolled at U.S. institutions in SY 2016–17, about 10,000 fewer than in SY 2015–16." (See Zong and Batalova.).

11. Ibid.

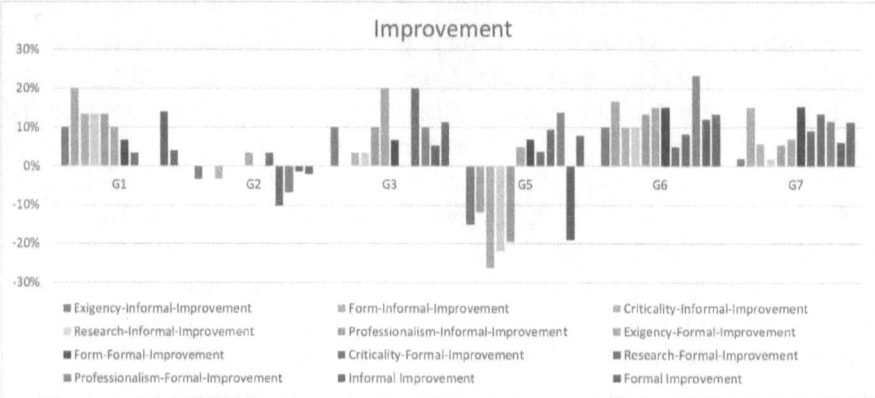

Figure 1.

Given the benefits of the GWTA for GTA populations on campus, we plan a second pilot. For the second year, we are seeking to increase the number of departments that participate. We hope to include graduate students from two or three of the following programs: biology, business, educational leadership, and industrial engineering. To broaden our reach, we are seeking funding from the campus diversity office and from the departments themselves. Diversity participants would assist us in broadening the range of writing concerns to include more in-depth conversations on audience awareness and expectations. We also plan to deepen our involvement with the graduate school, not only preparing oral presentations for delivery within the graduate professional development program, but also establishing an archive of taped presentations, further developing the peer mentor program we began this year. Finally, we seek institutional recognition of the GWTA program by increasing the interaction with classrooms beyond those that the GWTAs manage, by establishing a web page, and by seeking publicity for GWTA program activities.

Our broader mission to reinvigorate our university's WAC program will only be attained if faculty from other disciplines take notice of our achievements in improving student writing at both the undergraduate and graduate level. The dire note rung in the first pages of this essay regarding recent faculty disinterest in WAC initiatives should not be taken to mean that faculty needs to be withdrawn from WAC, but rather that we might imagine new ways of engaging and encouraging faculty to participate in our programs by proxy. A "stealth WAC" program, in other words, does not mean—at least in the way we borrow the phrase—an invisible WAC program. What we hope is that, in shining a light on the "invisible" world of TAs in the disciplines, and making graduate students the centerpiece of our program, university departments will have a greater appreciation for their students as communicative experts in their discipline.

Anticipating the argument that utilizing graduate students in this capacity will only further their exploitation and liminal status, we submit the following: graduate students are already tasked with the bulk of teaching in many disciplines across our university. Not acknowledging this fact will only further alienate students, particularly international students, by failing to offer them proper pedagogical training. Anecdotally, we know of many graduate students who, thrust into the classroom during their first year of graduate school, are frankly terrified by the prospect of teaching. Our program aims to lessen graduate student apprehension, offer them additional monies to supplement their stipends, and improve their own research writing in the process.

Our second pilot year will build on the momentum we have already established. As mentioned above; our GTAs are already assisting faculty in designing and implementing undergraduate writing curriculum. The expansion of this program will mean that graduate students will play an outsized administrative role in their disciplines and receive greater recognition as teaching assistants. The benefits of our initiative for undergraduate students and WAC seem self-evident to us at this point. We look forward to letting our programs evolve and adapt to encourage the culture we are working to create: a reciprocal give-and-take between WAC programs and GTAs that builds support for writing from a not-quite-so-invisible middle.

Note

1. The authors wish to thank Dan Frank and Eda Ozyesilpinar, our graduate assistants from the Rhetorics, Communication, and Information Design (RCID) program, who coded and analyzed the data from student papers. We also wish to thank the anonymous peer reviewers for their generous and insightful comments, which greatly helped in shaping the final draft.

Works Cited

Anson, Chris. "Mistakes in Social Psychology." *The WAC Casebook: Scenes for Faculty Reflection and Program Development*. Anson, ed. New York: Oxford University Press, 2002, pp. 212–22.

Champlin, Dell P., and Janet T. Knoedler. "Commodification of Labor, Teaching, and Higher Education." *Association for Evolutionary Economics @ Harry Trebing Session*, San Francisco, CA, January 2016. www.aeaweb.org/conference/2016/retrieve.php?pdfid=1200 Accessed 29 Jun 2018.

Cole, Daniel. "What if the Earth Is Flat? Working With, Not Against, Faculty Concerns about Grammar in Student Writing." *The WAC Journal*, vol. 25, Fall 2014, pp. 7–35.

Falconer, Heather. "Assessing Writing in Undergraduate Biology Coursework: A Review of the Literature on Practices and Criteria." *The WAC Journal*, vol. 28, Fall 2017, pp123–38.

Fulwiler, Toby, Michael E. Gorman and Margaret E. Gorman. "Changing Faculty Attitudes Toward Writing." *Writing Across the Disciplines*. Toby Fulwiler and Art Young, eds. Upper Montclair, NJ: Boynton/Cook Publishers, 1986, pp. 53–67.

Gardner, Grant E., and M. Gail Jones. "Pedagogical Preparation of the Science Graduate Teaching Assistant: Challenges and Implications." *Science Educator*, vol. 20, no. 2, 2011, pp. 31–41. files.eric.ed.gov/fulltext/EJ960634.pdf. Accessed 2 Jul. 2018

Hiller, Judith. "How Does That Work? Developing Pedagogical Content Knowledge from SubjectKnowledge." *Teacher Education and Practice*, vol. 26, no. 2, 2013, p. 323. *Opposing Viewpoints In Context*. link.galegroup.com/apps/doc/A514683037/OVICu=clemson_itweb&sid=OVIC&xid=fb1681e3. Accessed 2 June 2018.

Jablonski, Jeffrey. *Academic Writing Consulting and WAC*. Cresskill, NJ: Hampton Press, 2006.

North, Stephen. "The Idea of a Writing Center." *College English*, vol. 46, no. 5, 1984, pp. 433–66.

Rodrigue, Tanya K. "The (In)Visible World of Teaching Assistants in the Disciplines: Preparing TAs to Teach Writing." *Across the Disciplines*, vol. 9, no. 1, 2012, pp. 1–14. *WAC Clearinghouse*. wac.colostate.edu/docs/atd/articles/rodrigue2012.pdf. Accessed 19 Mar. 2018.

Schaefer, Katherine. "'Emphasizing Similarity' but not 'Eliding Difference': Exploring Sub-Disciplinary Differences as a Way to Teach Genre Flexibility." *The WAC Journal*, vol. 26, Fall 2015, pp. 36–55.

Swanson-Owens, Deborah. "Identifying Natural Sources of Resistance: A Case Study of Implementing Writing Across the Curriculum." *Research in the Teaching of English*, vol. 20, 1986, pp. 69–97.

Swilky, Jody. "Reconsidering Faculty Resistance to Writing Reform." *WPA: Writing Program Administration*, vol. 16, no. 1–2, Fall/Winter, 1992, pp. 50–60.

Walvoord, Barbara. "The Future of WAC." *College English*, vol. 58, p. 199.

Ward, Irene, and Merry Perry. "A Selection of Strategies for Training Teaching Assistants." *The Longman Sourcebook for Writing Program Administrators*, edited by Irene Ward and William J Carpenter, Pearson Longman, 2008, pp. 117–38.

Young, Art, and Toby Fulwiler. "The Enemies of Writing Across the Curriculum." *Programs that Work*. Young and Fulwiler, eds. Portsmouth, NH: Boynton/Cook Publishers, 1990, pp. 287–94.

Zong, Jie, and Jeanne Batalova. "International Students in the United States." *Migration Policy Institute Spotlight*, 9 May 2018, www.migrationpolicy.org/article/international-students-united-states. Accessed 29 Jun. 2018.

Appendix: Assignments from the GWTA Course

Writing Assignment Design (WAD)

This paper has three components: 1) identify an assignment of focus for this "design" project; this can be an assignment already scheduled in the syllabus (lab report, essay, project) 2) develop a rubric that adheres to your particular disciplinary conventions, while acknowledging the broader goals of improving undergraduate student writing that we have discussed on in class, and 3) explain how and why you've chosen to focus on these particular aspects of writing and how you expect your students to achieve mastery within the context of your rubric. For example, you may have a "Conclusion" section in your rubric worth 10% of student's total grade on this assignment. But, more importantly, how will you explain what a section that works as a conclusion is supposed to accomplish? Will you offer examples? Will you suggest certain templates? Why do you think these will be successful? 25 Points (25% of Final Grade)

Presentations

Over the course of the final two class periods, we will ask you to show how you implemented your Writing Assignment (see above) and discuss the results. What were your students struggling with in their writing initially? What did you want them to accomplish? How did your rubric address these particular struggles? What were the results? Where did you see the greatest improvement? In what areas do they continue to need improvement. The presentations will take the form of 5-10 minute Powerpoint presentation. 20 Points (20% of Final Grade)

Analysis

In lieu of a final, due during finals week and using two sets of collected papers from your undergraduate students (one early, one in response to the WAD, above), identify 3-4 students from each class that exemplify progress in their writing over the term. Compare their two papers, noting 1) what changed from paper 1 to paper 2, 2) why, in your estimation, are these changes significant, and 3) what is your conclusion about your WAC/WID efforts from this representative sampling. 15 points (15% of Final Grade)

Evaluation

At the end of the semester, write a 2-page evaluation of what you learned from the course. Furthermore, discuss how you have applied the writing concepts and lessons to your own respective courses. This paper should be written in narrative form. 10 points (10% of Final Grade)

The chart below shows one possibility for arranging your data.

Student A	Paper 1 Analysis	Paper 2 Analysis	Significance
Student B			
Student C			
Conclusion (This conclusion should be an analytical reflection on the results demonstrated by your student papers and your thoughts on the effectiveness of the WAC/WID teaching methods.)			

Review

C.C. HENDRICKS

Tarabochia, Sandra L. *Reframing the Relational: A Pedagogical Ethic for Cross-Curricular Literacy Work.* Urbana, IL: NCTE, 2017. 208 pages.

While many have recognized the challenges of working across disciplinary boundaries, few address these challenges as generatively as Sandra L. Tarabochia does in *Reframing the Relational: A Pedagogical Ethic for Cross-Curricular Literacy Work.* WAC scholars have long explored the complex—and sometimes problematic—dynamics of cross-curricular partnerships. For instance, Toby Fulwiler recognized the difficulty of assessing WAC. Chris Anson provided a glimpse into common issues that arise when faculty from across the disciplines come together to discuss writing in *The WAC Casebook: Scenes for Faculty Reflection and Program Development.* Similarly, Martha Townsend identified the "vulnerabilities" of WAC programs. More recently, these reflections have shifted into criticisms of "missionary" (Jablonski, 2006; Mahala and Swilky, 1994) narratives of WAC that gloss over these issues. Responding to these criticisms, Tarabochia conducts a cross-institutional study that asks: "What challenges to cross-disciplinary communication do faculty face in CCL [cross-curricular literacy] contexts? How do dilemmas manifest discursively through interaction? How do participants discursively respond to the challenges they face?" (Tarabochia 6).

What I found most innovative and compelling about Tarabochia's study is how she grounds her claims within "the conversational realities" of her participants (6). Building upon the discursive strategies already employed by her participants, she crafts a *pedagogical ethic* that can "help writing specialists adjust communication strategies to foster productive conversations with faculty in other disciplines, build sustainable relationships, and revise writing curricula amid complicated, ever-changing dynamics" (Tarabochia 6). By employing a pedagogical lens, Tarabochia effectively reframes WAC's often dilemmic moments as opportunities for reciprocal learning and collaborative meaning-making. She draws attention to the often overlooked challenges faced by WAC practitioners while also convincingly demonstrating how a *pedagogical ethic* can help to mitigate these challenges.

Tarabochia's methodology and theoretical frameworks are most clearly outlined in her introductory chapter. She applies an understanding of pedagogy as *epistemic* (Berlin, 1987), *reflexive,* and *relational* as an "interpretive frame" to analyze participants' experiences (7).

Over a ten-month period, Tarabochia collects data from five participant groups from four post-secondary institutions of various sizes: a public and private college, and two research universities. Each group includes at least one "writing specialist" and one "disciplinary context expert." She recruits writing specialists who planned on meeting with faculty from another discipline at least twice during the Fall 2012 semester to discuss writing by contacting WAC/WID administrators and circulating calls on WPA and WAC listservs. Using snowball sampling, she enlists six writing specialists with different degrees of CCL experience, including an undergraduate writing fellow, graduate teaching associate, and non-tenured and tenured faculty and writing program administrators. The five disciplinary content experts—who include a graduate student, tenured professors, and an associate dean—come from a variety of disciplines, such as communication science, chemistry, computer science, and education. By not enforcing strict requirements in her recruitment of participants, she includes the perspectives of a variety of WAC stakeholders, and offers meaningful insight into how CCL work operates across different contexts.

The breadth of data that Tarabochia gathers in one study is impressive; she collects a variety of data from each participant group: two surveys, at least two recorded meetings, and at least two semi-structured participant interviews (Tarabochia 21). She investigates how participants navigate the complex dynamics of *expertise* (chapter two), *change* (chapter three), and *play* (chapter four). More specifically, she identifies the discursive moves employed by participants to overcome unexpected challenges, which include *negotiating expertise, openness to change, willingness to play, reflexive practice*, and *relationship building*. Tarabochia provides examples of each of these moves in subsequent chapters.

In chapter two, Tarabochia explores one of the most complicated dynamics at play within cross-disciplinary partnerships: expertise. She asks, "How do writing specialists claim and validate our writing-related expertise and also urge disciplinary colleagues to recognize their own writing expertise and take responsibility for teaching writing in their disciplines?" (Tarabochia 29). Examining the communicative strategies participants use to "claim" or "share" expertise, Tarabochia argues for an understanding of expertise as ever-evolving, collectively distributed, and in constant negotiation. In addition to drawing attention to the sophisticated moves CCL workers make surrounding expertise, Tarabochia models a distributed view of expertise that can cultivate a co-construction of knowledge between "teacher-learners."

Tarabochia explores how participant groups discuss and encourage change as instances of liminal learning in chapter three. She contends that, "While the objects, agents, and goals for change vary across stages of the WAC movement, a largely limited, one-directional view of change remains constant" (Tarabochia 69). Working against hierarchical or linear views of change, Tarabochia highlights moments of mutual change between participants. She associates change with "deep" and "transformative" learning, effectively disrupting unrealistic narratives of progress that can impede efficacious cross-curricular partnerships.

One of Tarabochia's most unique contributions to WAC is her investigation into play in chapter four. She "identif[ies] cognitive and relational functions of playful moves in CCL exchanges and explore[s] their potential for supporting faculty experiences of liminality in the process of transformative learning" (127). Tarabochia analyzes three forms of play employed by participants to communicate and relate across difference: *metaphor, storytelling,* and *silliness*. From this analysis, she persuasively demonstrates how play can promote intellectual openness and reciprocal cross-disciplinary cooperation. In addition to making constructive connections between WAC and learning theory, Tarabochia offers important details on the "face-to-face exchanges so vital for cultivating productive cross-disciplinary relationships" (3). Instead of focusing on the products or effects of CCL partnerships as many other WAC studies do, she provides insight into the everyday processes of those partnerships in action.

These processes inform the tenets of Tarabochia's *pedagogical ethic,* which she most clearly defines in chapter five. She organizes the culminating chapter around three guiding principles of this *ethic*: (1) *commit to reflexive practice,* (2) *maintain a learner's stance,* and (3) *approach CCL conversations as pedagogical performance.* For each principle, she identifies the discursive strategies used by participants to enact it. Some of these strategies include making the theories and best practices of writing studies more accessible to others, withholding advice, and reflecting on the differences and similarities between one another's learning experiences. From these strategies, she builds practical heuristics for addressing common challenges that arise in CCL work. After articulating the interdisciplinary applications of her findings, she identifies writing center tutor training and graduate education as two areas in writing studies that would find a *pedagogical ethic* particularly valuable. Like WAC's attention to students' learning processes, Tarabochia emphasizes that "faculty members come to CCL exchanges as complicated people and multifaceted learners" (153). She urges us to approach our cross-disciplinary relationships with the same critical and ethical care that we devote to our classroom pedagogies.

Tarabochia successfully manages both her large dataset and the various interdisciplinary theoretical lenses she employs. Yet, I did want to know more about the contexts surrounding the participant groups. While Tarabochia states that "the impetus for the conversations varied across groups," she provides more information on some groups than others (Tarabochia 15). For instance, in the case of Alicia and Ann, there is not much explanation on the impetus for the particular meetings Tarabochia analyzes, only on how they originally met. It seems that participants' willingness to decenter their expertise and openness to new learning would be influenced by whether they chose, were required, or had incentive to meet. Relatedly, I wondered how the presence of a WAC program—or another CCL initiative formally endorsed by the institution—might correlate with Tarabochia's findings. She provides some of this institutional context in her description of the participant groups. However, more attention to the influence of these initiatives in her analysis could potentially provide support for arguments about the value of WAC programs. In addition, as Tarabochia directly acknowledges in both her introductory and final chapters, her study raises questions of power and difference that she does not address. However, I do see the potential in a *pedagogical ethic* for inspiring productive and critical discussions about the relationships between power, learning, and cross-disciplinary alliances.

Tarabochia ultimately calls for more critical reflection on "how we perceive, pursue, and measure the success of faculty exchanges in WAC/WID" (168). In this way, she echoes other scholars' efforts to evolve WAC practices to better address new contexts, including community engagement (Guerra, 2008; Kells, 2012), linguistic diversity (Zawacki and Cox, 2014), and technological advancements (Lunsford, 2009). Her call is particularly resonant right now, given the ever-shifting dynamics of higher education. For instance, traditional disciplinary boundaries continue to blur, evidenced by the average number of different occupations a student will have upon graduation and the increasing rate at which faculty and administrators are required to engage in cross-disciplinary collaboration. In addition, globalization necessitates approaches to WAC that interrogate how learning occurs across difference. Victor Villanueva speaks to this need in "Politics of Literacy Across the Curriculum:" "While we all explore ways of helping students translate their ways with words into the conventions of particular disciplines, we can also listen and learn from other disciplines about the political economies that give rise to difference" (174). Like Villanueva, Tarabochia emphasizes WAC's potential for mitigating myopic models of cross-disciplinary collaboration through cooperative learning. As a result, she contributes a sustainable model of WAC that is responsive to new and ever-emergent exigencies.

While anyone involved in cross-disciplinary or cross-curricular conversations would benefit from reading Tarabochia's text, WAC practitioners will find her contributions especially pertinent. Firstly, Tarabochia's presentation of CCL work as mutually pedagogical could prove useful to consultants and administrators as they make arguments about the value of WAC programs. For instance, her assertion that effective partnerships require change from both the writing specialist and content expert can help to dissuade perceptions of WAC as invasive. Secondly, Tarabochia contributes insight into an important quandary within WAC: "How do writing specialists teach expert processes and practices while maintaining respect for specialized writing expertise?" (53). This question is especially important given the history of writing studies' professionalization. By resisting finite metrics for assessing expertise, Tarabochia offers strategies for expanding the locus and responsibility of writing instruction while maintaining our own disciplinary capital. Thirdly, Tarabochia's inquiry into play provides inventive approaches for establishing the long-term, cross-disciplinary partnerships that are so integral to WAC's longevity. Finally, the heuristics for engaging in cross-disciplinary dialogue provided throughout the text and in the Appendices are applicable in a variety of WAC initiatives. In particular, new WAC consultants, or those unfamiliar with cross-disciplinary work, would find these heuristics beneficial.

Tarabochia's study is an exemplar of what can be gained from in-depth analysis of the unpredictable, day-to-day processes of WAC. Overall, she successfully reframes CCL work as a "pedagogical activity," and offers an innovative approach to WAC that is amendable to a variety of contexts and stakeholders.

Works Cited

Anson, Chris M. *The WAC Casebook: Scenes for Faculty Reflection and Program Development*. New York: Oxford UP, 2002.

Fulwiler, Toby. "Evaluating Writing Across the Curriculum Programs." *New Directions for Teaching and Learning*, no. 36, 1988, pp. 61–75.

Guerra, Juan C. "Cultivating Transcultural Citizenship: A Writing Across Communities Model." *Language Arts*, vol. 85, no. 4, 2008, pp. 296–304.

Jablonski, Jeffrey. *Academic Writing Consulting and WAC: Methods and Models for Guiding Cross-Curricular Literacy Work*. Cresskill, NJ: Hampton Press, 2006.

Kells, Michelle H. "Welcome to Babylon: Junior Writing Program Administrators and Writing Across Communities at the University of New Mexico." *Composition Forum*, vol. 25, 2012.

Lunsford, Karen J., ed. "Writing Technologies and Writing Across the Curriculum: Current Lessons and Future Trends" [Special Issue]. *Across the Disciplines*, vol. 6, 2009.

Mahala, Daniel, and Jody Swilky. "Resistance and Reform: The Functions of Expertise in Writing Across the Curriculum." *Language and Learning Across the Disciplines*, vol. 1, no. 2, 1994, pp.35–62.

Townsend, Martha. "WAC Program Vulnerability and what to do about it: An Update and Brief Bibliographic Essay." *WAC Journal*, vol. 19, 2008, pp. 45–61.

Villanueva, Victor. "Politics of Literacy Across the Curriculum." In *WAC for the New Millennium: Strategies for Continuing Writing-Across-the-Curriculum-Programs*, edited by Susan H. McLeod, Eric Miraglia, Margot Soven, and Christopher Thaiss. National Council of Teachers of English, Urbana, IL, 2002, pp. 165–78.

Zawacki, Terry M., and Michelle Cox. *WAC and Second Language Writers: Research Towards Linguistically and Culturally Inclusive Programs and Practices*. Anderson, SC: Parlor Press, 2014.

What We Mean When We Say "Meaningful" Writing: A Review of *The Meaningful Writing Project*

MARY HEDENGREN

Eodice, Michele, Anne Ellen Geller, and Neal Lerner. *The Meaningful Writing Project: Learning, Teaching and Writing in Higher Education*. UP Colorado, 2017. ($22.95; 170 pp., paperback)

One of the difficulties of research into student experience is that it tends to focus on faculty and administration perceptions of student experience. In *The Meaningful Writing Project*, Michele Eodice, Anne Ellen Geller, and Neal Lerner follow Richard Haswell's (2005) recommendations for replicable, aggregable, and data-supported research in their study on *student* perceptions of meaningful writing. The focus on empirical writing research is not surprising, considering Lerner's classic assessment apologia "Counting Beans and Making Beans Count" (1997) and follow-up adjustment "Choosing Beans Wisely" (2001), but perhaps this emipircal focus is tempered by the kind of practice-based pragmatism found in Eodice and Geller's *The Everyday Writing Center* (2007) or their recent anthology, *Working with Faculty Writers* (2013).

The resulting book-length study is both approachable and methodologically attractive. *The Meaningful Writing Project* begins with plenty of methodological discussion, then takes a graphic interlude to present the methods, sites, and results in infographic form. After the infographic section, the authors discuss three key terms in a chapter each: *agency, engagement*, and *learning for transfer*. Each of these chapters includes a review of the literature, findings from the Meaningful Writing Project (and, when applicable, other studies), and a case study of a representative student. These three student-centered chapters are followed by a chapter on the instructors behind those meaningful writing projects. Finally, the last chapter presents conclusions and applications for stakeholders across the university.

The study is based primarily on asking seniors to "Think of a writing project from your undergraduate career up to this point that was meaningful for you" (p. 148) and then answer a series of questions about those meaningful writing projects. They and their undergraduate and graduate research assistants next interviewed twenty-seven of the students, asking them to elaborate about their projects, the classes where those projects occurred, and their writing more generally (pp. 154–55). To correlate their findings, the researchers also interviewed sixty of the instructors who assigned the meaningful projects. The researchers are conscious about the differences between their institutions. The University of Oklahoma, rural and public, with an eighty-one percent acceptance rate, looks very different than Northwestern University, urban, private, and seventy-six percent white, and from St. John's University, Catholic, highly diverse and with a third fewer undergraduate students than the other sites. The differences between these sites foreshadow the variety the researchers discovered in what kind of projects are deemed meaningful.

What the Authors Did Not Find

The researchers were expecting to find clear patterns of who assigned meaningful writing projects and where. Instead they found that the meaningful projects were scattered across "nearly five hundred faculty . . . most named only once" (p. 109). Some of the instructors were veterans, some were novices, some were full professors, some were lecturers, and some were adjuncts.

There was also no pattern on *where* these projects were taking place. Meaningful writing projects occurred in big classes and small, required courses and capstones, and in no courses at all (pp. 130–31). Some of the projects took place in online classes, when an instructor and student had "never met face to face" (p. 128). Nearly half of the reported meaningful writing projects occurred during the students' senior year (and a quarter in their junior year), but roughly ten percent occurred in freshman, sophomore, and "middler" years (p. 30). It's possible these numbers are depressed because seniors may have an easier time recalling recent assignments. All of this variety is itself enlightening—it breaks down some of the assumptions faculty may have about what kinds of classrooms and instructors lead to "meaningful writing"—but the study also provides insights into what these various projects all have in common.

What the Authors Did Find

While there were not definitive patterns in where, when, or by whom these meaningful projects were assigned, the researchers did discover some unifying characteristics. These characteristics include some of the key terms in composition scholarship.

For instance, in the chapter on "Agency and the Meaningful Writing Project," the authors draw on Marilyn M. Cooper (2011) and Shari Stenberg (2015) to define agency as "a result of social interactions among instructors, peers, and subject matter . . . infused with power and authority" (p. 34). In a case study on agency, student Leah claims, "I get very frustrated with writing" (p. 47), but she valued a writing project that allowed her to exercise her agency. That term, "allow," was frequently used by students, but not in opposition to being "required" or "forced"—in fact, the terms were often used to describe the same writing project (p. 38). Because of this, the authors do not suggest that it is enough to write an assignment prompt that lets students write anything on any topic. Students, especially while writing in unfamiliar disciplines, may lack the necessary content knowledge and falter, unable to come up with a meaningful area of research. The findings of *The Meaningful Writing Project* encourage a "balance between *allow* and *require*" (p. 48).

Agency, the authors argue, is an outcome, but "engagement is a process" (p. 55). Social engagement may include practices like peer review, but it can also be engagement with content, or students' future selves. Some students said their projects were meaningful because they were able to publish or present their work, but other students found other measures of accomplishment, such as doing a lot of work or writing in a foreign language (p. 64).

Writing for transfer of knowledge and skills was strongly linked to making personal connections. More than one in three of the students from the survey mentioned "personal connection" as the reason why the assignment was meaningful (p. 31, 85). These personal connections sometimes draw on prior experiences and interests, like a project that allowed one student to research and write about an injury that had killed a high school friend (p. 87). Other projects look to the future of the student. Almost seventy percent of the students in the study said that the meaningful writing project was related to what they expect to do in the future, usually in prospective jobs (p. 41). They said things like "As a teacher, I must write lesson plans that are creative," and "As a career artist I ... must be able to write about my work when I submit it to juried exhibitions" (p. 41). Recognizing connections to their future lives invigorates writing for these students and clarifies the connections between their past, present, and future. As the authors put it, the meaningful projects were "holistic—not merely about content or genre or process but also about mind and body, heart and head—and to act as a kind of mirror in which students see their pasts and futures, enabling them to map those on to their writing projects to make meaning" (p. 107). It's not overstating to characterize these meaningful writing projects as meaningful experiences—period.

What Readers Will Find

There are a few shortcomings in this otherwise landmark study. One is whether the description of what students find meaningful naturally leads to a prescription of the kind of assignments instructors should design. Some readers may wonder if designing assignments with "personal connection" might not feed into an unhealthy narcissism, where students expect every assignment to be about *their* past and *their* future careers instead of encouraging them to look outward to people and phenomena around them.

Additionally, the school-writing focus of the study may hamper the results. This study may highlight the variety of meaningful writing projects that can occur within universities of all stripes, but it is handicapped by a focus on formal, in-class writing assignments. It is difficult to ask seniors in a school setting about "a meaningful writing project from [their] undergraduate career" (p. 148) without those seniors reading the prompt as implying a *school* project.

The authors mention that some of the meaningful writing projects took place without classrooms, teachers, or grades (p. 131), but there's not much discussion of those projects, because very few of the participants chose to respond to the question in that way. A full ninety-four percent of the participant seniors responded to the prompt with an in-class writing project (p. 108). This is hardly the authors' preference, and they express disappointment that more students didn't mention out-of-class writing, including transitional work-writing. The context of the survey (sent to students' school email, with an informed consent letter from their school's IRB, and beginning with a series of questions about their major, minor, and college) could play a large part in participants answering the question in relation to their classwork, as could the wording: "undergraduate career" implies school assignments more strongly than "over the last five years" and a "writing project" is not the phrase one uses to describe one's movie review channel on YouTube or application essay for medical school.

These concerns pale in comparison to the incredible work this project does, not only in its conclusions, but also in its student-centered research methods. *The Meaningful Writing Project* is a book well-structured for a WPA-led faculty and staff book club, particularly for WAC/WID coordinators who want to focus on improving writing assignments. It is written in a way accessible to the lay reader, with plenty of representation of student voices. One of the most satisfying and accessible sections is the robust "infographic" section at the beginning of the text. The infographic section includes conclusions-at-a-glance, helpful for any book club member who might not have done *all* of the assigned reading. The ecumenical conclusions and examples demonstrate that any kind of instructor, in any discipline, teaching any kind of class can create meaningful writing experiences.

The last chapter includes practical and reflective suggestions for instructors who wish to design more meaningful assignments, assignments that provide for agency and personal connection and encourage transfer to future writing tasks, but faculty aren't the only audience for these suggestions. Because all three of the researchers are also committed to writing center research, writing center consultants and other tutors are also addressed, as the authors recommend moving questions away from "Do you think this is meeting your professor's assignment?" towards "What is your professor hoping you will learn and do in this assignment and what are you hoping to learn and do?" (p. 139). By focusing all members of the university writing community on connection and transfer, the authors encourage a full, holistic approach to develop not just meaningful writing projects, but meaningful writing experiences.

The researchers of *The Meaningful Writing Project* suggest that instructors have been too cavalier about writing assignments' impact on students. "We (faculty, tutors, and mentors) have likely been underestimating our potential influence on student agency, engagement, and learning for transfer; you might assign that same project every semester, but to the students it is a one-time experience" (p. 135). Reframing assignment design as giving each student a once-in-a-lifetime opportunity to do a meaningful writing project can impart faculty with a greater sense of meaning in their own work. More research in writing studies should follow the example of *The Meaningful Writing Project*, laying aside our teacher-based assumptions and instead reaching out to a wide variety of students to discover insights into their college experience, which, compared to ours, is both formative and fleeting.

References

Cooper, M. M. (2011). Rhetorical agency as emergent and enacted. *College Composition and Communication, 62*(3), 420–49.

Geller, A. E., & Eodice, M. (2013). *Working with faculty writers*. Boulder, CO: University Press of Colorado.

Geller, A. E., Eodice, M., Condon, F., Carroll, M., & Boquet, E. (2007). *Everyday writing center: A community of practice*. Boulder, CO: University Press of Colorado.

Haswell, R. H. (2005). NCTE/CCCC's recent war on scholarship. *Written Communication, 22*(2), 198–223.

Lerner, N. (1997). Counting beans and making beans count. *Writing Lab Newsletter, 22*(1), 1–3.

Lerner, N. (2001). Choosing beans wisely. *Writing Lab Newsletter, 26*(1), 1–5.

Stenberg, S. J. (2015). *Repurposing Composition*. Boulder, CO: University Press of Colorado.

Contributors

Cameron Bushnell is Director, Pearce Center for Professional Communication and Associate Professor, English at Clemson University. She is author of *Postcolonial Readings of Music in World Literature: Turning Empire on its Ear* (Routledge 2013).

Michelle Cox directs the English Language Support Office in the Knight Institute for Writing in the Disciplines at Cornell University. She chairs the CCCC WAC Standing Group and the Association for Writing Across the Curriculum. Her scholarship focuses WAC program administration, graduate student writing, and second language writing.

Matthew Davis is Associate Professor of English at the University of Massachusetts Boston, where he directs the Center on Media & Society. His work focuses on composition theory and pedagogy, digital rhetoric, and literacy studies, and has appeared or is forthcoming in *CCC, Computers and Composition, enculturation, South Atlantic Review, WLN,* and several edited collections. He is the incoming co-editor of *Composition Studies*.

Jeffrey R. Galin is Associate Professor in the Department of English at Florida Atlantic University. He teaches academic and multimedia writing and is founding director of FAU's University Center for Excellence in Writing, WAC program, and Community Center for Excellence in Writing. His most recent co-authored book is *Sustainable WAC: A Whole Systems Approach to Launching and Developing Writing Across the Curriculum Program*. He is currently outgoing chair of the CCCC WAC Standing Group, outgoing chair of the newly formed Association for WAC, and co-chair of the WAC institute in June 2019.

Anne Ruggles Gere is Arthur F. Thurnau Professor of English and Gertrude Buck Collegiate Professor of Education at the University of Michigan, where she serves as Director of the Sweetland Center for Writing. Her most recent work is *Developing Writers in Higher Education: A Longitudinal Study* (University of Michigan Press).

Austin Gorman is the Director of the Writing Center and Writing Fellows Program at Clemson University, where he also serves as a lecturer in English. He has previously published in the *American Studies Journal*.

Mary Hedengren teaches writing and rhetoric at the University of Houston, Clear Lake. Her research in disciplinarity and writing centers has appeared in *Writing Center Journal*, *Praxis* and *Pedagogy* among other journals.

C.C. Hendricks is currently a doctoral candidate in Composition & Cultural Rhetoric at Syracuse University, where she also teaches and consults in the writing center. Her research interests include rhetorical history, feminist rhetorics, affect studies, WAC/WID, and Writing Program Administration. Her work has appeared in *The WAC Journal*, and *Across the Disciplines*.

Bradley Hughes has been the director of the Writing Center since 1984 and director of Writing Across the Curriculum since 1990 at the University of Wisconsin-Madison. The WAC website that he and colleagues at UW-Madison have developed (writing.wisc.edu/wac) is widely used at many universities, and he has been a WAC and writing center consultant at universities around the US and in other countries. He has received several awards from the IWCA for his research publications and service.

Neal Lerner is Professor of English at Northeastern University, where he teaches undergraduate and graduate courses on writing, teaching writing, writing centers, and creative nonfiction. His book *The Idea of a Writing Laboratory* won the 2011 NCTE David H. Russell Award for Distinguished Research in the Teaching of English, and he is the co-author of *The Longman Guide to Peer Tutoring*, 2nd ed.; *Learning to Communicate in Science and Engineering: Case Studies from MIT*, winner of the 2012 CCCC Advancement of Knowledge Award; and *The Meaningful Writing Project: Learning, Teaching and Writing in Higher Education*.

Naitnaphit Limlamai is a doctoral student at the University of Michigan, where she studies secondary English methodologies. Her most recent essay, "What language communicates: Surfacing language ideology with high school students" was published in *English Journal*.

Anna V. Knutson serves Assistant Professor of English and Director of Composition at East Tennessee State University. She has collaboratively authored articles published in *Across the Disciplines*, *College English*, *Kairos*, and *WPA: Writing Program Administration*. With her co-authors, she won the 2016 Computers and Composition Ellen Nold Award for "Sites of Multimodal Literacy: Comparing Student Learning in Online and Face-to-Face Environments," published in *Computers and Composition*. Interested in writing program administration, learning transfer, and digital literacies, Anna is currently exploring writing knowledge transfer between social media and academic contexts among intersectional feminist college students.

Dr. Michelle LaFrance directs the Writing Across the Curriculum program at George Mason University. She has published on peer review, e-portfolios, e-research, writing center and WAC-pedagogy, and Institutional Ethnography. She is the co-editor of

Peer Pressure/Peer Power: Theory and Practice in Peer Review, with Steven J. Corbett and Teagan Decker (Fountainhead Press in 2014) and *Peer Review and Peer Response: A Critical Sourcebook*, with Steven J. Corbett (Bedford St. Martin's 2017). Her monograph *Institutional Ethnography: A Theory of Practice for Writing Studies Researchers* (Utah State University Press) will be released in early 2019.

Ryan McCarty is a PhD candidate in the Joint Program in English and Education at the University of Michigan, where he studies the ways that learners think about their processes of translating in and across contexts. Recently, his work has appeared in *Discourse Studies*, *Composition Studies*, and *Across the Disciplines*.

Dan Melzer is an associate professor at the University of California, Davis, where he serves as the director of the first-year composition program. He has published the book *Assignments Across the Curriculum* and, with the authors of this article, *Sustainable WAC*. His articles have appeared in *College Composition and Communication*, *WPA*, and the *WAC Journal*.

Elisabeth L. Miller is an assistant professor of English at the University of Nevada-Reno where she researches and teaches about literacy, disability, and WAC/WID. She served as Assistant Director of WAC at University of Wisconsin-Madison. Her recent publications have appeared in *College English*, *Writing Lab Newsletter*, and *Community Literacy Journal*.

Justin Nicholes is an assistant professor at the University of Wisconsin-Stout. His teaching and research center on writing's role in constructing disciplinary identities, enhancing disciplinary learning, and supporting retention efforts.

Sarah Peterson Pittock is an Advanced Lecturer in Stanford University's Program in Writing and Rhetoric. She currently serves as the Coordinator of Writing in the Major and as Director of Bing Honors College. From 2013 until 2018, she served as the Associate Director of the Hume Center for Writing and Speaking.

Justin K. Rademaekers is an assistant professor of English at West Chester University of Pennsylvania where he serves as Writing Across the Curriculum Director. His research has appeared in *Across the Disciplines*, the *Journal of Technical Writing and Communication*, and the *Best of Rhetoric and Composition Journals* series.

Liane Robertson is Associate Professor and Director of Writing Across the Curriculum at William Paterson University of New Jersey. She is co-author of *Writing Across Contexts: Transfer, Composition, and Sites of Writing* (2014), winner of the CCCC 2015 Research Impact Award, and the Council of Writing Program Administrators 2014 Best Book Award. Her recent work appears in *Composition,*

Rhetoric, and Disciplinarity (2018), *Understanding Writing Transfer: Implications for Transformative Student Learning in Higher Education* (2017), *Critical Transitions: Writing and the Question of Transfer* (2016), *A Rhetoric of Reflection* (2016), and *Naming What We Know: Threshold Concepts of Writing Studies* (2015).

Alisa Russell is a PhD Candidate (ABD) in Rhetoric and Composition at the University of Kansas. Her research interests include rhetorical genre studies, writing across the curriculum, publics, language rights, and composition theory. She has published in *Composition Forum* and *The Clearing House*, and her current dissertation project explores the role of genre in shaping membership, inclusion, and access in local government.

Jenna Pack Sheffield is Assistant Professor of English at the University of New Haven, where she directs the Writing Across the Curriculum Program and serves as the Assistant Dean for the College of Arts & Sciences. Her research focuses on digital composing and writing program administration, and her work has appeared in publications such as *Computers and Composition International*, *Computers and Composition Online*, *Composition Forum*, and *College English*.

Kara Taczak is Teaching Associate Professor at the University of Denver where she also directs Faculty Development and ePortfolio Initiatives. Her research centers on composition theory and pedagogy, specifically teaching for transfer. Her publications have appeared or are forthcoming in *College Composition and Communication*, *The WAC Journal*, *Composition Forum*, *Teaching English in the Two-Year College*, and *ATD: Across the Disciplines*; she received the 2015 *CCCC* Research Impact Award and the 2016 *CWPA* Book Award for her co-authored book *Writing across Contexts: Writing, Transfer, and Sites of Writing*. She is the incoming co-editor of *Composition Studies*.

Emily Wilson is a doctoral candidate in English and Education at the University of Michigan. She is on the research team at the Sweetland Center for Writing, and she is one of the authors of the forthcoming book *Developing Writers in Higher Education: A Longitudinal Study*.

Erin Workman is Assistant Professor in the Writing, Rhetoric, and Discourse Department at DePaul University, where she directs the First-Year Writing Program and leads the Teaching Apprenticeship Practicum. Her research focuses on writing program administration, visual concept mapping, reflection, and composition theory and pedagogy, and is forthcoming in *College Composition and Communication* and *South Atlantic Review*.

Kathleen Blake Yancey, Kellogg W. Hunt Professor of English and Distinguished Research Professor at Florida State University, has served in several national leadership roles, among them Chair of CCCC and President of NCTE. She is currently the PI for an 8-site research project focused on the Teaching for Transfer writing curriculum documented in her co-authored *Writing Across Contexts* and awarded the CCCC Research Impact Award and the Council of Writing Program Administrators Best Book Award. Author/co-author of over 100 articles and book chapters and author/co-author/editor of 15 books, she is the recipient of several awards, including the Purdue University Distinguished Women Scholar Award and the CCCC Exemplar Award.

How to Subscribe

The WAC Journal is published annually in print by Parlor Press and Clemson University. Digital copies of the journal are simultaneously published at The WAC Clearinghouse in PDF format for free download. Print subscriptions support the ongoing publication of the journal and make it possible to offer digital copies as open access. Subscription rates: One year: $25; Three years: $65; Five years: $95. You can subscribe to *The WAC Journal* and pay securely by credit card or PayPal at the Parlor Press website: http://www.parlorpress.com/wacjournal. Or you can send your name, email address, and mailing address along with a check (payable to Parlor Press) to

>Parlor Press
>3015 Brackenberry Drive
>Anderson SC 29621
>Email: sales@parlorpress.com

Pricing

One year: $25 | Three years: $65 | Five years: $95

Publish in The WAC Journal

The editorial board of The WAC Journal seeks WAC-related articles from across the country. Our national review board welcomes inquiries, proposals, and 3,000 to 6,000 word articles on WAC-related topics, including the following:

- WAC Techniques and Applications
- WAC Program Strategies
- WAC and WID
- WAC and Writing Centers
- Interviews and Reviews

Proposals and articles outside these categories will also be considered. Any discipline-standard documentation style (MLA, APA, etc.) is acceptable, but please follow such guidelines carefully. Submissions are managed initially via Submittable (https://parlorpress.submittable.com/submit) and then via email. For general inquiries, contact Lea Anna Cardwell, the managing editor, via email (wacjournal@parlorpress.com). The WAC Journal is an open-access, blind, peer-viewed journal published annually by Clemson University, Parlor Press, and the WAC Clearinghouse. It is available in print through Parlor Press and online in open-access format at the WAC Clearinghouse.

PARLOR PRESS
EQUIPMENT FOR LIVING

New, in Living Color!

Type Matters: The Rhetoricity of Letterforms ed. Christopher Scott Wyatt and Dànielle Nicole DeVoss (**BEST DESIGN AWARD-Ingram**)

Rhetoric and Experience Architecture ed. Liza Potts & Michael J. Salvo

Suasive Iterations: Rhetoric, Writing, and Physical Computing David M. Rieder

New Releases

Networked Humanities: Within and Without the University edited by Brian McNely and Jeff Rice

The Internet as a Game by Jill Anne Morris

Identity and Collaboration in World of Warcraft by Phillip Michael Alexander

Best of the Journals in Rhetoric and Composition 2017

Rhetorics Change / Rhetoric's Change edited by Jenny Rice, Chelsea Graham, & Eric Detweiler (Rhetoric Society of America

Congratulations, Award Winners!

Strategies for Writing Center Research by Jackie Grutsch McKinnie. **Best Book Award, International Writing Centers Association (2017)**

Antiracist Writing Assessment Ecologies: Teaching and Assessing Writing for a Socially Just Future by Asao Inoue, **Best Book Award, CCCC, Best Book, Council of Writing Program Administrators (2017)**

The WPA Outcomes Statement—A Decade Later edited by Nicholas N. Behm, Gregory R. Glau, Deborah H. Holdstein, Duane Roen, & Edward M. White, **Best Book Award, Council of Writing Program Adminstrators (2015)**

www.parlorpress.com

www.ingramcontent.com/pod-product-compliance
Lightning Source LLC
Chambersburg PA
CBHW020236170426
43202CB00008B/99